I0759682

PRAISE FOR *NORDIC SOCIALISM*

"Dragsted provides a compelling vision of an economy built on solidarity—one rooted not in abstractions but in the real successes of Nordic economies. His book makes it clear that in our search for a better world, we don't have to choose between the inequalities of capitalism or the inefficiencies of command economies."

—Bhaskar Sunkara, author of *The Socialist Manifesto: The Case for Radical Politics in an Era of Extreme Inequality*

"A powerful and incisive analysis of modern capitalism, and an inspiring assessment of the forces aligned against it. Dragsted demonstrates that democratic socialism is the only way out of the mess we're in—and shows how we can all start building it right now."

—Grace Blakeley, author of *Vulture Capitalism: Corporate Crimes, Backdoor Bailouts, and the Death of Freedom*

"Dragsted offers a thought-provoking exploration of the critical role of democracy in societal well-being—something overlooked by many self-professed capitalists in the U.S. What he calls 'Nordic socialism,' I call 'Nordic capitalism,' laying the foundation for a great debate on our economic and democratic future."

—Robert Strand, author of *Nordic Capitalism: Lessons for Realizing Sustainable Capitalism*

NORDIC SOCIALISM

The Path Toward a Democratic Economy

Pelle Dragsted

Translated by William Banks

THE UNIVERSITY OF WISCONSIN PRESS

publication supported by a grant from
The Community Foundation for Greater New Haven
as part of the Urban Haven Project

publication of this book has been made possible, in part, through support
from the Society for the Advancement of Scandinavian
Study and the Danish Arts Foundation

The University of Wisconsin Press
728 State Street, Suite 443
Madison, Wisconsin 53706
uwpress.wisc.edu

Printed in the United States of America
This book may be available in a digital edition.

Library of Congress Cataloging-in-Publication Data

Names: Dragsted, Pelle, 1975– author | Banks, William, 1970– translator
Title: Nordic socialism : the path toward a democratic economy /
Pelle Dragsted ; translated by William Banks.
Other titles: Nordisk socialisme. English
Description: Madison, Wisconsin : University of Wisconsin Press, 2025. |
Includes bibliographical references and index.
Identifiers: LCCN 2025001931 | ISBN 9780299353605 (hardcover)
Subjects: LCSH: Socialism—Scandinavia | Socialism—Denmark
Classification: LCC HX318.5 .D7313 2025 | DDC 320.53/10948—dc23/eng/20250506
LC record available at https://lccn.loc.gov/2025001931

Contents

Foreword

Matt Bruenig

In the run-up to the 2020 U.S. presidential election, a student attending a Fox News town hall asked Senator Bernie Sanders how democratic socialism differs from the authoritarian systems in places like the Soviet Union. Sanders answered by referencing the socialism of the Nordic countries as exemplifying its democratic incarnation: "When we talk about democratic socialism . . . I'm talking about Finland, I'm talking about Denmark, I'm talking about Sweden."[1]

Admiration of what the Nordic countries have achieved politically and economically is nothing new. In 2013, *The Economist* magazine ran a cover story titled "The Next Supermodel" that celebrated the Nordic model as one that other countries should consider adopting.[2] In a gathering of Nordic leaders at the White House in 2016, President Barack Obama remarked that these countries were "extraordinary" because they created "opportunity for all people, through education, health care, and equal opportunity" and because they had "some of the least income inequality in the world." Obama further mused that these achievements perhaps explained why "they're some of the happiest people in the world, despite not getting much sun."[3]

Because the Nordic countries consistently rank at the top of the world on most indicators of individual and social well-being, there has been a considerable amount of public debate in America about how best to characterize their economies. Unsurprisingly, participants in that debate typically say that the Nordic economies should be understood as versions of whatever their own economic ideology happens to be.

Thus, Sanders, a socialist politician, claims that the countries are "socialist," the social democrat academic Lane Kenworthy argues they are "social democratic capitalist," and neoliberal pundit Jonathan Chait describes the Nordic model as being an "an amped-up version of what left-wing critics derisively call 'neoliberalism.'"[4]

In this book, Pelle Dragsted skillfully cuts through these dueling characterizations. According to Dragsted, the Nordic countries, like all countries, organize production and ownership in a variety of ways. Disputes about how to characterize the countries arise because commentators invariably attempt to place their entire national economies into one category or another rather than acknowledge their hybridity. That politicians and pundits make this mistake is understandable. Their jobs require them to simplify political and economic phenomena in order to appeal to the general public. But even academics writing for sophisticated audiences can fall into this trap.

In his 2022 book *Would Democratic Socialism Be Better?*, Kenworthy, one of America's foremost authorities on the Nordic model, uses the successful track record of these countries to push back against the recent resurgence of socialist politics in America. Kenworthy categorizes these countries as capitalist rather than socialist because "firms that are owned by the government, citizens, or workers" employ less than two-thirds of the total population and account for less than two-thirds of their total output. He does acknowledge that "two-thirds is an arbitrary cutoff" but maintains "it's as sensible as any other."[5]

Dragsted, on the other hand, makes a compelling case that the arbitrariness inherent in sorting hybrid economies into socialist or capitalist categories indicates that efforts to do so are, in fact, not sensible. Hybrid economies can and do contain both capitalist and socialist elements, and so it makes more sense to think of countries as being more or less socialist rather than as being socialist or not.

Reorienting our thinking this way helps us see that the Nordic countries are notable because they organize a remarkably large portion of their economy in socialist ways. This means that Bernie Sanders and other democratic socialists around the world are right to take inspiration from the Nordic countries, as they have shown that it is possible to have a successful economy that is far more socialized than the economies found in the United States, the United Kingdom, and most other developed countries.

Turning this inspiration into practical political action requires more than just knowing that the Nordic countries rank high in measures of public ownership and collective ownership. It also demands detailed knowledge about what Nordic socialism looks like both historically and now.

After explicating his high-level understanding of what socialism is, Dragsted goes on to provide an excellent account of socialist production in the Nordic economies, primarily focused on Denmark, where Dragsted is a member of parliament representing the socialist Red-Green Alliance. The Nordic region is home to hundreds of state-owned enterprises, enormous social wealth funds, large-scale public services, and one of the most robust consumer cooperative sectors in the world. In Dragsted's parlance, these types of enterprises make up the "democratic sector" of the Nordic economies. The goal of socialists around the world and in the Nordic countries, he argues, should be to carefully shift an ever-larger share of production out of the capitalist sector and into the democratic sector.

Dragsted's pluralistic approach to socialism, which embraces and promotes a variety of socialist organizational forms from worker cooperatives to government-operated companies, is similar to the "checkerboard" strategy advocated by the American socialist Gar Alperovitz in books like *America Beyond Capitalism*. Both offer hope precisely because in their view socialism is not a totally different system that we can only implement via a revolutionary leap into the unknown but rather already exists in pockets of the economy that can be built on.

Quite a few books have been written that attempt to provide an introduction to the Nordic countries to American and other English-speaking audiences, including Anu Partanen's *The Nordic Theory of Everything* and George Lakey's *Viking Economics*. But these books invariably downplay the socialism of the Nordic countries, preferring instead to focus on the impressive welfare systems found in this region.

The Nordic welfare states are an incredible achievement in their own right and they deserve all the attention they receive. But child allowances, disability benefits, and old-age pensions are not socialism, and you cannot understand what is so exceptional about these countries if you ignore or minimize the ways that they organize production and the ownership of wealth.

Preface

The reason I have written this book is to describe a democratic alternative to the economy we have today. And no less important to show how we can get there.

The goal of the book is to resurrect the debate over democratic socialism. I have no doubt that developing a more democratic economy informed by socialist ideas is necessary to confront the immense crises we face as human beings in the twenty-first century: escalating inequality, climate destruction, and the collapse of political legitimacy that threatens the foundations of democratic governance.

At the same time it is obvious that we socialists have not been able to win popular backing for our ideas. In my view it is we ourselves who bear much of the blame for this. Centrist social democrats, on the one hand, have abandoned the main ideas of socialism itself, giving in to the false claim that capitalism constitutes the end of history. The left, on the other hand, has struggled to produce a program with real persuasive power, either because it is written off as utopian and unrealistic or because it does not provide answers to the many questions and objections it raises.

For my part, I do not believe that history has come to a conclusion. The world can be changed. We are not powerless. We can build a society in which wealth is not hoarded at the top but rather the fruits of our labor fall to all of us. A society where democracy does not stop at the doorstep of our workplaces, where we need not fear that losing our jobs will lead to ruin or that a foreign asset management giant like Blackstone will throw us out of our homes. We can take back power and influence from an unelected economic elite and return it to democratic institutions so that we in common can democratically determine how society and the economy will develop. And this will allow us to build a more secure, equal, and free society, to put a stop to climate change and to protect our forests, our fjords, and our wildlife. This is what democratic socialism is about: empowering ordinary people with the democratic powers needed to build the kind of world we desire.

Yet if the next chapter of our history is to be democratic and socialist, we will need a vision that can persuade the large majority to get on board, one that is less utopian and more practical than in the past with less sloganeering and more concrete proposals for reform. And such a vision must be grounded in our considerable prior experience with establishing a democratic and communal economy outside of and opposed to capitalism. This is what I wish to accomplish with this book.

I am certain that the ideas in this book will be met with criticism. The right will denounce it as a left-wing extremist fantasy that would surely lead to totalitarianism and economic ruin. And for its part, sections of the left will view it as a reformist betrayal of authentic socialist teaching.

I look forward to such critique, as the mere fact that we will once again be discussing the utility of socialist ideas will in and of itself be evidence of immense progress. I consider my own contribution to be the beginning rather than the conclusion of the debate over the nature of a modern democratic socialism because it hardly addresses all of the critical issues demanding the attention of today's left. First and foremost, this book centers the matter of economic power; issues of racial, gender, and sexual discrimination are only mentioned sporadically. This is by no means because I do not think these kinds of discrimination are important or because I believe that the many conflicts of society can all be reduced to class conflict. On the contrary, it is because the left has for many years been almost wholly on the defensive in the struggle against concentrated economic power. While we have made significant progress toward gender and sexual equality, for the entirety of my lifetime we have experienced defeat after defeat in the effort to change the balance of economic power between elites and the people.

Another limitation of this book is that the stage for the social struggle it describes is primarily national. The reader will search in vain for proposals for the reform of international institutions. While the current political and economic global order does largely dictate the extent of political maneuverability in Denmark and elsewhere, the national state is still the most powerful democratic means through which to create change. It is within the borders of Denmark that we Danes have achieved our greatest successes, and it is matters of national and local concern that most engage the ordinary citizen. The struggle for change, therefore, must begin here at home. And yet many of the reforms I propose cannot be realized if we act alone. We must somehow persuade other countries to begin a similar process of democratic change, and together with them we must seek to reform the international institutions, laws, and regulations that now so limit democratic governance at home. Importantly, this book is also primarily written with an eye to countries like Denmark, that is, relatively wealthy nations with strong democratic institutions. Less wealthy countries lacking such institutions face very different challenges that require their own solutions.

This book has long been in the making, at least within my own head. And in the years since it was conceived, many good things have happened. Since the 2008 financial crisis, a new generation of democratic socialists has appeared in Europe and the United States that has largely left behind older leftist sacred cows such as the binary distinction between reform and revolution. This new generation is more interested in practical solutions than theoretical debates, consciously seeks real political power, both at the national and local levels, and, curiously enough, takes many of its ideas from our own Nordic welfare society. The attention our little corner of the world has received from abroad has in fact bolstered my faith in the central idea of this book: that the building of a modern democratic socialism can take inspiration from our experience with establishing democratic alternatives here in Denmark and elsewhere in Norden.

And thus I must acknowledge a debt of gratitude to the young international left that has provided so much inspiration and so many new ideas. Peoples' Policy Project founder Matt Bruenig's many writings on Nordic socialism have been particularly important, as have the socialist reform proposals of Joe Guinan of the Democracy Collaborative and Thomas Hanna of Common Wealth. I must also thank the staff of *Jacobin* magazine, which has become such a critical point of reference for democratic socialists the world over. And finally I must acknowledge the late Erik Olin Wright, whose undogmatic and eminently curious approach to social change and socialism remains a model for us all.

Thanks are also due to many folks here at home, such as my publisher, Gyldendal, for many years of encouragement, my editor, Anne Weinkouff, for holding my feet to the fire and for her many efforts to improve the prose, and everyone who has provided invaluable critiques and suggestions for improvements, both with respect to content and to language, including Rune Lykkeberg, Andreas Møller Mulvad, Pil Christensen, Esben Bøgh Sørensen, Anders Lundquist, Rune Møller Stahl, Jonas Kylov Gielfeldt, Anders Dybdal, Thomas Bredsdorff, Hans Erik Avlund Frandsen, Lars Engberg, Mai Villadsen, Niels Dragsted, Jørgen Bech, Jonas Algers, Rune Lund, Frank Aaen, Jakob Sølvhøj, Peter Westermann, Jakob Legarth Sandorff, Dino Knudsen, Mikael Nyberg, Sebastian Gjerding, and Anne Folke Henningsen.

Special thanks are also due to Ejvind Larsen, that lion of the democratic left. Our many conversations over the years about Marx, Grundtvig, the cooperative movement, economy democracy, and so many other things have yielded innumerable insights for me.

And last but absolutely not least, a hearty thanks to my partner, Janne, my severest and best critic. Without you, your patience and your faith in me and your many invaluable suggestions, this book would not have happened.

Responsibility for the book's content and conclusions are mine alone.

Note to Readers of the English Edition

It is with great joy that I present my book on Nordic socialism to an English-speaking audience. Over the past decade, I have observed how the Nordic model—our experiences with strong social welfare programs, public ownership of public goods, and a robust cooperative sector—has increasingly inspired a new wave of democratic socialists in both the United States and the United Kingdom. In turn, the ideas and policies put forth by this new generation, including figures like Bernie Sanders and Alexandria Ocasio-Cortez, have been a profound source of inspiration for my own work as a Danish socialist parliamentarian.

I hope the publication of this book will contribute to an ongoing exchange of ideas and insights between the Nordic left and the Anglophone left. As we reflect on our shared past experiences, it becomes clear that our futures are even more interconnected—and the political developments in the United States over the coming years will have far-reaching consequences for the rest of the world. It is my sincere hope that this book can play a small part in the push toward a more democratic and less oligarchic United States.

One important note for readers: This book was originally written for a Nordic audience. Therefore, you will occasionally find collective references to "our" society, which reflects the Nordic context in which the book was first conceived.

NORDIC SOCIALISM

Introduction

Nordic socialism. I first encountered the concept in the fall of 2018. Sitting in my office at Christiansborg, the home of the Danish parliament, I stumbled on a report that had just been published by the administration of Donald Trump.[1]

The report was a warning to Americans against the openly declared democratic socialists within the Democratic Party, Bernie Sanders, Alexandria Ocasio-Cortez, and others, and more broadly against a new generation of activists who have identified Denmark and the other Nordic countries as an inspiration for their version of democratic socialism.[2] One of the report's sections, titled "Nordic Socialism," aimed to prove that Nordic economies are both inefficient and hostile to freedom and that we Nordics are less well-off and must put up with higher taxes and prices.

A few months earlier, Fox Business Network host Trish Regan had also castigated Denmark in a segment on the contagion of socialism. According to Regan, Denmark's high taxes and support for the unemployed and for students discourage people from working or from completing their studies, since they would rather open cupcake cafés. "This is the reality of socialism," she said, rolling her eyes.[3]

Both the White House report and Regan's Fox Business segment were filled with factual errors regarding the Danish economy, and their arguments were met with dismissal from across the whole of the Danish political spectrum.

Danes were particularly incensed with the suggestion that the Nordic welfare society has anything at all to do with socialism. "Completely absurd," declared then–Liberal Alliance foreign minister Anders Samuelsen, while Venstre finance minister Kristian Jensen described such talk as "idiotic." The Social Democrats and their allies on the left, for their part, also acknowledged that Denmark is indeed a capitalist, free market economy.[4] We have our welfare systems, surely enough. But socialism? Not at all.

One of the central assertions of this book, however, is that Trump, Regan, and the American right are actually correct when they call the Nordic countries socialist, or at least more correct than previously acknowledged. And furthermore that our inability to recognize the socialist characteristics of our economy in part explains why it seems so difficult to imagine, describe, and argue for a persuasive and realistic alternative to the capitalist economy.

It is self-evident that the economies of Denmark and the other Nordic countries are not *entirely* socialist. Far from it. But is not the opposite assertion—that they are *entirely* capitalist—just as absurd and idiotic?

The Danish encyclopedia defines capitalism as an economic system based on wage labor in which "the production of goods and services are characterized by an arrangement according to which the means of production, capital—for example land, raw materials and machines—as well as the products themselves, are owned by capitalists, who produce for a market in competition with other capitalists."[5]

According to this definition, large parts of the Danish economy can hardly be considered purely capitalist: our public sector makes up fully a quarter of our economy. Here the means of production—hospitals, schools, roads, railways, preschools, nursing homes, libraries—are owned and managed by democratically chosen organs, whether at the national, regional, or municipal level—that is to say, indirectly by the whole of the citizenry.

Nearly a third of us are employed in these democratically governed sectors that do not produce for the market. Our debit cards can remain in our wallets when we go to the hospital, the preschool, or the nursing home. The benefits are funded through a solidaristic tax system; each of us contributes a part of our income to a common fund that pays for the salaries of public employees and other expenses, which in turn permits us to receive equal access to the benefits of a welfare society—free health care, education, and other services. These characteristics of the Danish system stand in sharp contrast to the Danish encyclopedia's definition of a capitalist market economy.

Moreover, this democratic ownership model, according to which the means of production are owned in common rather than by a small group of capitalists, is hardly limited to the public sector in Denmark. Large pockets of democratic ownership are also found in the private sector, where groups of citizens own and manage enterprises. Our second largest grocery chain, Coop, is a cooperative owned by some 1.8 million members. These members elect the three thousand local steering committee members and the upper management. No capitalist profits from our consumption because we ourselves are the owners.

In our utility sector, democratic ownership is more the rule than the exception. Our electricity, water, and heating are produced and dispensed predominantly by cooperatives that we ourselves own. Surpluses from these enterprises do not go to the owners of capital but are either returned to the customers or reinvested for their benefit. Here too the customers themselves choose the leadership and exert direct influence through our local housing associations.

Even our much maligned financial sector has a strongly democratic and noncapitalist component. We have cooperative banks owned and overseen by the customers. Our largest mortgage lender, Nykredit, is owned by a collective constituted by all the borrowers of NyKredit and Totalkredit. We have a wide variety of insurance mutuals owned by policy holders. And our democratic pension funds manage billions in capital, securing returns for wage and salary workers.

There are many challenges facing our democratically managed enterprises. In the public sector, citizens do not exert much real influence, and in the private sector, the role of members has been reduced owing to centralization. But these enterprises that make up these sectors are still fundamentally distinct from capitalist ones because their goal is not to earn money for absentee shareholders.

The situation is the same in the other Nordic countries. In Norway, Sweden, and Finland, the state owns critical enterprises and controls a significant portion of investment capital. And like Denmark they share a long tradition of democratic cooperatives.

Are these public and private democratically managed enterprises really just a part of capitalism, even though they are definitionally opposed to the idea of it? Or are they defined more by socialist ideas of collective ownership and democratic administration?

Not according to modern social democrats, who understand socialism as state ownership and planned economy as in the Soviet Union, nor to the revolutionary leftists, who argue even if more democratic enterprises exist, they are subordinated to the capitalist economy and have nothing to do with socialism because socialism can only happen after the existing capitalist economy has been overthrown. Both social democrats and the revolutionary left alike thus view capitalism as a totalizing and all-encompassing system that structures our entire economy. Nothing is outside of it. All is capitalism.[6]

I believe that it is precisely this binary conception of capitalism as all-encompassing and socialism as a utopian project of the future that has long handicapped the efforts of the left to create a more solidaristic and more economically just society. The way we have formulated our task has precluded its fulfillment.

Do Not Believe in an Alternative

"It is easier to imagine the end of the world than the end of capitalism," philosopher Slavoj Žižek notes in frustration over the fact that despite rising discontent with the capitalist economy and its human and environmental consequences, the left has been unable to develop a convincing strategy for a way toward a noncapitalist society.

And he has a point; we find ourselves in the midst of a historical rupture in which more and more people are critical of the consequences of the capitalist economy, among them steeply climbing inequality between elite and masses, periodic economic crises that throw millions out of work, the gradual undermining of the welfare society and of the economic security built up by the generations before us, the erosion of safe working conditions, and not least the climate crisis that threatens our continued existence on the globe.

In the wake of the financial crisis of 2008, powerful new opposition movements have emerged from the 15-M movement that saw the occupation of public squares by young activists in Southern Europe to Occupy Wall Street, Black Lives Matter, and the climate movement that under the slogan "System Change, Not Climate Change" has taken to the streets from Sydney to Berlin. There is desire for change, and hope has been awakened that we can create a world in which people are more equal, free, and secure and in which we can live in harmony with nature and one another.

Opinion polling reveals rising opposition to capitalism. One poll from 2015 showed that 65 percent of British citizens regard capitalism as unjust. In Germany no less than 77 percent are skeptical of it. Among young Americans between 18 and 29, attitudes toward socialism are now more favorable than toward capitalism.[7]

Yet despite rising discontent and growing doubts about our dominant economic model, despite the desire for change, the left has up to now failed to procure support for an alternative to capitalism from a majority of the population. There have been local victories and support for alternatives has grown, but nowhere has the neoliberal status quo been challenged in earnest.

The question is why. I believe that the main reason is that the majority of people have difficulty believing in a better alternative. Dissatisfaction with the present is not in itself enough to provoke change; there must also be an alternative that is perceived as both possible and realistic. But socialists have plainly been unable to persuade a majority that it is possible to create a new, more just economy and society. That social democrats now embrace a politics largely identical to that of the right has bolstered the impression that there is in fact no alternative to existing capitalism. And far-left calls for the overthrow of capitalism or a socialist seizure of state power are viewed by the majority as unworkable, unrealistic, or perhaps even a little frightening, since they associate socialist ideas with the command economies of the Eastern European past. In his book *Capitalist Realism*, British activist and author Mark Fisher describes just such a reality, the wholesale acceptance of the idea that "not only is capitalism the only viable political and economic system, but also that it is now impossible even to imagine a coherent alternative to it."[8]

I cannot begin to count the times, whether during political meetings or in social media debates or in conversations on the train or bus or in the supermarket, I have been struck by the skepticism toward the idea that there is an alternative to capitalism. I have met so many people, young and old and from all layers of society, who evince a burning discontent with what the world has become and yet have difficulty imagining that it is possible to arrange society and the economy in a more just and democratic manner.

My suggestion is that our inability to imagine alternatives to capitalism and to articulate concrete ideas that are perceived to be realistic and attractive is largely the result of two factors: our aforementioned blindness to the seeds of socialism that already exists in our society and the conception of capitalism as an all-encompassing system marking the end of history. In my view it is especially the latter point that has, on the one hand, led social democrats to surrender to capitalist realism, and on the other, kept the left entranced by the utopian vision of socialism as revolution.

Socialism Is Here

But what if capitalism is not so powerful and so extensive? All through its history, after all, people have succeeded in banding together and creating alternatives that defy its narrow division of power and ownership. The fact is that we have already taken steps toward a more democratic economy and therefore are closer to socialism than we had believed.

What if instead of cramming all sorts of widely diverging social and economic phenomena into a box we call capitalism, we acknowledge that capitalism is not the sum of our economy, that it has always shared the scene with more democratic and socialistic forms of ownership and distribution, and that Trump is actually right when he asserts that the Nordic economies are characterized by strong socialist tendencies?

This acknowledgment is important precisely because understanding our economy as a hybrid of many different modes of production provides us, as this book demonstrates, with new and better ways to think about and argue for social change.

In the first place, this understanding concretely grounds socialism in the reality we know and in the social progress we have already instituted. By identifying and acknowledging the areas of our economy and society that already are noncapitalist, we can see that socialism is not a utopian vision of the future but already here.

In the second place, it also frees us from the binary choice between a more or less regulated capitalism and a complete and all-encompassing overthrow of the existing economic system—a strategy that has never succeeded in all of history. Instead of viewing economies and societies as *either* capitalist *or* socialist, we can instead view them as *more* or *less* capitalistic and *more* or *less* socialistic. This opens the possibility of gradually rendering our society more socialistic and less capitalistic by expanding the areas of the economy that are democratically owned and managed and by reducing the scope and the influence of the market economy—not as a sudden rupture but as a gradual transformation.

The Experience of Socialism in Nordic Countries

The acknowledgment that capitalism is not all-encompassing is especially relevant in Denmark and the other Nordic countries. This is why I suggest we embrace Trump's concept of Nordic socialism, that we make it our own, that we turn it into a signifier of a new, modern, and democratic socialism, inspired by our own experience with socialist ideas that have demonstrated their worthiness throughout our history.

This is evident in our welfare society, which demonstrates every day that we can democratically manage important parts of the economy without anyone profiting from them. We have chosen to make vital sectors such as health care, education, and childcare part of a communal rather than market economy, where in good socialist fashion we contribute according to ability and receive according to need.

It is also apparent from the many successes of our cooperative movement. Small farmers established their own dairies and slaughterhouses to ensure that they rather than landowners or merchants profit from their labor. Citizens worked together to found locally and community owned waterworks, consumer cooperatives, and savings banks. And our public cooperative housing sector guarantees that it is not the size of your wallet that determines whether you have a view of the sea.

It is further evident in our strong labor movement, in which wage earners organize because they understand they are the foundation of our prosperity and thus should have much more say in their working lives and a much larger share of the wealth they create. And in our folk high schools, our independent schools, libraries, and all the other civil society associations.

In short, our experience with socialist ideas is attested in all the places we as citizens work together to create value not in order to make a few rich and powerful but to be stronger and freer together. It is within this tradition that we will find the ideas and inspiration for a new democratic socialism. Not in the Soviet Union's *kolkhozes* (the collective farms established after the Russian Revolution) but in the democratic associations of the cooperative movement. Not in the utopian designs of a perfect future society but in the lived and proven experience of our own history. Not in Lenin and Mao but rather in and Borgbjerg and Branting.[9]

In their attempts to defend the inequality and unsustainability of the capitalist system, the right always poses the question "Where has socialism ever worked?" "Right here," should be our answer, "in the Nordic countries," where the forces of our democratic enterprises and welfare society, rather than those of the market and the narrow interests of capital, set much of the agenda. This is our point of departure, our building block. And the reason to believe we can create a new and more democratic economy. A Nordic socialism.

To speak of a specifically "Nordic" socialism is not to say that our ideas and experiences cannot be employed in other parts of the world. It is hardly coincidental that many of the new progressive movements and democratic socialist organizations around the world point to the Nordic countries as a source of inspiration for a more just society. But Nordic societies have not developed in isolation from the surrounding world, and the ideas that underpin both the labor and cooperative movements as well as the welfare society have been constantly influenced by those from abroad. I am not therefore advancing a kind of Nordic essentialism but only acknowledging that our part of the world has made important contributions to the democratization of the economy, contributions that socialists around the world can learn from and build on.

A Pluralistic Socialist Economy

By acknowledging that societies and economies are always hybrids, we can see that we need not choose between free market capitalism and a planned state socialism. Between these two extremes are a wide range of mixed alternatives, and just as capitalism is dominant but not all-encompassing today, so could socialism be in the future.

In my mind this way of conceiving social change is emancipatory, since it allows us to dismiss comprehensive visions of an ideal social order that can contain the seed of totalitarianism, insofar as the effort to realize a specific blueprint can force the entirety of society into a single economic model. And moreover, it encourages a more pluralistic vision of a socialist economy that supports different forms of ownership and that does not force us to choose between a market economy or democratic planning.

The main purpose of this book is to set forth ideas and suggestions for how we can develop such a pluralistic economy. How we can widen and deepen the democratic forms of ownership already known to us from our cooperative movement and public sector. How we can further democratize ownership in the form of employee funds that ensure co-ownership for wage earners and in a national wealth fund that distributes a part of the profits of capital among the whole population. How we can change the balance of power in our private enterprises so that those who labor also decide. And how we can create an economy in which we employ market mechanisms in those areas where they are beneficial and support an efficient and sustainable economy yet permit democratic decision-making to determine the framework, the rules, and the overarching goals.

The concept of a specifically Nordic socialism that I propose thus emphasizes how socialism is anchored in our previous experience with democratic enterprise, how it builds further on these experiences, and how distant it is from the countries that have historically called themselves socialist. It is pluralistic insofar as it rejects black and white distinctions between the state and civil society or the market and democracy but recognizes that the complexity of society and the multifaceted nature of human beings demand complex and multifaceted solutions. It is oriented toward civil society, skeptical of centralization, bureaucracy, and growing state power, and predicated on the idea that the democratic engagement of ordinary people at all levels of society is a precondition for socialist development. Most importantly, it is a *democratic* socialism, anchored in Nordic democratic governance with stable institutions, a strong civil society, and the protection of individual freedoms.

It is a socialism that rejects any hint of totalitarian pretense to the violent overthrow of society or to authoritarian rule, but it is still an ambitious socialism that consciously and progressively works to replace the existing capitalist economy with a socialist alternative that centers democratic management and collective ownership, that does not accept the idea that the economy and our working lives are not entitled to the same freedoms and democracy as is the rest of society, and that recognizes that as long as the ownership of banks, corporations, land, and data remains as concentrated as it is today, economic elites will be able to exercise what I later will define as oligarchic power, which undermines and hollows out democratic governance.

The idea of the gradual development of a more socialist economy rooted in our prior experiences with democratic planning and collective ownership is not based on a naive understanding of social change as a harmonious and frictionless process. The development of society is never linear. There will always be regression, conflict, and tests of strength as well as progress, in part because the emergence of a more democratic economy will surely be met with resistance from the economic elites that enjoy the privileges of the capitalist economy's uneven distribution of wealth and power. Just as the generations that fought to replace monarchical power with parliamentary democracy were met with derision and resistance, their ideas labeled utopian, unrealistic, and radical, so will our generation encounter the same opposition as we work to make the principle of self-government applicable to the economic sphere. We will be told that it cannot be done, that the existing economy is the end of history. That there is no alternative.

A Decisive Moment

The story we have been told—about the eternal nature of capitalism and the impossibility of alternatives—is the most critical ideological fundament of today's capitalist economy.

It is why we still accept an economic system that distributes the fruits of our labor so narrowly, that gives so much economic and political power to so few, despite the fact that no one has voted for them, that separates the economic sphere and the whole of working life from the democratic principles that apply to the rest of society, and that is on a direct collision course with the natural world. It is because we have bought the line that history is over.

But history is never over. No system is eternal. In our own history we have shown that when people band together we can change our society and our life conditions. It was through such collective action that we created our political democracy as well as our welfare society after the crisis of the 1930s.

The capitalist economy is once again in crisis. Growth has slowed, and what growth there is benefits only a tiny elite at the top, while the majority receives less and less. Economic contraction is socially regressive, as every economic slowdown results in new cuts to the welfare society for which generations before us struggled. This further leads to discontent, feelings of powerlessness, and suspicion of the political system. And it now threatens even the democratic system and the freedoms we take for granted. The experience of an economic system that does not work for the majority engenders apathy and disillusion, and is powerful fodder for authoritarian political figures like Donald Trump, Matteo Salvini, and Viktor Orbán.

But fortunately right-wing populism is not the only response to political mistrust. In Southern Europe new social movements and political parties have been established and have begun to acquire influence. Across the world we witness youth movements such as Sunrise and Fridays for Future demanding radical change. In the United States a declared democratic socialist was close to being a major candidate for the presidency, uniting millions of engaged young people in the wake. In Britain an otherwise dying Labour Party was over the course of a few years reanimated by left-wing ideas. While none of these newer formations have managed to take power, it is clear that socialist ideas have immense drawing power, that people want something more than market competition that only makes the rich richer and everyone else more precarious, that there is growing faith in the possibility that we can make change and create a society in which the people in collaboration set the agenda rather than the blind forces of the market.

In other words, we find ourselves at a crossroads. The current political breakdown could lead in several directions. Either it could permit the triumph of anti-liberal and authoritarian forces through the promise of strong leadership and the scapegoating of ethnic and sexual minorities or it could foster the birth of a new left that overcomes its impotence and begins to transform the economy and society.

This is why it is critical to provide a socialist alternative that can inspire enthusiasm, hope, and dreams and yet that is also realistic, persuasive, and concrete, because it builds on the socialist elements in our existing society. We must not proffer slogans but provide substantive answers to the difficult questions that the development of a more democratic and sustainable economy will raise.

This book is a contribution to just such a process. It attempts to address the two great questions that anyone who seeks social change must answer: where shall we go? and how can we get there?

In chapter 1, "Diagnosis," I argue for the necessity of a new democratic and socialist economy. It is increasingly clear that an economy dominated by a small ownership class not only contributes to steadily rising inequality and injustice but also undermines the foundation of democracy, since it secures for a tiny economic elite an oligarchic power that circumscribes the space of democratic governance. At the same time, the capitalist economy, with its narrow profit motive, has also proven itself incapable of addressing our generation's greatest threat—the climate crisis. My position is that these problems cannot be resolved within the confines of the currently existing capitalist economy. What is needed is a democratization of the economy that distributes ownership and power among the many and further democratizes decisions on investment and the goals and direction of the economy.

In chapter 2, "Change," I discuss strategies for social transformation and review the ways the left has historically attempted to challenge capitalism. Neither modern social democrats nor the left, of which I myself am a part, have been able to offer sufficiently realistic and convincing ideas about how we can create a more solidaristic and democratic economy. Among other things this is due to a persistent tendency to regard capitalism as an all-encompassing system. I suggest a new conception of society as a hybrid between multiple modes of economic production and show that such an understanding can facilitate a society in which the capitalist part of the economy is gradually diminished in favor of a democratic and socialist economy based on democratic ownership and governance.

In chapter 3, "The Communal Economy," I show that the capitalist economy in Denmark and the other Nordic countries has always faced competition from a democratic and collectively owned alternative. This takes the form of the producer and consumer co-ops that have constituted a significant portion of the economy and the democratically governed welfare society that has reduced the scope and influence of market forces. I also discuss what we can learn from our century and a half experience of this vital democratic sector and how we can build on it.

In chapter 4, "Nordic Democratic Socialism," I explore how a modern democratic socialist economy can be instituted. How can the economy be managed more democratically? What does it mean to democratize ownership, and who will own what? What role should market mechanisms play, and how do we create an economy that secures the most possible freedom and democratic participation for each individual? I dismiss the state socialist models of the past and instead argue for a socialism based on a pluralism of ownership forms. At the same time I argue that the left must do away with the binary distinction between market and planned economies and instead find a balance that preserves the positive qualities of market mechanisms but reduces their scope, ensuring that the marketized sectors of the economy are subject to democratic oversight and are compelled to work within the limits of our planet's resources.

In chapter 5, "Ten Reforms," I present ten concrete reform proposals that constitute the first steps toward establishing a new democratic economy, a Nordic socialism. In various ways these reforms transfer power and influence away from a narrow elite by virtue of the democratization of the ownership of production, investments, land, data, and information, by communalizing still greater parts of the economy, making us less dependent on the market when it comes to the fulfillment of our most basic needs, and by replacing the unplanned and arbitrary functioning of the market with a much more comprehensive democratic planning.

In the epilogue I consider some of the questions and objections the book will surely raise. Are my proposals sufficiently comprehensive to resolve all the problems we confront? Which social forces can instigate such change? Is gradual socialist development even possible in an economy dominated by globalized capitalism?

I hope that my book can help create a new faith that change is not only necessary but also entirely possible and that it will stimulate not only debate and discussion but even more so the engagement and the collective action that in the end is the foundation of all democratic social change.

Enjoy the book.

1

Diagnosis
Capitalism Is Oligarchic and Unsustainable

In the summer of 2020, amid the global COVID pandemic, the American stock index reached its highest level ever recorded. The same was true of the fortunes of the U.S. billionaire class, which also mushroomed. During the same period the number of the newly unemployed surpassed forty million, and the lines at food banks stretched for miles. And here in Denmark the stock and property markets likewise boomed as the economy suffered its worst contraction in nearly a hundred years, with thousands losing their jobs.

That same summer the carbon content of the atmosphere once again peaked—the drop in emissions resulting from the COVID crisis was hardly sufficient to slow the rising trend.[1] California was in flames, as smoke and ash colored the sky red over San Francisco, making it look like something out of a science fiction film. On the other side of the world, the Siberian tundra was also aflame as a consequence of the highest temperatures ever recorded. And in the fall the United Nations was compelled to concede that the comprehensive eradication of plant, animal, and insect species had continued despite international agreements to protect biodiversity.

This is a picture of a system in crisis. Or rather multiple, simultaneous crises, all of which stem from certain inherent characteristics of the capitalist economy. The first is a strong tendency toward increased inequality and concentrated wealth in the hands of a tiny economic elite. And the second is that the relentless drive to maximize capital accumulation coupled with the unplanned nature of market forces effectively prevents us from making the changes needed to halt the destruction of our climate and the mass extinction of species. It is to these characteristics of capitalism that I now turn.

Capitalist Oligarchy

The Workers' Museum of Copenhagen is located on Rømersgade near Nørreport station. The red-brick building that houses it is the old meeting hall of the labor movement. I have visited the museum many times with my children and with guests from abroad, since the permanent exhibition, in a series of images and text, provides the distinct impression of social life in Denmark over the past one hundred and fifty years. Room by room, the evolution of the life conditions of ordinary working people unfolds, from early industrialization, when the working class, deprived of rights and subject to the whims of employers, endured profound misery, to the crisis of the 1930s, when families still lived packed together in darkened tenements but also when a social safety net was gradually created, to the postwar economic boom that, combined with the rising political and trade union power of the working class, lifted ordinary people out of poverty and granted new rights such as sick leave, apprenticeship supports, universal public pensions, and early retirement. The exhibition thus relates an optimistic and affirmative narrative of continual progress, a story of how ordinary people, through union organizing and political struggle, changed their life conditions by securing for themselves a steadily rising share of the value they created through their labor, and of how each generation won new rights.

The paradox is that if the Workers' Museum developed a new exhibit following events up to the present, it would in many ways tell the opposite story. Instead of a steady increase in workers' rights, it would describe how hard-won rights have been rolled back. Instead of continual strengthening of the social safety net, it would show how larger and larger holes have been opened up and how social security has been eroded. And instead of tracing a continually rising labor share of national income, it would reveal how it has declined as riches have been concentrated at the top.

For the first time since the birth of the labor movement, wage earners in the Nordic countries today will enjoy fewer rights and less security than their parents. If they receive a pink slip, the road to financial ruin is much shorter. If they fall ill or are injured on the job, they cannot be assured that they will receive support from the state while they recover. They will likely have to work into old age, as the opportunity to receive early retirement benefits has largely been eliminated. At the same time the risk that they end up in at-will employment has greatly increased, and with the growth of Uber, Amazon, and other gig-work firms, more and more workers will find themselves without fundamental rights.

In other countries, conditions are even worse for the majority of workers. In Germany, the so-called working poor, that is, people who still live in poverty despite full-time employment, now amount to a tenth of the labor force, and there are twelve million working poor in the United States.[2] Poverty has also increased among the British working classes, where more than half of the poor are poor despite at least one parent being employed.[3]

These developments have resulted in a rising awareness that the future will no longer promise progress and betterment for ordinary people. In 2017, Denmark's largest labor union, 3F, conducted a survey of its members regarding their expectations for the future. More than two-thirds, 70 percent of the membership, did not believe that their children would be better off than themselves. Only 27 percent saw the future as bright.[4]

The paradox here is that society has not become poorer, nor is it the case that the same rights and the same standard of living can no longer be afforded. On the contrary, in Denmark, for example, national wealth is higher than ever and continues to rise year after year. In other words, we as a society are more able than ever before to afford early retirement benefits, welfare, and sick leave.

It is therefore not the economy that prevents us from continuing the movement that resulted in greater freedom and security for ordinary wage earners for decades and thus benefited the large majority. Why, then, are we moving backward? A well-functioning democracy, after all, ought to look after the interests of the majority. So why is a new generation coming of age with reduced social rights and diminished welfare?

The answer is that an inherent characteristic of the capitalist economy, what I refer to as the oligarchic tendency of capitalism, concentrates wealth and thereby political influence among an economic elite with no democratic mandate.

Exploitation—Capitalism's Dirty Little Secret

As is well known, the capitalist mode of production is characterized by the fact that a relatively small class, the capitalists, own the means of production and distribution, that is, factories, banks, container ships, supermarkets, social media platforms, and all the other kinds of companies that sell goods and services on the market.

Opposite this small class is the great majority of the population, which either owns nothing or at most an insignificant share of the apparatus of production and instead lives off the sale of labor to capitalists: the working class—or wage earners, as we call this group today.

The division of the citizenry into a small class that owns the means of production and a majority class that sells its labor to the former is the foundation of the inherent tendency of capitalist production to concentrate wealth and thereby increase inequality. The concentration of riches is due to the exploitative relation between the capitalist and all those who sell their labor.

This is capitalism's dirty little secret, which Karl Marx discovered during those long nights at the British Library. Marx describes how a single mechanism accounts for the concentration of wealth, namely, that when wage earners sell labor to capitalists, they earn back less in wages than the value they have created through their labor. The remainder, which Marx calls the surplus value of the wage earners' labor, is appropriated by capitalists, by employers. To simplify, a wage earner is paid back the full value of all labor performed from Monday through Wednesday, while the value created on Thursday and Friday is appropriated by the capitalist and transformed into profit.

This profit is then invested into new enterprises, securities, or property that provides still more returns for capitalists, thus deepening the inequality between the capitalist class and the rest of the population.

The society we inhabit today is of course much more complex than in Marx's time. We no longer all work at the same job at the same textile factory. The economy has become much more diverse, and the feedback loop by which wealth is concentrated has become obscurer and more opaque. The evolution of a steadily more globally integrated economy and a financial sector that has assumed ever greater significance, the expansion of patent rights, big data, and intellectual property, and the growth of public sector employment have rendered the open exploitation of labor power Marx describes in the Victorian mills more complex and less immediately apparent.

Such conditions have bolstered claims that it is passé to speak of classes and of class contradictions, that we have entered into a postindustrial knowledge economy to which Marx's theories of surplus value and exploitation no longer apply. Yet regardless of the complexity of the modern economy, the foundation of wealth remains the same: the labor of human beings. The only thing that can create wealth in any society is human beings who go to work and produce something that other people need or want. It is as simple as that. If all of us stayed home from work tomorrow, no wealth would be created. No goods or services would be produced or exchanged. Derivative forms of accumulation, that is, those of speculative finance and the tech monopolies, likewise would wither away without the underlying production of goods and services provided by those who go to work.

It therefore follows that the accumulation of riches, despite the complexity of today's economy, ultimately rests on the fact that someone has expropriated the labor of others. Behind all the obfuscation, the fundamental contradiction is the one between the great majority who go to work and create value and the small minority that, by virtue of its ownership of the means of production, captures an inordinate share of that value.

In recent decades, many have sought to downplay this contradiction by declaring the death of class struggle. Yet the unequal distribution of value persists regardless of whether it is publicly acknowledged or whether class struggle takes place openly or in the shadows. In the capitalist firm the most important task of the employer is to generate the greatest surplus for its shareholders by keeping costs down, not least the cost of labor. And for their part, wage earners naturally desire the highest possible wages.

Often this clash of interests takes place out in the open, as when after a couple of years we return to the bargaining table to negotiate how much of the firm's revenue shall go to wage earners. Here the contradiction is crystal clear: one cent more for the wage earner is one cent less for the owners.

This same contradiction is what leads to continual labor disputes, strikes, and lockouts when no agreement can be reached or when employers choose to rely on casual employment, import underpaid labor power from abroad, or outsource production to reduce labor costs. And it has also featured in recent political debates, such as when reformers have cut sick leave or cash transfers, thereby reducing the incomes of workers who become unemployed even more. The results for employers, on the other hand, are wholly advantageous, because such reforms reduce the bargaining position of wage earners, for whom a pink slip can have more serious consequences.

These struggles constantly determine the distribution of a firm's value creation between wage earners and ownership. When wage earners and their organizations and political parties are strong, workers will receive a larger slice of the pie, while in those periods in which they are hard pressed, it will be the capitalists who walk away with the largest part. Purely statistically, this phenomenon can be seen in the relation between the so-called wage share, which measures the proportion of national wealth captured by labor, and the capital share, which measures that which goes to profit, a relation that for many years has steadily tilted toward capital and away from workers.

The Financialization of Capitalism

The concentration of wealth under modern capitalism, however, is not only based on the exploitation of labor power. A significant and growing number of capitalists acquire their fortunes through the ownership of goods and services that others must pay to access—so-called economic rent seeking. Speculators own land and homes, capital funds own vital infrastructure, banks control money creation and debt issuance, tech giants control mass data, and big pharma owns patents. In many cases it is not the capitalists themselves who develop the new goods or services; instead, they extract wealth from others through control of them. Rising property rents, interest and fees on debt service, the sale of mass data and income from patents, and the expansion of intellectual property rights increasingly drive the distribution of wealth. Marxist economist Grace Blakeley describes this so-called rent seeking as "unproductive transfers from one group to another based on an asymmetry of power."[5]

According to Blakeley, the rent-seeking share of wealth has grown markedly in recent decades, up from 5 percent in 1970 to 15 percent in 1990 in Britain and up 20 to 40 percent during the same period in the United States, the result of the economy having become *financialized*.[6] Financialization, as defined by economist Gerald A. Epstein, refers to "the increasing role of financial motives, financial markets, financial actors and financial institutions in the operation of the domestic and international economies."[7] The performance of the economy is thus less determined by what is created in the real world and more by what happens in the financial markets. The financial sector's share of the global economy has grown steadily larger since the 1980s, including here at home. In his book *Danish Capitalism*, political economist Anders Lundkvist shows that the share of Danish wealth captured by finance increased eightfold between 1957 and 2014.[8]

But financialization does not only affect the growth of the financial sector; nonfinancial firms too have become more financialized and have invested a rising share of their income in financial markets rather than in capital improvements for their own activities. Financialization has also spread into other areas and even into our daily lives, especially with respect to our homes. Far from being the place we live, our homes have increasingly become speculative objects for private investors, who extract income from them. Over the past ten years, global asset managers such as Blackstone have entered the Danish housing market and have bought up hundreds of properties. These global property speculators then raise rents and thereby earn more in rental income, and thus the fruits of social investment in the improvement of the land are concentrated in the hands of global property speculators. Our agricultural land has also, as in so many other countries, become a speculative asset, after a majority in the parliament made it legal for foreign firms to own Danish farmland. The ever more powerful information economy is the basis of another form of rent seeking, based on the control of intellectual property rights. The pharmaceutical industry, for example, enjoys enormous profits because comprehensive patents provide it with monopolies over products essential to medical care, which can then be sold at inflated prices. The four largest tech concerns, Microsoft, Apple, Amazon, and Alphabet (which owns Google), are now also the world's four largest companies, and their market cap continues to grow annually.[9] Tech giants do not generate their wealth primarily through the exploitation of labor but by using social media platforms or services to harvest our data without our knowledge or consent. The information regarding our behavior and preferences is then sold to a steadily growing advertising market. So-called data brokers with names like Experian, Epsilon, and Altegrity have annual revenues of USD 200 billion.[10] In her book *The Age of Surveillance Capitalism*, the American scholar Shoshana Zuboff calls income from data harvesting the "surveillance dividend" because firms earn money from an intimate knowledge of our habits, preferences, attitudes, and behavior.[11]

In financialized capitalism, therefore, wealth is concentrated not only through the exploitation of labor but increasingly through the rent seeking of a narrow elite that accumulates wealth through financial firms, ownership of land and property, and control of information, knowledge, and data. Financialization thus accelerates inequality beyond what the exploitation of labor alone does.

Rising Inequality

As French economist Thomas Piketty has demonstrated, the rising capital share of wealth and the rising profitability of rent seeking have resulted in a situation in which capital income growth now outpaces that of wage earners. This escalates inequality, since those who own capital will see their incomes rise much more rapidly than the majority who do not.

The United States offers a dramatic example, as real wages for ordinary citizens have largely stagnated, rising a mere 12 percent since 1978, while CEO compensation has exploded. The CEOs of the largest 350 firms now earn around three hundred times as much as the median employee. For the CEO of McDonald's, Steve Easterbrook, the figure is one thousand.[12] With respect to the distribution of capital income, the gulf is even wider; 97 percent of capital income in the United States goes to the wealthiest 10 percent.

Unprecedented income inequality has further led to inequalities of wealth not seen in more than a century. Since 1982 the wealth of the Walton family, for example, has risen by 10,000 percent, while the average American family has less wealth than it did in the mid-1980s.[13]

Although the U.S. case is extreme, the pattern is the same across the world. OECD figures show that the labor share of national income is falling. While wages have historically trended up along with rising national wealth, over the past fifteen years they have been decoupled, and the labor share in nearly all the member countries has fallen. Thus society becomes richer and richer, yet those who create value and who live off their labor get less and less.[14]

In Denmark and other Nordic countries income inequality is still lower than in many other places, but it has risen sharply in recent years. According to the think tank Kraka, Denmark is second after the United States with respect to the growth of inequality since 2004, as measured by Gini coefficient.[15]

In a series of analyses, the Danish labor movement think tank Arbejderbevægelsens Erhvervsråd shows how incomes at the top and the bottom have diverged dramatically in the first two decades of the new century.[16] Since 2002 the wealthiest 10 percent of Danes have seen their real after-tax incomes rise DKK 203,000. Among the top 1 percent, this figure is DKK 704,000—a 77 percent increase. During the same period, the bottom 10 percent of Danes saw their real after-tax incomes fall DKK 1900. And since the financial crises of 2008 the income of the bottom 40 percent of Danes has largely stood still.[17]

The same has occurred with respect to wealth. According to the OECD, Denmark has the third highest wealth disparity among member nations; the richest 10 percent own 64 percent of national wealth.[18] Other Nordic countries show similar wealth disparities.[19]

Wherever we look in the world, then, we see rising inequality, with all its resulting negative social consequences. Copious research has shown that unequal societies fare worse than more equal societies on a host of measures. Crime and insecurity are higher, public health is worse, and trust between people is lower.[20] But the most serious consequence is that rising economic inequality also leads to rising inequality in political power and influence, which undermines the foundation of what we understand as democracy. And as we shall now see—and this explains the previously noted paradox—despite rising national wealth our welfare and social rights have been steadily hollowed out.

Economic Power Means Political Power

It's pretty simple: concentration of wealth leads to concentration of power. When income and wealth distribution are steadily more skewed toward a narrow capitalist class, political and social influence are also rendered less equal. Individuals and groups with large fortunes can use their wealth and their control over operations, firms, and banks to exert decisive influence over the political development of both state and international institutions.

The obvious way of turning wealth into political power is through direct donations to political parties and politicians, media organizations, and think tanks, all of which serve to protect the interests of the well-off. Here at home, financial support from economic elites for right-wing parties has grown in recent decades.[21] The figures from the 2019 election have yet to be finalized, but in 2015 the difference between private contributions to the right and left blocs was larger than ever. While the Venstre, Conservatives, and Liberal Alliance received upward of DKK 50 million, the Social

Democrats, Socialist People's Party, and the Red-Green Alliance took in around DKK 17 million.[22]

An example of how the political contributions of certain firms or sectors are interwoven with political outcomes that benefit the very same groups is found in the 2003 decision of a narrow parliamentary majority to authorize oil exploration in the North Sea, which provided Danish shipping and logistics company A.P. Møller-Mærsk with advantages unheard of in other developed countries. The annual records of the parties that supported the agreement reveal that all of them received contributions from the firm, as they also did when a new and equally lucrative agreement was negotiated in 2015.[23] According to leading economists, annual tax revenues would have been DKK 10 billion higher if we had taxed the Danish oil industry at the same rate that Norway did during the same period.[24] Similarly, the parties that passed the multibillion kroner rescue package for the banks after the 2008 crisis promptly received abundant donations from the political arm of the finance sector.[25]

Above and beyond such eye-popping quid pro quos, the financial support of economic elites for political parties remains a problem for democracy in general, for providing the parties who represent the interests of wealthy patrons more cards to play than the parties who serve the wage earners and the less wealthy distorts the democratic process.

The economic elite also uses its wealth to finance both lobbying and longer-term efforts to influence public opinion. A right-wing think tank like CEPOS, financed primarily by the same elites that benefit from its work, exerts a decisive influence on public discourse. Another example is the recent debate over inheritance taxes on family-owned firms. In 2016, a number of Denmark's largest firms joined together to form the front group Growth through the Generations, which spent more than DKK 1 million to hire a professional PR firm to conduct a long and lavishly funded campaign to persuade the then-ruling government and its largest party to lower the amount of inheritance tax they paid on family-owned companies. The Løkke government promptly secured a tax rebate for them, reducing their inheritance tax to a mere 5 percent, while the remainder of the population continued to pay 15 percent.[26] This amounted to a savings of billions for these firms.[27]

If we consider the EU, the lobbying of economic elites is even more widespread. In the years after the financial crisis, when the EU threatened regulation of the banks, the European finance lobby retained up to seventeen hundred lobbyists to influence EU institutions, four times the number of employees in the EU's finance division.[28] The lobbying effort was effective, and plans for the thoroughgoing regulation of the finance sector were quickly dashed. The same systematic lobbying can be found in other sectors.

But the United States, where candidates even for lesser offices are deeply dependent on abundant donations to run campaigns, surely offers the most disturbing example of how wealth can be turned into political influence. And by far the majority of donations come from the wealthiest fraction of the population.

Capitalists also transform wealth into power through control of the media and of channels of communication. The best example is the Italian media tycoon and politician Silvio Berlusconi, who leveraged his control over a number of TV stations and media outlets to further his political and personal ambitions.

There are many less colorful but no less effective examples of economic elites purchasing media companies in order to forward their interests and fight back against the forces challenging the status quo. The former leader of the British Labour Party, Jeremy Corbyn, was subjected to a yearlong smear campaign by the privately owned media, not the least that of ultra-rich media baron Rupert Murdoch. Day after day Corbyn was depicted as extreme and irresponsible, groundlessly accused of having cooperated with the KGB and of supporting terrorism. A report from British researchers revealed pronounced media bias in coverage of his campaign against Boris Johnson, with many more negative stories on him than his opponent.[29]

In sum, concentrated wealth is converted into political influence through numerous channels, securing for wealthy elites a disproportionate impact on public opinion and political processes.

The Structural Power of Capitalists

Another, far more effective means by which economic elites exercise power over politics is rooted in the very core of the capitalist economy: their ownership of the means of production. Because the prosperity of every society depends on the production of goods and services, the social economy is wholly dependent on capitalists' continual maintenance and development of productive activities. And since corporations are owned and directed by small groups of capitalists, this dependency can be transformed into political influence, providing a powerful means of pressuring democratically elected representatives.

Capitalists can either individually or collectively put the brakes on production by reducing their investments, denying credit, or moving jobs or capital or operations abroad, all of which damage the national economy and the well-being of the public. Such measures quickly result in a fall in tax revenues, making it harder to pay for welfare and social programs, and a rise in unemployment and general impoverishment. These consequences in turn put pressure on governments, which must either try to appease the capitalists or be voted out in the next election.

This structural power has increased significantly in recent decades because of economic globalization, which has liberalized capital flows and on the whole made it easier for firms to move their production and/or headquarters to other countries, with all the attendant consequences for employment and tax collection in the countries they abandon. Democratically elected politicians thus increasingly find themselves competing against each other for the favor of the capitalist class.

The evolution of corporate tax codes reveals how structural power is deployed. In order to attract investment, states all over the world engage in tax competition, resulting in a rapid downward spiral. In just a few decades the corporate tax rate in OECD countries has tumbled from an average of 48 percent in 1985 to 23.5 as of 2019. In Denmark it has come down from 50 to 22 percent.[30]

Many other forms of taxation on capitalists have either been reduced or eliminated entirely. Whereas many developed countries levied taxes on large fortunes in the past, very few do so today. Governments have lowered inheritance taxes and progressive income tax rates in an effort to to win the favor of elites. A number of states go even further to attract capital, carving out tax shelters to lure investors. And it works. French economist Gabriel Zucman claims that USD 9.2 trillion, corresponding to 12 percent of global GDP, is currently housed in tax shelters of one sort or another.[31] Countries that consciously help wealthy individuals and corporations avoid taxes are thus roundly rewarded with investments and capital.

On the other hand, governments that step out of line by enacting new laws and regulations against the interests of economic elites are immediately punished. "Markets react negatively," so it is always said, when capital punishes states that challenge the servile deference to corporations and investors.

Corporations and wealthy investors pressure recalcitrant governments to adopt a politics that serves their interests in innumerable ways. Countries that elect progressive governments that attempt to roll back privatization or introduce new regulations are routinely disciplined through capital flight and capital strikes, as is understood all too well in Greece, Spain, and Argentina. When, for example, a majority of Spaniards elected a new socialist government in 2019 with the help of the leftist party Podemos, the Spanish stock index fell drastically, as capitalists, seeing their interests threatened, sold off their shares in Spanish firms.[32]

Capitalists barely make much of an attempt to conceal the efforts to compel democratically elected politicians to backtrack when they presume to intrude upon their interests. A galling example is a July 2019 editorial in the *Financial Times* that reveals just how normalized such a power relation has become. After criticizing Mexico's newly elected president, the leftist Andrés Manuel López Obrador, for raising taxes and for halting the privatization of the state-owned oil company Pemex, the author only reluctantly acknowledges the president's solid majority in congress and his strong support from citizens. But fortunately, according to the *Financial Times*, there is another means of controlling the president's exercise of power than the Mexican people: "It is not too late for him to change before financial markets . . . force change upon him."[33]

Countries that challenge the privileges and concessions enjoyed by capitalists thus suffer falling investments and outright capital flight, which can quickly lead to reduced employment and subsequent reduced tax revenues. At the same time, investors' punitive measures can also result in the so-called credit agencies, such as Moody's or Standard and Poor's, rapidly downgrading the rating of the impacted country. Borrowing from abroad, whether to make new investments at home or to fill in the holes left by vanishing foreign investment and falling employment, in turn becomes more expensive.

The financial crisis of 2008 made this asymmetrical power relation between democratic states and the capitalists of the economic elite clearer than ever. As is well known today, the crisis was caused by a steadily more speculative and unscrupulous financial sector that had over several years artificially inflated the value of certain securities, especially those in the housing sector. Inevitably the bubble burst, the bankers losing confidence in one another so that lending between them ground to a halt. This meant that the big banks could no longer meet their debt obligations, in many cases facing insolvency and collapse. This was certainly the case with Denmark's largest financial concern, Danske Bank.

But the reach of the big banks was so large and their significance for the economy so comprehensive that in reality it was not possible to make them pay the price for their irresponsibility. Despite immense popular dissatisfaction, taxpayers across the world had to dig into their pockets to send trillions in rescue packages and state guarantees to save the banks from ruin.

The banks were saved, and in many cases their directors were rewarded with bonuses and salary increases. All over the world, the bill was sent to citizenries in the form of reforms that cut into unemployment benefits and minimum wage rates or raised the retirement age. Deep cuts hollowed out the various European welfare states during these years, and in order to pay for the rescue packages, a new wave of privatization of public enterprises and infrastructure was carried out.

The financial crisis revealed that the idea that competition in the free market, on the model of Darwinian natural selection, ensures that the most capable and the most innovative survive, while the weakest go to ruin, is a fairy tale. When firms are large and powerful enough, the state stands at the ready to rescue them, since the consequences of their collapse cannot be ignored. This implicit state guarantee leads to still risker behavior, as we have witnessed in the years since, during which new bubbles in real estate and financial activities that threaten to unleash the next crisis have formed.

The enormous structural power that concentrated ownership of firms and banks affords the economic elite, as we have seen, seriously constrains the freedom of maneuver of democratically elected governments. Governments that run afoul of elite interests are forced to accommodate it or are swept away, without so much as a shot fired. This has gradually resulted, especially in recent decades, in the gradual transfer of power from democratically elected governments to unelected economic elites. Democratic power has thus been replaced with oligarchic power.

Oligarchic Power vs. Democratic Power

In his classic work on the forms of statehood, Aristotle describes how oligarchies are distinguished from democracies: "Wherever men rule by reason of their wealth, whether they be few or many, that is an oligarchy, and where the poor rule, that is a democracy. But as a fact the rich are few and the poor many; for few are well-to-do, whereas freedom is enjoyed by all, and wealth and freedom are the grounds on which the oligarchical and democratical parties respectively claim power in the state."[34]

The basis of their power in wealth rather than a democratic mandate reveals how economic elites, who constitute a minority, wield power over the broad majority. It is not their numbers but the vast fortunes at their disposal. But since the foundational principle of democracy is that power rests in the people, the rise of oligarchic power increasingly undermines it. As the American scholar Jeffrey Winters notes, "Formal juridical equality is essential to human freedom. But full political equality, even in the most liberal democracy, is impossible as long as concentrated wealth places grossly unequal political influence in the hands of a few citizens."[35]

My contention is not that we live under an oligarchy but that there are two competing power sources in our society: a democratic power based on a majority mandate and an oligarchic power anchored by the wealth of a narrow elite.

The problem is that the power of the oligarchy is self-reinforcing. Economic elites use the wealth that capitalist ownership accrues to them to exert pressure on political authorities and manipulate the political process in order to secure lower taxes or lower labor costs, which further permits them to appropriate an even larger proportion of national wealth that they then employ to acquire even more political influence. And so it continues . . .

The OECD, which can hardly be thought of as a left-wing organization, concludes in a 2017 report that "a key aspect of wealth accumulation is that it operates in a self-reinforcing way." "Wealth begets wealth," and furthermore, "wealth begets power, which may ultimately beget more wealth."[36]

It is precisely this vicious oligarchic circle that explains the apparent paradox with which I began this section, that despite rising national wealth and the desire of the majority for more equality, for a stronger welfare state and for greater security we have moved in the opposite direction, having witnessed the erosion of social rights and the decline of living standards. That this continues no matter who is in charge is due to the fact that oligarchic power has increasingly overwhelmed democratic power.

The Crisis of Political Legitimacy

In 2020, the United States found itself engulfed in demonstrations against police violence toward Black and poor communities, while in 2019, millions took to the streets in Chile, Lebanon, Ecuador, and Iraq, and in 2018, Paris erupted in flames when the Yellow Vests gathered tens of thousands to protest the French government. This new wave of protest unfolded only a few years after young Spaniards, inspired by the Arab Spring, occupied plazas and squares across the entire country, demanding democratic and social reforms. On the other side of the Atlantic, in the fall of 2011, tens of thousands of Occupy Wall Street protestors demanded a revolt against the power and the greed of finance capital.

These protests are only the visible expression of the immense turmoil that has challenged political normalcy in recent years. Older parties that had dominated the political landscape for a century have vanished or are in the process of vanishing, and new parties now define it. The election of Trump in the United States and the Brexit referendum in Britain are just two of the more noteworthy examples of this turmoil.

The causes of the recent turmoil are of course multifaceted and vary locally. But there is no doubt that the loss of legitimacy among older political parties is related to the changing power relations between democratically elected representatives and economic elites. Between democratic and oligarchic power.

The pressure to attract investments forces governments all over the world, regardless of political leanings, to implement policies favorable to the economic elite at the expense of the majority of wage earners and the self-employed. That the wealth of society as a whole steadily increases while the security and well-being of the individual worker steadily declines provides the ordinary citizen with the impression that little changes when a new government comes to power, since the new regime is just as beholden to oligarchic power as the old. This contributes to the rising suspicion that the political system cannot at all protect the interests of the majority and in the worst cases tends to undermine faith in democracy itself.

A 2018 Eurobarometer poll revealed that 59 percent of EU citizens are suspicious of their governments and that nearly 77 percent harbor suspicions of political parties. In the United States, a similar poll conducted by the Pew Research Center in March 2019 showed that only 17 percent of the surveyed expressed trust in the government, the lowest it had been in fifty years. A 2019 global poll from the German institute Dalia Research, which surveyed 177,000 citizens in fifty-four countries, demonstrated that 45 percent of those who live in democracies do not believe that their countries are actually democratic. And still more concerning, the number of citizens who consider it "critical" that they live in a democratically governed country has fallen among successive generations. A 2016 article published in the *Journal of Democracy* reported that in the United States, 72 percent of those born in the 1930s say that democratic government is critical, while for those born in the 1980s, the figure is 30 percent.[37]

The resolute actions taken by some governments during the COVID crisis has increased trust in the political system in those countries. But my sense is that this constitutes a short-lived deviation from the unfortunate trajectory of recent decades.

The democratic form of government cannot legitimate itself solely by recourse to the claim that democracy is a lovely idea. The decisive factor in the adoption of democracy in various countries over the past century and a half has been the ability to deliver results in the form of improved life conditions for the majority, since elected politicians generally seek to make their constituents happy and content. But the rising power of oligarchy challenges this form of legitimation, because politicians, pressured by the structural power of capital, are no longer capable of providing for the betterment of the majority; indeed, more often than not they tend to reduce the welfare and the security of the public.

Already in 2007, the former head of the U.S. central bank Alan Greenspan described the impotency of the democratic system: "Thanks to globalization, policy decisions in the United States have been largely replaced by global market forces. National security aside, it hardly makes any difference who will be the next president. The world is governed by market forces."[38]

One segment of the public reacts to this erosion of democratic power with apathy, giving up on democratic participation and attending only to their own private lives. Others react with anger and frustration, which in some cases results in new forms of popular protest. But in many places it has led to mistrust of democracy and an embrace of authoritarian political parties and leaders, who attempt to direct the anger over rising insecurity toward minorities such as Jews, Muslims, immigrants, and homosexuals or against their political opponents, whom they describe as elites or as traitors. In other words, the concentration of wealth and ownership in the capitalist economy increasingly threatens to undermine support for constitutional rule and even democracy itself.

The growing power of oligarchy, however, is not the only threat we face from the capitalist economy, for my children's generation not only confronts a future of diminished security and well-being but also stands at the edge of a veritable abyss: the threat of widespread, destructive climate change and the reduction of biodiversity. Since these changes are irreversible, they are without a doubt the steepest challenges we face. The welfare society can be rebuilt. Inequality can be rolled back. Social security can be reestablished. But if first we pass the climactic tipping point or bring about a widespread extinction event, then we will have done irreparable damage to our planet and thus decisively compromised the conditions of life for the generations that come after us.

Capitalism and the Climate Threat

Around Christmas 1988, at the age of thirteen, I attended a socialist youth gathering in a dimly lit classroom, where I listened to a presentation that made a powerful impression on me. The theme was something called the greenhouse effect, and the speaker described in vivid detail the destructive consequences that would follow if we continued to emit greenhouse gasses from our factories, farms, and vehicles.

For more than three decades we have thus been fully aware that we face a potentially devastating threat to life on Earth. Yet in the intervening years CO_2 levels have continued to increase, despite ever louder and more persistent warnings from scientific researchers that we are close to a point of no return.

And we have further been aware of what needs to be done, that it is necessary to make fundamental changes to all sectors of economy and society: a rapid transition from fossil fuels to renewable energy in our homes, industries, and transportation system; a transformation of agriculture away from meat production; and the restoration of much of our farmland to carbon absorbing forests. Just as is the case with rising economic inequality and declining social security, we here confront a problem we know we can resolve and that the great majority have a strong interest in resolving, and yet we have failed to change course. And like our inaction on the economy, the explanation for our failure to address the climate and biodiversity is to a large extent found in certain inherent characteristics of the capitalist system. Because the concentration of ownership provides a small elite with enormous power over the investments our society makes, decisions regarding whether we invest in coal and oil or in wind and hydroelectric power, in electric vehicles or gas guzzlers, in meat production or plant-based alternatives are made by an economic elite with no democratic mandate and who therefore cannot be democratically held to account.

These decisions have immense significance for all of us, but the majority has no democratic influence over them. It is a general problem for democratic governance when critical decisions are turned over to people for whom no one has voted. But the problem is obviously more serious when these decisions can impact the future of the planet and of humanity.

From a purely moral point of view it is obvious that these kinds of decisions should be made democratically and that those who make the decisions should be the ones who face the consequences. And even though democratic decision-making in and of itself is not enough to guarantee responsible outcomes, experience shows that a democratic majority makes more responsible and sustainable investment choices than capitalist elites. It is thus hardly an accident that it was the consumer-owned and democratically managed grocery Coop that initiated the market for organic foodstuffs that today constitutes an immense export success. Or that the member-owned pension funds that directly elect their leaders have been the first to divest from fossil energy, while private, non-democratic investors have continued to put their money into them.[39]

Capital Accumulation vs. Climate

It is not only concentration of ownership that pits the capitalist economy against climate action, for the very mechanism that drives decision-making under capitalism, capital accumulation, also serves to obstruct the implementation of necessary policies.

Accumulation of capital is itself the motor of the capitalist production mode. The motive for investment is the expectation of realizing a profit, a surplus. When corporations invest in new activities or when financial investors invest in corporations, they do so with an eye to securing the greatest possible surplus. This is not because they are particularly evil or greedy (although greed on the personal level can surely play a role) but because it is a condition of their survival. Large investor-owned firms are scrutinized daily for their capacity to generate surplus. If a company does not deliver the same surplus as its competitors, then investors pull out, share values fall, and, in the end, the firm goes under. As Gar Alperovitz, author and founder of the think tank Democracy Collaborative, puts it, "If a corporate executive does not show steadily increasing quarterly earnings, the grim quarterly-returns reaper will cut her down sooner or later."[40]

This "grow or die" logic can hardly be regulated away. It is at the very core of the capitalist mode of production, the characteristic that defenders of capitalism emphasize, since the pressure to amass the greatest possible surplus inevitably channels investment toward the most capable and most imaginative, who then produce new goods and services, and create new jobs and new wealth, which benefits society as a whole.

This is a much-debated claim, even among speculative investors themselves. But even if one believes that the dynamic of capital accumulation, purely economically speaking, will naturally lead to the largest returns, another problem remains—a blindness toward the ancillary consequences, or negative externalities, as economists call them. When the focus is single-mindedly on profits, the many negative effects on society that do not impact the earnings of the individual firm or its investors are given short shrift. This blindness to any perspective other than profit maximization constitutes a serious impediment to our ability to counteract climate change and the extinction of species. Since the short-term earnings of the individual firm are not impacted by climate change or declining biodiversity, investment decisions are generally made with little regard for such concerns.

Regulations such as levying carbon tax to motivate companies to reduce their CO_2 emissions can affect investment to a certain extent, at least according to the assumptions of economics textbooks. But even if such regulations are effective, they are difficult to implement, since the oligarchic power of capital is continually employed to block or to water them down. Between 2000 and 2016, American firms alone spent USD 2 billion on lobbying campaigns to prevent American politicians from regulating the fossil fuel sector, and in the EU oil companies spend billions on lobbying and for years have succeeded in blocking the adoption of an effective carbon quota system.[41] And here at home we also felt the impact of capital on the negotiations over the Danish climate goals, as heavy industry did everything it could to prevent the implementation of an ambitious plan.

Making demands or levying new taxes and penalties that could assure climate-friendly conduct becomes ever more difficult when the space for political maneuver is hollowed out by oligarchic power. As long as critical investment decisions are left to the few and as long as economic elites command the most influence over society, they will break the back of regulations and all efforts to institute the massive transformation of investments that is necessary if we are to live up to the Paris Agreement's goals of reducing emissions and preventing climate catastrophe.

Without Growth, No Accumulation of Capital

But the conflict between the logic of capital accumulation and environmental sustainability runs still deeper. This is because the precondition for capital accumulation is continuous economic growth. Without growth it is not possible for capitalists to receive returns on their investments they currently enjoy.

All previous experience demonstrates a close relationship between economic growth on the one side and the use of resources and the rate of carbon emissions on the other.[42] Thus up to now it has not been possible to maintain historical rates of growth without increasing the consumption of resources and the amount of emissions. A review of more than six hundred studies of the possibility of decoupling carbon emissions from growth undertaken by the European Environmental Bureau concludes as much: "Overall, the reviewed literature converges in saying that there has never been a global pattern of absolute decoupling of CO_2 from economic growth." The report also notes that the literature shows that resource consumption in general cannot be decoupled from economic growth: "Not only is there no empirical evidence supporting the existence of a decoupling of economic growth from environmental pressures on anywhere near the scale needed to deal with environmental breakdown, but also, and perhaps more importantly, such decoupling appears unlikely to happen in the future."[43] Economic growth results in increased consumption, and the production that satisfies the desire for increased consumption entails increased carbon emissions and resource use.[44]

It is important to understand that when economists speak of economic growth, they mean growth that is exponential, not just linear, which is to say that growth in dollars and cents is higher year after year. Assuming a GDP growth rate of 3 percent per annum, national production will have tripled by 2050, increased tenfold by 2100, and 240 times over by 2200.[45] This amounts to a tripling of consumption in each generation, and thus it goes without saying that such growth cannot be reconciled with our desire to protect our natural world and to prevent catastrophic global warming. It is simply not possible to sustain eternal exponential growth given the limitations of our planet's resources. And as long as we continue to overproduce, the hunt for resources and the push for increased production will continue to inflict irreparable harm on the climate and on biodiversity. A quote attributed to the heterodox economist Kenneth Boulding hit the nail on the head more than fifty years ago when he remarked that "anyone who believes that exponential growth can go on forever in a finite world is either a madman or an economist."[46]

Much indicates that whether by our own free choice to protect our habitat or simply because sooner or later we will have exhausted all resources, we must begin the transition to what American economist Herman Daly terms the steady-state economy. Such an "equilibrium economy" would maintain present levels of prosperity and leave open the possibility of limited, *linear* growth, but the wealthy part of the world would no longer be able to expect continued *exponential* growth.[47]

But rejecting exponential growth directly conflicts with the very motor of the capitalist mode of production, that is, with capital accumulation. Without general growth in the wealth of society, investors cannot expect future returns on their investments equivalent to those of today. A few especially fortunate or able investors may turn a profit, but if the overall economy is not growing exponentially then the logic of investment, based on the expectation of future growth, will cease to function. Putting a stop to exponential growth would completely overturn the way our economy works and necessitate the development of new mechanisms to ensure that capital and investment be directed wherever they would produce the greatest good for society.

A steady-state economy would certainly require investment. Human beings would not stop coming up with good ideas. Businesses would not cease to be innovative. Capital would be needed for investment in new technologies, new discoveries, and new products. But in the absence of economic growth it would no longer be assumed that the expectation of return on private investment would ensure that capital flows are directed where they are needed.[48]

In other words, democratizing investment decisions is not only desirable from the perspective of democracy. It could well become an absolute necessity, since if we are to avoid climactic destruction, we must plan for an economic future that would in fact make it impossible to continue to rely on capital accumulation as the central mechanism for allocating capital and investment.

The Solution Is Democratic and Socialist

In this chapter I have tried to show how the capitalist economic model that dominates our economy has obstructed the search for answers to the many crises we now confront. Regardless of whether we speak of escalating economic inequality, rising suspicion of liberal democracy, or the threat of destructive climate change, we can largely trace our problems back to certain inherent tendencies of this model.

The first is the tendency toward an ever more unequal distribution of wealth that provides economic elites with oligarchic power and influence over political development. The second is that critical decisions impacting the whole of society tend to be made according to short-sighted and narrow calculations of profit maximization, regardless of the consequences for the climate and biodiversity.

To a certain extent, these tendencies can be counteracted and balanced through political regulation. The implementation of a progressive tax system and a tax on capital gains, inheritance, and wealth may help curb the inequality capitalism generates, and further taxes or sensible regulations might influence the investment decisions of capitalists. These are doubtlessly important steps we must wholly embrace.

And yet as recent decades have demonstrated, it has become more and more difficult to mitigate the negative effects of capitalist ownership. Both the employment of the tax system and the regulation of climate-impacting industries are complicated by the international mobility of capital and thus the ability to play individual states against one another in the competition for investment. This oligarchic power is, as I have noted, self-reinforcing. Elites use their wealth to exert political influence to secure for themselves the best possible conditions for further increasing their wealth, which they then once again use to purchase more influence. In this way oligarchic power increases at the expense of democratic power.

It is against this background that we must understand the political and economic developments of recent decades, and not the least the "democratic paradox" according to which decisions are made against the interests of the majority despite the fact that democratic rule should ensure the opposite. As long as we have an economy in which ownership and power are so tightly concentrated, the decision-making power of democratic governments will gradually be hollowed out, the regulation of capitalist activity will be constantly undermined, and social progress will be forestalled.

In 1935, Hungarian economist and social scientist Karl Polanyi identified the contradiction between democratic rule and capitalism, concluding that "basically, there are two solutions": either "the extension of the democratic principle from politics to economics, or the abolition of the democratic 'political sphere' altogether."[49]

And he was right. There is a fundamental contradiction between the principal of democratic government and the concentration of economic and political power within a narrow elite. If democratic governance is to recover real power, if the majority is once again to enjoy the benefits of rising prosperity, and if we are to counteract global warming, then we must focus on the fundamental problem of the capitalist mode of production that dominates our economy: the concentration of capital ownership and the distortion of power and democracy that follows from it.

If we are to break the oligarchic power of the economic elite and establish the principle of the sovereignty and equality of the people, we must find ways to distribute ownership and thereby economic power outward to the majority. It is only by democratizing and diffusing ownership that democratic power can confront oligarchic power, thus ensuring that democratically elected politicians can govern in the interests of the broad majority.

A more democratic and distributed form of ownership would not only return power to democratic governance but would also ensure that we as citizens would have much more of a voice than we have today, both more narrowly with respect to our own lives and more broadly to the development of society. Workers who own the firm at which they work are subject to much less insecurity and arbitrariness. The threat of our jobs being sent to low-wage countries would be a thing of the past, for why would we send our own jobs overseas? Consumers who own their energy producer can democratically act to push the rapid adoption of green technologies and further avoid massive payouts to investors, thereby lowering their rates. And when capital is democratized we can make collective investment decisions that reflect a broad concern for society, nature, and the environment rather than allowing the desire for the maximization of profit in the short term to dictate our choices.

A hundred and seventy-five years ago we Danes took the first steps away from absolute monarchy and toward democracy in the political sphere. Gradually we wrested power away from a king without democratic legitimacy or basis in the new popularly elected institutions through which the people via free (and by now) equal elections could hold the powerful to account and thereby ensure that political decisions would reflect the interests of the majority. It is about time that we complete the journey toward popular democracy by rising up against the oligarchic power of the small economic elite that today largely controls the means of production.

But how do we make such a change? And what can we learn from the experiences of past socialist movements and parties that have confronted capitalism and attempted to create a more just and democratic economy? This is the subject of the next chapter.

2

Change
Reformed Capitalism, Revolution, or Erosion

It is March 5, 1872, and Blegdams Road is abuzz with activity, as workers, street kids, and craftsmen make their way to a demonstration being held at Sankt Hans Square in the Copenhagen suburb Nørrebro. Between them and the square stand several policemen with truncheons drawn. As the demonstrators shout and sing, surging forward and backward, galloping horse hooves are suddenly heard from the bridge as a squadron of hussars comes riding at speed. Blows from truncheons and the flat sides of sabers rain down on the demonstrators as they are driven toward Nørre Fælled, while rocks and horse droppings fly in the other direction. After several hours of struggle, the demonstrators, by now scattered, are forced to flee. This confrontation, known as Battle of the Fælled, was the first large working-class uprising in Denmark. But it was hardly the last.

Capitalism has always been met with resistance, from the moment workers in the darkened factories first met each other other's gazes, recognizing that they not only shared a common interest but also possessed the strength to change their situation, if only they would stand together and have each other's backs. This is what led to the formation of both trade unions and socialist parties, instigated a movement to oppose social injustice, terrible working conditions, and the compulsion of working life, and inspired the dream of a new organization of society that would make it possible for human beings to live in freedom and security and in which poverty and inequality would be a thing of the past.

Over time, and especially after the First World War, two distinct strategies emerged within the socialist movement. On one side was the social democratic or reformist wing whose goal was to redistribute wealth and tame the worst aspects of capitalism through state regulation. On the other was the revolutionary wing that sought to replace capitalism with an entirely new socialist society through a radical overthrow of the system. Both strategies have, for better and for worse, played decisive roles over the past century, but today much suggests that they have run their course. The capitalist system has recently faced its most serious crises in decades, and yet the left has been unable to mobilize popular dissatisfaction toward socialism.[1]

On the contrary, the old social democratic parties of Europe lie in ruin, and here in Denmark they remain a shadow of their former strength, if we set aside the cold comfort of the popularity of their handling of the COVID pandemic. And the revolutionary left has been unable to turn rising dissatisfaction with capitalism against its relentless advance, let alone win support for a more thoroughgoing break with it.

In this chapter, I explore why both wings of the socialist movement have stalled and consider whether there is a way forward that transcends the old binary distinction between reform and revolution.

Social Democracy: You Keep the Means of Production, We Divide the Wealth

The social democratic or reformist wing of the socialist movement was dominant throughout the twentieth century in Western Europe. The most important theorist of the original movement was the German Eduard Bernstein, who renounced the idea of a revolutionary road to socialism at the turn of the last century. Bernstein also rejected the Marxist contention that the internal dynamics of capitalism itself would result in either radical rupture or in steadily worsening conditions among the working class and argued that revolution was neither necessary nor desirable. He thus became the spokesperson for the idea that socialists could gradually build support for socialism if they could secure governing power in the newly democratic states and that a step-by-step institution of reforms would eliminate capitalist exploitation.[2]

Reformism was thus originally a strategy for the evolutionary development of a socialist society that retained the goal of breaking with the market economy and the property rights of private firms but would achieve this in stages through the democratic parliamentary process. The manifestos of social democratic parties continued to call for the establishment of a socialist society well into the twentieth century. The democratization of the economy remained a stated goal in the Socialist International's statement of principles, the Frankfurt Declaration, until 1989, and it was not until 1992 that economic democracy (ØD) and collective ownership of the means of production were removed from the Danish social democratic party's platform.

But even if the goal of systemic economic change was maintained in theory, strategy in praxis had long since shifted. As social democratic parties came to power across Western Europe in the interwar and postwar periods, not least here in the Nordic region, plans for the substantial socialist transformation of society were gradually replaced by a strategy of regulating markets through the use of governing power, setting limits on the power of capitalist firms, and distributing wealth more broadly through progressive taxation. And all of this was to be achieved, importantly, without implementing fundamental changes in property relations.

As social democratic finance minister Per Hækkerup suggested, it wasn't necessary to kill the goose that lays the golden egg, that is, to challenge the ownership of the means of production, when it was possible to assure that the wealth generated by capitalist firms was distributed across a broad spectrum of the population through political power.

The idea that capitalists could still own the means of production but that social democrats would distribute the surplus became the underlying basis for the social democratic class compromise, which over the decades came to define postwar social democratic parties.

The prominent Swedish social democratic economist Gunnar Adler-Karlsson summarized the social democratic strategy at the end of the 1960s:

> Swedish socialists fully recognize that there are contradictions in society and especially so with respect to what in socialist language is termed the conflict between the capitalist and working classes. . . . But we also know that this conflict is not all encompassing. On the contrary, we are convinced that market society involves a measure of harmony. This is evident in the fact that all members of society have a common interest in economic growth. . . . When the capitalist acquires larger surpluses he is more willing to share with his employees, and when workers see that their standard of living is steadily

> rising they are more willing to continue peacefully cooperating with existing social conditions. . . . All parties in this economic process come to the understanding that the most important economic task is to increase the size of the pie, so that everyone can satisfy themselves with a larger bite. . . . It could be said that we have preserved the *goals* of socialism but have chosen other means for their realization than the socialization of production.[3]

Functional Socialism

This new social democratic strategy that for all practical purposes abandoned the goal of socializing ownership of the means of production was based more on direct experience than theoretical considerations. While the theoretical literature of the revolutionary Marxist left is abundant, more theoretically oriented presentations of the social democratic reformist strategy are surprisingly few and far between.[4]

Of these, Adler-Karlsson offers one of the best theoretical treatments of the social democratic reformist strategy in his concept of functional socialism. Its core contention is that ownership is not an absolute concept, that we can intervene in and reform the right to private property without fundamentally altering the formal nature of property rights. As an example, he points to the housing reforms instituted by social democratic governments in the twentieth century. Private landlords, at least in the formal sense, did own the properties they rented out, but rent was regulated by law and renters were protected against eviction. Planning and preservation laws determined whether a property could be torn down and if so, what could be built in its stead. And the profits of rental income and the sale of properties were taxed. Functional socialist reforms thus did not change the formal terms of ownership, but as Adler-Karlsson notes, they "have indirectly socialized a number of the functions of property ownership that the owner would have controlled had there been no restrictions." Sweden has therefore not, he continues, "instituted a total socialization of private property, but instead sought a selective socialization of certain aspects of the most significant functions within the totality of functions within what we call property rights," making it harder for "the owners of the means of production to employ their resources in an antisocial manner."[5]

From the interwar period and especially in the three decades following the Second World War, a long series of such functional socialist reforms were instituted in the welfare states of Western Europe. This occurred both by statute as well as, especially in the Nordic countries, through collective agreements between employers and workers. Laws securing paid vacation, regulating the workday, workplace conditions, and termination limited the power of employees to dispose of their labor forces as they saw fit, and new laws and collective agreements determined wage scales. Industrial policy and planning set the direction for overall economic and industrial development and environmental regulations sought to mitigate the negative impact of firms on their surroundings. The financial sector was subject to strict regulations, such as lending caps and the prohibition on financial institutions engaging in a broad range of activities, and capital movement across borders was strictly controlled. Macroeconomic policy was employed to achieve full employment through state intervention, and strongly progressive taxation distributed wealth and security broadly.

Three Decades of Success

The reformist, social democratic wing of the left came to dominate the labor movement in most Western European countries. And there was a good reason for this: the functional socialist strategy worked.

In the decades after the Second World War, social democratic governments managed to make substantial and lasting improvements in the lives of working people. Labor relations were improved, wages rose, and working families were able to move out of tenements and enjoy the light and clean air of sanitary living conditions. Increasing wages and progressive taxation led to a considerable decrease in inequality. For twenty to thirty years, unemployment, the bane of capitalism, was held at bay.

At the same time, social democratic coalitions built up a welfare state that secured free and equal access to health care and education and a social safety net that provided financial security in sickness and old age. The welfare society not only made workers freer, more secure, and more self-assured but also gave them much more bargaining power when they negotiated with employers over wages and working conditions. These changes strengthened democratic power and weakened oligarchic power.

Naturally enough, the spires of the welfare society did not reach into the heavens. A low-wage sector persisted, and large income and wealth inequalities remained. Yet on the whole the reformist strategy in the decades after the Second World War seemed like it could deliver permanently improved living conditions to ordinary working people, fight back against the worst excesses of capitalism, and reduce social insecurity. The capitalist class was compelled to accept the class compromise that limited their power to make use of their property rights. The existence of a communist bloc and the constant competition from the more radical sections of the labor movement constituted a threat that pushed capitalists to accept reforms in order to avoid something worse for them. At the same time, historically high growth rates throughout the 1950s and 1960s made it possible to raise wages and to fund a growing public sector while maintaining the profitability of capitalist enterprises. In other words, the success of reformist social democracy was based on certain unique historical, political, and economic conditions.

Elites Strike Back

Yet in the early 1970s the ideology of steady progress based on the strict regulation of capitalism began to crack up when the capitalist economy entered a profound international crisis. Unemployment and inflation exploded, while debt and budget deficits deepened. And the typical Keynesian remedy of debt-financed public investment was unable to resolve the crisis. While the dramatic increase in oil prices implemented by the OPEC countries no doubt played a large part in instigating the crisis, it was perhaps also a result of the success of the reformist strategy itself. The many social reforms and the strength and assertiveness of the working class had begun to cut into the profits of capital, and this along with the oil crisis dampened the enthusiasm of capitalists to invest, which resulted in falling growth and rising unemployment.

Regardless of causes, the crisis presented elites with the opportunity to strike back and to change the balance of power that undergirded the success of social democracy. With Margaret Thatcher and Ronald Reagan in the lead, capital in Western Europe and the United States launched the political and economic counteroffensive that has since become known as neoliberalism. One by one the reforms of functional socialism were rolled back and the limits on the power of capital were eliminated. The privatization of public companies, the deregulation of the financial sector, and the lowering of taxes on the wealthiest led to the spike in inequality we have all witnessed whereby wage workers in large parts of the West are denied their share of the general prosperity. With the collapse of the Soviet Union and the Eastern bloc in the late 1980s and early 1990s, neoliberal capitalism emerged triumphant and free of challengers, engendering a widespread sense that history had reached its conclusion, that there were no longer alternatives to the capitalist market economy. In the decades following and up through today, the neoliberal ascendancy has resulted in the strengthening of oligarchic power at the expense of the democratic.

Social Democrats Surrender

The counteroffensive from economic elites and the end of functional socialism are critical to understanding what came after. The success of social democracy was built upon class compromise, on the acceptance by economic elites that the general prosperity would be redistributed and on the understanding that their ownership of the means of production would be conditioned by comprehensive democratic control over their activities. But with the rise of neoliberalism in the late 1970s the capitalist class annulled this compromise. When the opportunity to free themselves from regulation and redistribution emerged, economic elites struck back.

Yet social democrats have evidently found it difficult to understand or acknowledge that the class compromise the capitalists agreed to has been annulled by neoliberalism. Their failure to recognize this new reality has resulted in an asymmetric marriage in which social democratic governments across Europe, like a submissive spouse, accommodate an ever more brutal and arbitrary economic elite. When they are told to jump, they ask how high, permitting the raising of the retirement age, reductions in the social safety net, lowered corporate taxes, and the leveling of progressive tax rates. And they have resigned themselves to rising inequality and to markedly increased social insecurity among wage workers.

This accommodationist strategy has gone by many names. In the UK, Tony Blair called it "the third way." His government continued the policies of welfare retrenchment, deregulation, and marketization begun by his predecessors. In Germany the social democrat Gerhard Schröder oversaw the so-called Hartz reforms, which created a new class, more than one million strong, known as the "working poor," that is, those who work one or more jobs but remain in poverty because of low wages. And here in Denmark social democrats Helle Thorning-Schmidt and Bjarne Corydon have embraced the idea of the "competition state," leading them to introduce a series of reforms that have undermined the social security of working people and redistributed wealth upward.

Regardless of what they call themselves or where they come from, modern social democrats are all in agreement that they must please economic elites in order to attract investment and create jobs because the capitalist economic model is the only possible model and that this is all entirely natural.

This surrender has played a key role in the recent collapse of European social democracy that has reduced social democratic parties in France, Greece, and the Netherlands to a shadow of their former selves. Disillusion with the fact that the old worker's parties can no longer ensure progress and security has driven large numbers of working-class voters to parties of the right or to political apathy. The wave of immigrants into Western Europe in the new millennium has doubtless also been a factor here. And yet all the attention that has been directed toward immigration is also related to the depoliticizing of economic policy. In his book about the Norwegian anti-immigrant Progress Party, *The Progress Party Code*, Magnus Marsdal asserts that when voters do not see any difference between the economic policies of the center right and center left, they tend to focus on other issues, like immigration, which then becomes the difference that makes the difference.[6]

Social Democrats Try Again

In the years since the financial crisis of 2008, a number of social democratic parties have broken with precedent and begun to critique the consequences of neoliberal capitalism.

Here in Denmark, Mette Frederiksen, who became the social democratic party leader in 2015, is far more critical of neoliberalism in both interviews and in print than her predecessors. In a 2018 article for the *Financial Times*, she acknowledged that social democratic parties bear responsibility for their own decline and for the growth of right-wing populist parties: "People feel abandoned by the traditional parties of labour, believing them to have failed in a period of prolonged economic crisis and increased pressures on workers' rights. The Social Democratic party in Denmark, like its counterparts elsewhere on the continent, has suffered a loss of popular trust."[7] And in an interview in the newspaper *Information*, she called for a renewal of the social contract: "The principal cause of the present political and economic upheaval is a weakening of the social contract between capitalism and justice. . . . The great political and economic struggle of the 21st century is to strengthen this contract; in reality, we must save capitalism from its own worst impulses—indeed, perhaps even from destroying itself."[8]

In his book *Sick Capitalism*, the young social democrat theorist Peter Hummelgaard eviscerates the neoliberal-fueled rise of finance that threw the world into crisis, increased inequality, and hollowed out the social contract, and similar sentiments have been echoed by social democrats in a number of other European countries.[9] A new generation has thus rediscovered a more critical attitude than that of the old third-way social democrats, setting itself the tasks of healing an ailing capitalism and renewing the social contract that undergirded the golden decades of the postwar era.

Forget About the Concentration of Ownership

That a new generation of social democrats has become more conscious of and more critical toward the many negative consequences of the capitalist economy is a very positive sign. And yet it is noteworthy that when they offer concrete proposals for the restoration of social justice, they wholly avoid the question of the concentration of ownership and the oligarchic power that naturally results from it.

Hummelgaard does acknowledge that economic injustice is tied to "the old questions of property rights, exploitation and distribution" and thus also to that of "who owns the means of production."[10] He further concedes that "wealth is power and that extreme concentration of wealth is synonymous with extreme concentration of power."[11] But in the concluding chapter of his book, in which he proposes a series of reforms to restore the balance, we search in vain for measures that would address either the concentration of power or of the ownership of the means of production. The same lack is evident from the first years of Frederiksen's premiership. Nothing suggests that the new generation of social democrats has a strategy for democratizing the economy that might alter the balance between oligarchic and democratic power. In the aforementioned interview, Frederiksen in fact specifically dismisses any effort toward more collective ownership, which she considers a "drawing board project."[12]

This lack of interest in confronting oligarchic power is evident in the 2017 Danish Social Democratic manifesto, the first in the history of the party to blot out any vision for broadening ownership and economic power. This is remarkable in an era when capitalist monopolies dominate a greater and greater proportion of finance, technology, and the broader economy at large. And it is also disturbing insofar as it indicates a lack of understanding of how the skewed distribution of property and power relations prevents the realization of its declared desire for a socially just economy, or at least one that would prove durable and lasting.

Can Capitalism Be Saved?

The strategy of the social democrats, which presumes that capitalism can be healed or saved from itself, is grounded in a belief that contemporary neoliberal capitalism is an anomaly, that the normal state of capitalism is the regulated capitalism of the golden age of the 1950s and 1960s. The goal appears to be to turn back to the original class compromise and to revive the social democratic and functional socialist model that found such great success in the postwar era. Mette Frederiksen has specifically pointed to evidence of this in Nordic history, arguing that capitalism can be regulated in order to work to the advantage of all.[13] Hummelgaard makes this explicit: "History has shown that a powerful contract between capital and labor can in fact rein in the capitalist economy."[14]

But there are good reasons to believe that neoliberal capitalism is the norm and that the brief period of the class compromise was the historical exception, not least because the social democratic class compromise was contingent on the specific historical conditions, as previously suggested.

First, the capitalist class feared the prospect of more thoroughgoing reforms. The existence of a socialist bloc and of a strong working class with a radical wing pressing for radical change served a disciplinary function on economic elites. A new study by the Brazilian economists André Albuquerque Sant Anna and Leonardo Weller thus demonstrates a direct link between social democratic reforms and the existence of a communist threat: "the more national elites were under the threat of communist revolution, the more the state introduced policies that reduced top income shares."[15]

Second, the class compromise was built upon a unique economic epoch, characterized by historically high growth rates and productivity gains. This meant that it was possible to improve the lives of working-class people without seriously impacting the profits of capital. The pie grew rapidly, and everyone could claim a big slice, to employ Adler-Karlsson's language. But economic growth has never returned to such high rates. With the climate crisis and the depletion of the earth's resources, we must as noted look forward to a future with much lower or no economic growth at all.

Because of these reasons, I am much thus less optimistic than Frederiksen and Hummelgaard that the old class compromise can be reinstated. But even if it were possible to use political means to restore the pre-neoliberal balance of power, experience shows that it is always fragile and temporary, as long as the influence of oligarchic capital remains uncurbed.

Hummelgaard acknowledges that "one of the keys to understanding how capitalism became sick over time is that the social contract has at best been weakened and at worst altogether voided."[16] But he provides no explanation of how this happened. What both he and Frederiksen fail to see is that it was no accident that the success of the social democratic class compromise was so short lived. On the contrary, it was due to a foundational weakness within functional socialism, namely, that as long as the ownership of the greater part of the economy remains in the hands of a small group of capitalists, the class compromise will always remain fragile.

As long as the basis of oligarchic power of capital remained intact, it was only under certain favorable conditions that the balance of power permitted policies that ensured the betterment of all. When the opportunity presents itself—for example, during economic crises—elites unleash their oligarchic power to roll back social progress.

As long as capitalists can pressure popularly elected governments with threats of capital strikes or offshoring through their control of the means of production and investment, real reform remains vulnerable.

Certain social democrats already saw the writing on the wall in the 1970s, warning that if the social gains of the postwar period were to be preserved and expanded, then the central question of ownership had to be addressed. In the mid-1970s, leading social democratic economist Rudolf Meidner put it this way: "The concentration of wealth in a highly advanced industrial society is however not only a question of justice, but still to a greater degree one of economic power. . . . The economic history of the modern Western world abounds with examples of intervention against monopolies, cartels, and abuses of power of all kind. And yet at the same time it cannot be denied that economic development has in its essence been directed by capitalists and according to their interests."[17] For Meidner, therefore, functional socialism was just one step on the path toward resolving this contradiction.[18] As long as capitalists maintained control over the means of production, they would have a "gun pointed at the heart of the labor movement."[19]

It was this acknowledgment in Sweden as well as in Denmark that prompted extensive but ultimately fruitless debates over how reforms could secure for wage earners a measure of ownership and power within private firms.

In sum, it is difficult to overestimate the immense progress made by the social democratic wing of the left across the twentieth century. It is indisputable that social democrats created the best, the freest, and the most just society in the history of the world. Yet the reverses of the final decades of the century—the rising inequality and increased social insecurity—demonstrate that the social democratic strategy of class compromise, because it did not confront the concentration of ownership, could only produce fragile and precarious gains for working people. If the betterment of the many is to be durable and lasting, we must change the nature of ownership and of power relations.

But if the fact that the struggle against ownership has been abandoned accounts for the current crisis of social democracy, then why has the other half of the labor movement, that is, the revolutionary wing that has remained committed to fundamental change in the economic system, thus far had so little success in challenging capitalism?

The Revolutionary Alternative

Social democratic ideas have never held a monopoly over the socialist labor movement. They have always coexisted and competed with a revolutionary current that, unlike reformism, insists on foundational changes to property relations.

The definitive split within the labor movement occurred with the outbreak of the First World War, when social democratic parties across Europe reneged on their pledge to oppose participation in the war. In Denmark and many other countries, this led to a breakthrough for the more radical subset of the left, which proceeded to found its own revolutionary socialist and communist parties. The Russian Revolution and the establishment of the new International, the Komintern, deepened the fissure between communists, who gave their support to the new "workers' state," and social democrats, who kept their distance from the Soviet Union.

Throughout the twentieth century, the revolutionary wing further fractured into a number of competing parties. A growing awareness of the authoritarian and repressive nature of the Soviet bloc, especially after the

USSR's suppression of democratic uprisings in Hungary in 1956 and in Czechoslovakia in 1968, resulted in a split in Denmark between a more pro-Moscow wing, the Danish Communist Party (DKP), and a new left movement critical of Soviet socialism, represented by the Socialist People's Party (SF), the Left Socialists (VS), and various other formations.

In most of the advanced industrial countries of the West, the revolutionary wing has always been the junior partner, never managing to win the majority of support necessary to advance its program of fundamental social change. During the social democratic golden age, most workers supported the reformist agenda, since it delivered marked improvements in life conditions decade after decade. But even the decline of social democratic reformism in recent decades, together with the loss of social rights and an ever more brutal form of capitalism, has not breathed new life into the idea of revolutionary systemic change.

I believe that the revolutionary wing's failure to win support for more foundational change owes largely to its theory of social change. While different parties over time have proposed varying strategies for overthrowing capitalism, two central points have remained conspicuous. First, they have all agreed that existing institutions cannot be used to build socialism, that a socialist society can only materialize through a revolution from below. And second, that socialism cannot be instituted through gradual reforms but instead must take the form of a comprehensive overthrow of the system, in which private ownership of the means of production is abolished and the market economy is replaced with planning.

Extraparliamentary Revolution

Revolutionary socialists in the early twentieth century insisted on extraparliamentary revolution on the grounds that otherwise the political system of capitalist society would always remain the handmaiden of capitalists. Marx describes the capitalist state as a committee for the management of the common interests of capitalists, a view elaborated on by Russian socialist leader Vladimir Lenin, who argues in his classic work *The State and Revolution* that "the state is an organ of class rule, an organ for the oppression of one class by another," because "the liberation of the oppressed class is impossible not only without a violent revolution but also without the destruction of the apparatus of state power, which is created by the ruling class."[20] Thus according to the revolutionary left it is not possible to use the existing system, parliaments or otherwise, to establish socialism. Instead it must build up competing institutions alongside the "old" state—a system of "dual power" in the form of democratic councils in the workplace and in other areas of society. Sooner or later, Lenin explains, when the capitalist economy enters into one of its periodic crises, the majority will lose trust in the old "bourgeois" state apparatus and a revolution will bring down the existing state, vesting power in the councils and in a new socialist state. The new socialist society will thus be built upon the ruins of the old.[21]

It must be emphasized that historical experience with this form of revolutionary upheaval has been anything but positive. Despite the courage, self-sacrifice, and noble intentions of those in the past who attempted to establish a socialist society on the Leninist model, they never produced the democratic and egalitarian society they envisioned. To speak plainly, all have ended in either despotism or brutal oppression. Segments of the left have offered several explanations for these failures. Some point to specific historical conditions, such as the economic backwardness of the young Soviet Union or the relative absence of a large working class, while others blame the pressures resulting from the foreign intervention. Still others resort to counterfactuals: What if Lenin had not died? What if Trotsky had triumphed over Stalin? All such explanations thus presume that it is not the idea of extraparlianmentary revolution itself that is the problem but other, historically contingent factors.

But at least in the case of the Leninist model, it is more likely that the concept of extraparliamentary revolution itself accounts for the totalitarian drift that is often the outcome. The idea that a revolution can be grounded in dual power, in which two centers of power compete against one another, must necessarily end in a period of extralegality. Lenin is explicit on this, speaking of the workers' councils as possessing a "power bound by no laws." But history has shown that the suspension of democratic legality is notoriously dangerous, since it is far from certain that the democratic forces will emerge triumphant when the rule of law is reestablished in the postrevolutionary situation or even that the rule of law will be reestablished at all.

There are certainly societies, both past and present, where all democratic pathways to change have been closed and where revolutionary change has served as a vital step toward a more democratic society, not the least in the various countries of the Global South. But there is good reason that the majority of citizens in democratic countries have been skeptical of running the risk of despotism so long as the smallest possibility of gaining power through the ballot box remains.

The twentieth century also demonstrated that the idea that the state is the unambiguous instrument of capital is both distorted and even outright wrong. Perhaps it was in tsarist Russia, but the establishment of universal equal suffrage elsewhere fundamentally changed its nature. In many countries, labor parties won outright majorities or came to power in coalitions, and as we have seen, they employed state power to build up a comprehensive welfare state and to redistribute wealth. Economic elites have always influenced politics, but at the same time there has always been a democratic counterweight.

This more nuanced view of the state became dominant in the 1960s with the rise of the New Left and Eurocommunism. As theorized by Nicos Poulantzas, the state was reconceived as a site of contestation, the character of which is determined by the power relations between classes at any given moment. The concept of extraparliamentary revolution was thus, whether openly or implicitly, gradually abandoned, in favor of the idea that radical social change comes out of the interplay between struggles in legislative bodies and the building up of powerful social movements outside them.

The Rejection of the Gradualist Path to Socialism

Even though the majority of the left gave up on the idea of extraparliamentary revolution, the non–social democratic left continued to maintain that socialism could not be instituted through gradual reforms, that a new socialist society could only take form after the overthrow of the existing system. This did not mean that the revolutionary parties did not still work for and contribute to critical improvements within capitalism. The revolutionary left in Denmark played a decisive role in both social movements and in local and national governments and thus can claim much of the credit for many of the rights we take for granted today, including tenants' rights, apprentices' rights in the trades, and the right to a thirty-seven-hour workweek. Parties like the DKP and the VS also developed thoroughgoing reform programs and thus in praxis came close to embracing the concept of gradual change. Yet they generally operated with a sharp distinction between improvements within capitalism and the larger vision of a truly socialist society, which could only happen if capitalism was overthrown.

Socialism could not be the sum of a series of reforms but demanded a radical rupture.

I believe that this particular conception of socialism has contributed to the failure of the left to win comprehensive backing for its program within the modern democratic system. The prospect of an overthrow of the system seems to many too utopian, too unrealistic, and maybe even a little frightening, either because of historical memory of previous social revolutions or simply because very few people desire to throw themselves into the unknown so abruptly. Persuading a majority to get on board with revolution is a bit like proposing a trip to Mars.

—Will you come along on our spaceship to Mars?
—Hmmm, that sounds a bit wild. Have you figured out how we live up there?
—Yeah, we'll figure that out once we get there.
—But has anyone tried this before?
—Oh yeah, but it all went to hell, but don't sweat it. It won't happen this time.
—How do you know that?
—We just do!
—Thanks for the offer, but I think I'll pass.

This dialogue is admittedly a little slanted, but in the end I think that it shows how immense the challenge would be to make the case for the abrupt overturning of the existing system in favor of a wholly new society. Except for societies suffering brutal oppression and with little opportunity for things to improve, most people will regard the idea of making sudden changes skeptically, given that the consequences are unknown.

Another reason to be skeptical of a sudden overturning of the system is that the economy in our part of the world is highly developed and complex. An abrupt change such as the immediate seizure of the banks and large private firms would inevitably put the brakes on the economy, bringing production and distribution to a halt. A period of economic contraction and a falling living standard for the majority would follow. Such a deep and lasting economic recession in a democratic society would make it all but impossible for a socialist government to survive the next election. The most likely outcome would be victory for nonsocialist parties, and any changes that had been instituted in the interim would likely be partially or fully rolled back.

The Two Blind Alleys

It could thus be argued that the strategies of both branches of the socialist movement have turned out to be blind alleys, as neither has been able to address the question of how we are to break out of a steadily more destructive capitalist system.

Social democrats attempt to "heal capitalism" by reviving the class compromise that long ago was rejected by the other side and which rested on certain historical conditions that no longer apply. And even if it were possible to revive it, experience has revealed it to be fragile and temporary, since it did not confront the matter of unequal property and power relations.

In the meantime, the alternative of the revolutionary overthrow of the system appears neither realistic nor attractive to the majority. Memories of earlier revolutions frighten, and the idea of an abrupt and total makeover of society seems utopian and unrealistic.

And yet it is arguable that both blind alleys share a common origin, namely a shared sense that capitalism is an all-encompassing system that determines the whole of society and the economy and that we face a binary choice, between either preserving capitalism by regulating its worst impulses or seeking a revolutionary break and the replacement of the whole package with an entirely new form of society. Thus the choice between socialism and capitalism is understood as a choice between black and white, an either/or.

The central question is whether reality actually corresponds to this. Is capitalism a totality that has conquered the whole of the economy? An all-encompassing form of society with which we must make do through regulation or which we must replace with something wholly new? Or is this binary opposition rooted in an incorrect understanding of societies, of economies and of social change? I believe the latter.

A New Understanding of Society and Social Change

I myself was brought up with the belief that we must choose between gradual reform and revolutionary overthrow. In my family we were on the side of the revolutionaries. When as a child I rode in the loudspeaker car during the Mayday parade, as Søren Sidevind's songs blared over Nørrebrogade, I was with the communists. I learned that those over on the other side of Fælledparken were wrong in their belief that capitalism could be reformed and that only when we put an end to capitalism and replaced it with a new system would the world be a better place.

Into my adulthood I continued to believe that we had to choose between the social democratic way of reform *within capitalism* and the revolutionary way of building socialism only *after capaitalism*. And like so many others on the left, regardless of which side they take, it has shaped my understanding of society and social change.

But twenty years ago I came upon an article written by two American feminists that reframed the question in a whole new light. The two authors, who wrote under the collective pseudonym J. K. Gibson-Graham, ask how as feminists they could be a part of process that gradually moved society in a less patriarchal direction while, at the same time, as anticapitalists and socialists, they were wholly unable to push forward social change and instead had to wait for a great revolutionary breakthrough that hardly seemed realistic.[22]

Their answer, which was eye-opening for me, is that what makes capitalism appear so invincible is our own tendency to understand it as such. It is not a material object, like a chair or a lightbulb, that can be defined by its physical or chemical composition. It is rather an abstract sociological concept we use to describe a complex social reality. According to Gibson-Graham, the very manner in which the left, and not only the left, conceives of capitalism attributes to it certain characteristics that make it seem far more powerful than it in fact is.

The groundbreaking aspect of the article is its critique of the understanding of capitalism as a social totality. When today we describe our society, we customarily say we live in a capitalist society and under a capitalist system with a capitalist market and, at least according to many leftists, a capitalist state. Linguistically, we speak of society, the economy, the state, and the market as totality, as specifically a capitalist totality. Society *is* capitalist. The economy *is* capitalist, the market *is* capitalist, the state *is* capitalist. In this way we render capitalism all-encompassing. Capitalism is everywhere. Capitalism runs everything. Nothing can escape capitalism. There is nothing outside of it.[23]

This conception of capitalism as an all-encompassing system to which the whole of society is subordinate, as a ubiquitous and ever-expanding totality, defined how the left has understood it throughout the past century. Its origins are found in the historical materialism of Marx and Friedrich Engels, which portrays historical development as a series of societal formations determined by the nature of the means of production: from slavery to feudalism to capitalism. And from capitalism to socialism.[24] According to this conception, at least in the popular understanding, the economy of each social formation is directed by certain logics and social relations that are reflected in the material development of society. When one social formation replaces another, a new set of logics and social relations follow. Society is thus governed and determined by the specific mode of production.[25]

Although there are moments when Marx also hints at the idea that various means of production can coexist, the left has in general stuck with the view that capitalism is all encompassing and ever expanding. A recent example is Paul Mason's *Postcapitalism*, which claims that capitalism is "much more than just economic structure or a set of laws and institutions. It is the *whole* system—social, economic, demographic, cultural, ideological. . . . Capitalism is an organism. . . . It is a complex system, operating beyond the control of individuals."[26]

Given such an understanding of capitalism as a cohesive and and organic system equivalent to the whole of society and economy, it is hardly surprising that it appears impossible to overthrow. If there is nothing outside of capitalism, then there is hardly space for the building up of alternatives. As Gibson-Graham concludes: "If capitalism takes up the available social space, there's no room for anything else. If capitalism cannot co-exist, there's no possibility of anything else. . . . If capitalism functions as a unity, it cannot be partially or locally replaced."[27]

There Is Something Outside of Capitalism

But does it really make sense to conceive capitalism this way? What if instead of equating capitalism with the whole of society and economy, we narrow our definition to only that part of the economy in which capital exploits labor? What if we define capitalism as only those sectors in which a small elite owns the means of production and thereby accumulates wealth and power by appropriating a measure of the value of labor power that the majority sell in order to survive?[28]

Capitalism understood as such merely connotes that part of society and economy defined by this form of ownership and by these power relations, that is, the firms and sectors that exchange goods and services on the market where the labor power of workers is exchanged and where profits and investment decisions are controlled by a narrow group of capitalists.

Such an understanding of capitalism opens our eyes to all the areas of society and economy that are not based on capitalist ownership and the exploitative exchange relation between a small group of capitalists and wage laborers, such as consumer and worker cooperatives, single-proprietor firms, small family farms, and not the least to our public sector, which does not cater to the profit seeking of the economic elite and whose services are not exchanged via a market but are provided through a solidaristic tax system.

Thus even though our society and economy are currently dominated by the non-democratic capitalist mode of production, they also have always had room for other, noncapitalist enterprises and modes of production. Instead of viewing society as wholly capitalist or socialist, we must consider individual institutions, relations, and firms as either the one or the other.

This does not mean that the two separate modes of production operate independently of one another. On the contrary, they continually interact with and influence each other. In an economy dominated by the logics of the capitalist market, democratically run enterprises will often face challenges, such as how to secure capital, but these enterprises can also exert pressure on price setting in the private sector.

That society and economy are not capitalistic through and through, that there is indeed something outside of capitalism, is especially evident here in the Nordic region, where we have a strong cooperative sector and a welfare state that takes significant sections of the economy out of the market, thereby transforming them into public goods.

A Lack of Understanding Has Led to the Two Blind Alleys

The misconstruing of capitalism as an all-encompassing system, importantly, has largely blinded the left to those sectors of the economy that do not follow its logics.

In order to maintain the conception of capitalism as all-encompassing, we have indeed resorted to intellectual violence in the effort to subordinate the whole of society to the capitalist system. Despite the fact the labor movement overcame powerful opposition from economic elites to create the welfare state, leftists have often written it off as merely an integrated and subordinate aspect of capitalism itself, a means of reproducing the working class through the national health service, childcare, education, and so forth. While both social democrats and revolutionaries agree that strengthening the welfare state is beneficial insofar as it betters the lives of ordinary people, neither views its expansion into new areas as a step toward less capitalism but rather as just further reform within capitalism.

Paradoxically, we have thereby given credit for the welfare society to the capitalist economy, even though it was the outcome of the struggles of the labor movement and even though the welfare state is at its core noncapitalist and has reduced the economic field in which capital may operate.

Socialist strategists likewise tend to downplay the value of consumer and worker cooperatives because they operate within the confines of capitalist society. That our system of mortgage credit was nonprofit and member owned is hardly appreciated, since it is just another aspect of capitalism. Thus, with only a few exceptions, the left did not resist when beginning in the 1980s the large collectively owned portion of the Danish finance sector—mortgage-lending institutions and member-owned savings and loan banks—were gradually turned over to capitalists and thereby dedemocratized. Both social democrats and the revolutionary left were unable to see the many pockets of democratic management and noncapitalist modes of production that have always existed in our society.

Instead of learning and taking inspiration from our own experiences with democratic management, the Danish left took study trips to Albania, Moscow, and Beijing. While we studied the experience of collective ownership in the state socialist regimes, we closed our eyes to the pockets of socialism and democratic ownership right outside our windows. And this same blindness led social democrats to support the privatization of significant sections of the public sector, most recently the sale of DONG, Denmark's energy producer.

More than anything, the view of capitalism as a totalizing system has influenced our strategies for social change, in both the social democratic and revolutionary wings of the socialist family. The consequence of this is the conviction that socialism cannot be built gradually. It is an either/or. Either reform *within* capitalism or a total socialism *after* capitalism. It is precisely this that, on the one hand, leads Peter Hummelgaard to conclude that "the capitalist system as precisely an economic system has no better alternative . . . The world [cannot] make due without capitalism," and on the other, leads many of the revolutionary Left to deny that socialism could be instituted through gradual reforms.[29]

For social democrats this binary opposition has resulted in the abandonment of the idea that there is any alternative to capitalism. For the revolutionary wing it has transformed socialism into a utopian vision of the future that can only be realized after an absolute rupture with capitalism.

Societies Are Hybrids

But when we abandon the idea that capitalism is an all-encompassing totality and instead conceive it as only one among many competing modes of production in our society and economy, when we acknowledge that human beings, as long as capitalism has existed, have always created noncapitalist alternatives, we are able to recognize that the choice between capitalism and socialism is not an either/or and that society has never been completely capitalist or completely socialist but rather more or less socialist or more or less capitalist.

This helps explain the significant differences between the many countries we consider capitalist. While it is obvious that the economies of countries like Denmark, Norway, and Sweden are quite distinct from those of the United States or Dubai, we still describe them all as capitalist. The clear differences between the one and the other reflect how dominant the capitalist mode of production is in each society and the degree to which it is insulated from competition from noncapitalist forms of ownership, logics, and modes of production. The Nordic region is by all means more socialist than the United States, and it is precisely this that largely explains why we perform better than the more capitalistic countries on virtually every comparative metric.[30]

This further accounts for the difference between the kind of society we Danes had in the 1970s and what it has now become after thirty years of the neoliberal counteroffensive. Neoliberal reforms, privatization, and deregulation were instituted because of a desire to expand the field of the capitalist economy, such as when member-owned banks were replaced with private banks or when private capital was permitted to purchase agricultural land or rental properties.

And yet the fact that capitalism can colonize new sectors of the economy through political reform demonstrates that capitalism is not a totality, since that which has been colonized was once outside of capitalism. Thus we are able to recognize how capitalism has expanded and therefore also able to propose the opposite development, that democratic socialist forms of ownership begin to colonize currently capitalist sectors, thereby becoming more and more dominant.

The late sociologist Erik Olin Wright refers to this conception of change as "erosion," an alternative to revolution or reformist regulation. Instead of conceiving the economic system as a cohesive organism, as many Marxists have done, he argues that the economy is more like an ecosystem:

> Think of a lake. . . . A lake consists of water in a landscape, with particular kinds of soil, terrain, water sources, and climate. Collectively, all of these elements constitute the natural ecosystem of the lake. This is a "system" in that everything affects everything else within it, but it is not like the system of a single organism in which all of the parts are functionally connected in a coherent, tightly integrated whole. Social systems, in general, are better thought of as ecosystems of loosely connected interacting parts rather than as organisms in which all of the parts serve a function. . . . The strategic vision of eroding capitalism imagines introducing the most vigorous varieties of emancipatory species of noncapitalist economic activity into the ecosystem of capitalism, nurturing their development by protecting their niches and figuring out ways of expanding their habitats.[31]

The goal is thus that noncapitalist activities can spread outward from their niches, thereby transforming the ecosystem as a whole. This view of the transition from one economic system to another is also much more in alignment with how social change has historically occurred. All earlier economic epochs have been characterized by the coexistence of multiple means of production in which one gradually replaced the others. Capitalism did not emerge in one fell swoop but arose within a feudal economy and only slowly progressed. It began with relatively minor activity within the cracks and the corners of the feudal economy, gradually growing in strength before eroding the foundations of feudal structure and power. The bourgeois revolutions only came after the necessary material conditions and power relations had materialized, after capitalism had become the dominant mode of production. Socialists, however, typically see the transition to socialism in precisely the opposite terms, arguing that revolutionary rupture must *precede* social and economic transformation.

Olin Wright notes that it is much more likely that the transition to a socialist society will proceed in the same gradual way as earlier historical transitions:

> Alternative, noncapitalist economic activities . . . emerge in the niches where possible within an economy dominated by capitalism. These activities grow over time, both spontaneously and as a result of deliberate strategy. Some of these emerge as adaptations and initiatives from below within communities. Others are actively organized or sponsored by the state from above to solve practical problems. These alternative economic relations constitute the building blocks of an economic structure whose relations of production are characterized by democracy, equality, and solidarity. . . . Eventually, the cumulative effect of this interplay between changes from above and initiatives from below may reach a point where the socialist relations created within the economic ecosystem become sufficiently prominent in the lives of individuals and communities that capitalism can no longer be said to be dominant.[32]

This idea of the building of socialism through a gradual process of erosion of the capitalist mode of production is opposed to both the revolutionary idea of a sudden rupture and the modern social democratic embrace of the idea that the capitalist system constitutes the historical endpoint.

Historically there have been parties and theorists who have situated themselves between the reform of capitalism and its revolutionary overthrow. The so-called Third Way socialism, associated with the German labor leader Karl Kautsky and perhaps even more with the so-called Austro-Marxist school, combined fidelity to the ultimate socialist goal with a commitment to the peaceful and gradualist parliamentary achievement of it. In the 1970s, the Eurocommunists sought the same pathway. Here in Denmark we can include the Socialist People's Party and to a certain extent the DKP, whose conception of anti-monopolistic democracy constitutes a tradition that acknowledges the possibility of moving society in a socialist direction prior to a decisive break with capitalism.[33]

Yet despite these and so many other examples, the idea persists that socialism can only begin when capitalism has been overthrown, that it cannot already take root in our existing economy. But when we look at the early Danish labor movement, before the split between revolutionary and reformist, we see a clear understanding that socialism can do precisely this.[34] The socialist labor leader and newspaper editor Frederik Borgbjerg, with whom we shall become more familiar later on, saw the building up of a democratic and cooperative alternative economy within and alongside capitalism as a critical element of his strategy for socialist change. He describes the cooperative movement "as a kind of social modular building that takes place unnoticed within the deepest core of society and yet touches on that which is essential for all social democrats, namely the economic. At the inmost core of society new organs are being built that influence the essential economic structure of society, thereby contributing to the shaping and ordering of a new society." Through cooperatives, he argues, socialists can "establish *the kernel of a socialist economy that steadily expands outward while at the same time forcing the contraction of the capitalist sphere.*"[35]

Is Gradual Change Possible?

Many revolutionary socialists will surely be skeptical about the idea of such a gradual transformation of the economy. They will say that as long as capitalists hold the seat of power, as they do today, they will be able to put the brakes on such an undertaking. In a critique of Olin Wright's conception of society and economy as ecosystem, Dylan Riley argues that "the inauguration of socialism will not resemble the introduction of an invasive species for the simple reason that capitalist economies, unlike eco-systems, are backed by political institutions that are specifically designed to eliminate such species as soon as they begin to threaten the system. . . . As such, the strategy of eroding capitalism requires a prior political break—a decisive confrontation with the capitalist state."[36]

This is a legitimate critique, for the capitalist economy is indeed anchored in powerful institutions. But Riley's view is based on the same Leninist conception of the state I have already challenged. In my view he underestimates the changes in the character of the state brought about by universal suffrage and thus the possibility of employing state power to support the development of a noncapitalist sector.

Riley is, however, correct in noting that economic elites, who are possessed of the immense advantage that capitalism continues to be the dominant mode of production, will certainly oppose reforms and measures that could lead the way to a more democratic and collectively owned economy.

First and foremost, they can use their immense economic power to remove even very popular politicians. After socialist Françoise Mitterrand came to power in France in 1981 together with communists, he launched a process of the comprehensive socialization of the economy, including a large majority of the financial sector. But capitalists immediately responded with capital flight and investment strikes, which within a few years forced the socialist government to retreat. The leftist alliance SYRIZA that assumed power in Greece in 2015 on the promise of an end to austerity politics was likewise compelled to retreat.

How such a reaction can be avoided, or at least minimized, is an important question. Here we can perhaps learn something from the strategy of the neoliberal counteroffensive of recent decades. The neoliberal ascendancy was far from a natural development in which capitalism simply triumphed on its own virtues. It was rather a meticulously planned project, in which skillful politicians and business leaders, through many years of influencing public debates, the exertion of economic pressure from below, and political regulation from the top, managed to facilitate a process by which the capitalist mode of production gradually and purposefully undermined the noncapitalist and democratic sectors of the economy. Gradualist reforms, such as cuts to unemployment benefits or the liberalization of the currency supply, weakened the power of organized labor and the democratic state, paving the way for still more ambitious neoliberal reforms.

A strategy for socialist change must do precisely the same, but in the opposite direction and with other allies. It must take conscious steps on a deliberate path toward changing power relations through reforms that expand democratic power at the expense of oligarchic elites, thereby diminishing their ability to undermine the decisions of the democratic majority. The establishment of a democratic finance sector, for example, would limit the ability of private bankers to threaten a credit crunch to compel politicians to overturn the necessary regulations. And a powerful worker-owned sector within the economy would create an alternative for wage earners, which would reduce the threat offshoring.

On the Way Toward a More Socialist Society

To sum up this chapter, both the social democratic and revolutionary branches of the socialist family share the conception of capitalism as an all-encompassing organic system whose scope is equivalent to the whole of society. This has prevented them from acknowledging what Donald Trump, Fox News, and the U.S. left alike clearly understand, namely that the Nordic economies cannot at all be characterized as entirely capitalist but also exhibit strong socialist traits.

By recognizing that capitalism is not a totality but coexists with alternative, democratic institutions, we can see that socialism's materialization does not require a break with capitalism. Socialism is already present in our existing society and can be consciously deepened and expanded. Far from a utopian fantasy, socialism is a concrete alternative with which we are already familiar. And yes, we can also point to the fact that countries like the Nordics with more socialist attributes perform significantly better than the countries in which capitalism is dominant, with respect to both the well-being of the population and economic effectiveness.

We can also see that the choice does not have to be between total capitalism and total socialism. Instead we can conceive of more pluralistic economic systems and mixed economies that make socialist ownership and democratic planning dominant but not all-encompassing.

In my opinion this approach to social change is far more appealing, persuasive, and realistic than either the revolutionary conception of a total overthrow of the system or the social democratic overtures to a return to old class compromise. It preserves the commitment to foundational social change and the democratization of ownership, which can gradually reduce the oligarchic power of elites, but it abandons the idea that change can only occur "after capitalism" in favor of a strategy attuned to the already established noncapitalist sectors of our economy.

It is this understanding of society and social change that informs my vision of a Nordic socialism—and my ideas as to how we can bring it into being—that I present in the following chapters.

The first step is to identify the noncapitalist sectors of the economy, that is, the elements not based on concentrated and undemocratic ownership but on other, more egalitarian and democratic principles and then to consider what we can learn from these experiences, so that we can further develop and expand them to other areas.

Let us therefore take a tour of noncapitalist Denmark.

3

The Communal Economy
A Part of Our History

It is Saturday morning, and you wake up in your apartment in northwest Copenhagen, a property built in 1941 by the workers of the Danish Cooperative Housing Union (AKB). You are a renter but also a kind of owner, since the property is owned by the cooperative, and you are a member and thus participate in choosing the leadership. You are happy to live here, not least because the rent is affordable, and because you and your neighbors yourselves are the owners, only you can raise it.

You hop out of bed and head to the bathroom. The water in which you bathe is provided by HOFOR, a corporation owned by a conglomerate of municipal governments within the greater Copenhagen area. The same is true of the company that heats your apartment, and electricity is provided through a grid owned by the consumer cooperative Andel.

You decide to surprise your family with breakfast in bed, so you head out to Brugsen to pick up pancake mix, eggs, and bacon. Since you are a member of Coop you have helped to elect the representative from your neighborhood shop, and Coop, as is rarely appreciated, does not turn over its profits to a capital fund or ownership group that has nothing to do with the grocery business. You add a block of cheese to your cart from Thise, an organic producers' cooperative owned by seventy farmers in North Jutland. You pay with your Coop card from your account at Merkur Andelskasse, your member-owned bank. You left the privately owned Danske Bank after the latest scandal and are content that your savings are now invested sustainably, and you yourself can have a say in investment decisions by attending the general assembly, each member of which has one vote, regardless of how many shares members have purchased. The other day you had to visit the hospital because your youngest took a tumble at day care and broke a wrist. The nurses were busy but eminently professional. You think of your husband's American cousin. When his daughter fell ill with a serious blood disease, he had to sell the family home. Shortly after, he was fired from his job and thus lost his health insurance. You remind yourself to be thankful that we live in a country in which it is not the size of one's wallet that determines who receives treatment or whether one can get a good education or be assured a place in a retirement home. Market forces have their place, but some matters are too important to leave to them. And it is much better to pay for all this through a solidaristic tax system, according to which one pays according to ability but all have equal access to services.

On the way back from Brugsen, you stop by the newly built library on Rentemestergade to pick up the books you have reserved. It's nice that we have such libraries, where people can share books instead of having to buy their own copies.

This little story could have unfolded just about anywhere in Denmark. And I could have continued it by mentioning the summerhouse you have purchased with a loan from Denmark's largest mortgage lender, the member-owned Nykredit, the insurance policy from the 100 percent member-owned GF Forsikring, the construction workers of the worker-owned cooperative Logik & Co. who build homes for the housing cooperative, the grants issued by the government to cover the cost of education, and the pension contributions to your union's democratically run pension fund. But the point should be clear: every day we Danes come into contact with the democratic and noncapitalist sectors of our economy, including organizations that operate within the market like Thise and Coop as well as those we have chosen to take out of the market, such as our health-care and education systems. And it works, entirely without the profit motive, private capital, or speculators.

A collectively owned and democratically run economy is not a utopian fantasy. It is on the contrary a well-established and highly successful reality that for more than a hundred years has been an integral part of our society to the advantage of the broad majority.

But how did we get here? Let us take a deep dive into our long history of democratic management in the economy, so we may learn from this experience (while I focus on Denmark, the same history can be traced in in Sweden, Norway, and Finland).

The Roots of the Nordic Communal Economy

The year is 1866. A group of people have gathered at the city hall in the small town of Thisted. It is primarily made up of trade and factory workers. They listen intently to the local vicar, Hans Christian Sonne. He speaks passionately about how the attendees should band together and open a democratically run purchasing cooperative and retail store that would offer cheaper daily necessities for the town's workers.

Sonne had just visited Copenhagen, where he had heard tell of the cooperative that had sprung up in Britain in the northern city of Rochdale. There a group of weavers and other workers had established a completely new kind of company, a purchasing cooperative run according to the foundational democratic principle of one person, one vote. The organization was open to all who wished to join, and any future surpluses would be distributed fairly among the members instead of ending up in the pockets of the grocer or wholesaler.

Sonne was enthusiastic about the idea. He had witnessed how the workers of Thisted struggled to make ends meet and often had to pay extortionate prices to the local shopkeeper. The nourishment of the soul was not the first among the needs of the impoverished workers of his parish: "My congregants immediately made it clear that if I was to do something for them, I must first help them acquire their daily bread," he later wrote.[1] At the meeting in Thisted the parishioners were skeptical at first. Could they really do something like that? Could ordinary people get together and run a company in such a manner? But Sonne managed to persuade them, and Denmark's first consumer cooperative opened for business on November 1, 1866, on Store Torv in Thisted. It was the opening salvo in the cooperative movement, here in Denmark often referred to as "andelsbevægelsen," which for a century and a half has set a profound mark on the Danish economy and business world.

Andelsbevægelsen: Liberal but Anticapitalist

Unlike Rochdale, which had been an urban phenomenon, it was the rural population of Denmark that first took to the idea of democratically managed enterprises. Rural Denmark was in the midst of a historic social, cultural, and political awakening. For centuries the rural peasantry had constituted an oppressed and subjugated class, looked down upon by the rural gentry as well as the merchant bourgeois of the towns.

But by the late nineteenth century, change was in the air, due not least to the ideas of the great theologian N. F. S. Grundtvig, who had envisioned an independent and enlightened peasantry. Grundtvig had sought to uplift the rural peasantry through popular education and organizing, such that the small farmers might be able to stand on their own and be masters of their own homes. The key words were self-governance, independence, and the rejection of authority, whether it came in the form of the urban bourgeoisie or the state bureaucracy: "the sun rises with the farmer, not with the scholars," wrote Grundtvig. It was precisely this focus on self-governance and self-sufficiency that became a central force in the building up of the Danish cooperative movement, which grew from the bottom up through the solidarity of ordinary people.

Inspired by Thisted, consumer co-ops sprang up in hundreds of towns and villages in the years following, and the success of the movement sparked further interest in the idea of democratically managed and collectively owned enterprises.

In the winter of 1881, a group of farmers gathered together at the Ølgod tavern in the western Jutland town of Hjedding to discuss the possibility of establishing a dairy cooperative. They were frustrated with the terms imposed on them by the local private dairy processer. Three were tasked with drafting articles for the new enterprise. They worked through the night and by five in the morning the basic principles had been outlined. The influence of the Rochdale and Danish consumer co-ops was clear; the new dairy would be democratically managed—one man, one vote—regardless of the size of the members' herds. If the dairy turned a profit, the proceeds would be distributed among the members according to the amount of milk each had delivered. From now on, only the farmers themselves would profit from their labor. Shortly thereafter Denmark's first democratically managed and producer-owned dairy was established.

Dairy co-ops began to appear all over Denmark in the following months and years, like a wave from the North Sea, as Niels Pedersen, the principal of a folk high school in Askov, later put it. In 1888 alone no less than 244 dairy co-ops were founded, all based on the same foundation of democratic management and collective ownership.[2]

The concept of the cooperative soon spread to other sectors. On May 27, 1887, the *Horsens Folkeblad* published a statement from Peter Bojsen, the leader of the Horsens agricultural union and *højskole* principal, calling for the establishment of a cooperative slaughterhouse. This would, according to Bojsen, ensure that "the profits that now line the pockets of private shareholders" would by "the cooperative principal be divided among the producers." Bojsen would later recall his thinking on whether to adopt the democratic cooperative model: "Should this be a privately or cooperatively owned plant? This was the question I constantly asked myself. The first option would the easiest to finance, but the cooperative principle would get more on board. The capitalists had no such advantage."[3]

More than twelve hundred local farmers were quickly signed up. But resistance from the capitalist sector was fierce. Private banks would not provide loans to the cooperative, and opponents employed all sorts of bureaucratic trickery. And when the cooperative was finally established, the private processers engaged in a vicious price war to try and kill it off. Yet the opposition was in vain, as cooperative slaughterhouses were established across Denmark in the following years.[4]

In 1899 the consumer, dairy, and meat processing cooperatives banded together to form the Cooperative Council, which joined the international organization for cooperatives, the International Cooperative Alliance.

Since the rural population had strong connections to liberal Venstre party circles, it may seem surprising that the pioneers of the movement were highly critical of capitalist ownership. When in 1890 leading Danish capitalist C. F. Tietgen attempted to persuade the cooperative slaughterhouses to join with the private processors to form a shareholder-owned cartel, Bojsen rebuffed him, explaining that

> as far as I know, in publicly traded companies decisions are always made by the shareholders; when a single shareholder owns a very large number of shares, he also has a great number of votes. . . . We have a different way of voting in our cooperatives. He who can only deliver one hog per year has the same voting rights as he who delivers three hundred; our voters are people, not capital. . . . This, if I may, democratic foundation on which our cooperative system is based would be lost; if we were to join forces with a large publicly traded company, our people would hardly be among those with the most shares. Instead it would be the capitalist who could buy up the most

shares who would become the center of gravity and who would dominate the rest of us.[5]

Severin Jørgensen, a pioneer of the consumer cooperative movement, likewise critiqued the tendency toward the concentration of ownership in the capitalist economy: "The business world trends more and more toward to the centralization of ownership . . . which steadily increases the wealth of the few who possess capital. . . . And if the broad majority do not make use of the power they have to resist this increasing concentration of wealth and ownership . . . then prospects for future social progress are anything but bright."[6] He was explicit that the goal of the consumer co-ops was "to improve the economic and material conditions of working people and to oppose the rising power of capital, which is so damaging to the large majority of the population."[7]

The Socialists Hesitate

Given that the cooperative movement was highly critical of capitalism, one would expect that the early socialist labor movement of the 1880s would have immediately embraced it. Yet attitudes were quite mixed within the labor movement. Leading socialists viewed consumer cooperatives as an expression of a petite bourgeois mentality and the establishment of democratic enterprises as a distraction from the struggle for a socialist society. One of the central ideological standard bearers of the social democrats, Gustav Bang, criticized the Rochdale movement for poisoning the minds of the English working class: "And thus a petty capitalist desire for profits took root among all too many of England's workers." He was completely dismissive of the idea that the democratic governance of the consumer co-ops could function as the germ of a future socialist society: "Consumer cooperatives are not revolutionary in essence or in praxis, they do not shake up the capitalist mode of production that underpins our present society, they are not socialist at their core."[8]

Other early labor leaders, however, viewed the cooperative movement much more favorably, such as prominent socialist agitator Frederik Borgbjerg, who was himself from the countryside and who became the principal spokesperson for the idea that the labor movement should take inspiration from the experiences of democratic management established by the rural cooperatives: "The grandest expression of the cooperative idea, that which encompasses all kinds of production and social classes, is called socialism. . . . The whole people should do as the farmers have done: band together and organize production and trade according to the cooperative system so that no single person skims off the cream, and so every cooperative member, that is, every member of society who participates in the workings of society, enjoys a full and just dessert."[9]

The building up of consumer and producer cooperatives, according to Borgbjerg, should constitute a third thread in the labor movement, alongside the strengthening of the Social Democratic party and the labor unions. His views did eventually get a hearing, as they were incorporated into the official platform at the 1908 party congress. But by that point cooperatives were already a reality among the urban working class. Even before the end of the nineteenth century, a series of cooperative bakeries and consumer co-ops had been established in the cities by labor movement activists, and soon building trade cooperatives sprung up across the country.

The various cooperatives established by the labor movement joined together in 1922 to form the Union of the Cooperatives, today known as Kooperation. The cooperative movement in Denmark thus was, unlike in many other countries, split into two branches from the beginning, one tied to the rural population, the other to the urban working class and the social democratic party, each with its own national organization. Both the rural Cooperative Council and the urban Union of Cooperatives, however, joined the International Cooperative Alliance.

The Century of Democratic Enterprise

Denmark thus entered the twentieth century with a growing democratic, anticapitalist sector, propelled by farmers in the countryside and the labor movement in the cities. Over the course of the new century, this movement for democratic enterprise would play a critical role, spreading outward into new sectors. At its peak, the cooperative movement constituted about one-fourth of the Danish economy.[10]

Consumer Cooperatives

The most successful and eventually the most significant sector was most certainly the consumer co-ops; by 1899 there were already a thousand of them in Denmark.[11] While the principal aims were to secure cheap, essential goods for the members and to avoid handing the surpluses over to private merchants and wholesalers, the cooperative movement was also, according to Jørgensen, about community and solidarity: "Community is a necessary aspect of human life, indeed even of all creation, wherever life and growth is found. No tree, no flower, no blade of grass would be able to grow and to thrive alone on this earth, for they would be knocked over by the wind, pelted by the rain, or dried out by the blazing rays of the sun, if indeed they did not grow up together in common, mutually protecting and nourishing one another."[12] This sense of strength in community led to the establishment of a union of all the consumer co-ops, the Fællesforeningen for Danmarks brugsforeninger (FDB), which because of its size could negotiate favorable prices with national and international vendors.

Conflicts with private capital also pushed FDB to build its own production facilities for coffee, chocolate, tobacco, rope, soap, clogs, and margarine. In 1902, when a cartel of tobacco factories refused a reasonable price for a large order, the union established its own tobacco factory in Esbjerg. A number of these conflicts with capitalist cartels had international ramifications. In 1925, the largest global producer of incandescent lamps established the international cartel Phoebum, which used its monopoly power to jack up prices and thereby secure immense profits. The Swedish consumer cooperative movement responded by founding the pan-Nordic Kooperativa lumaförbundet, which then established a light bulb factory, quickly reducing the price of lamps by half.[13]

By 1971 all the consumer cooperatives had joined FDB, which would later be rebranded as Coop, as we know it today.

Agricultural Cooperatives

The agricultural cooperative movement also grew rapidly in the first half of the twentieth century, coming to dominate egg hatcheries, nurseries, fisheries, and furrieries. The movement also took steps to free itself from dependence on capitalist interests. Before the formation of the cooperatives, many of the products on which farmers relied—seeds, fertilizer, feed, and so forth—were imported or purchased from large private companies, many of them organized as price-fixing cartels. The Cooperative Council thus established the Danish Cooperative Fertilizer Company in 1902 in response to the formation of a fertilizer cartel. Co-ops for livestock feed, seeds, and exports were founded under similar circumstances.

These challenges to private interests resulted in a series of bitter clashes with capitalist firms. When, after a long struggle with the cement cartel led by the Foss family (the founders of Aalborg Portland), the Danish Cooperative Cement Factory was established, its new manager Anders Nielsen remarked that "never here in Denmark has the capitalist regime suffered such a severe defeat."[14] But there were many more to come, as the cooperative movement generally got the best of private capital, and by mid-century it dominated the markets for both agricultural implements and products.

Producer and Worker-Owned Cooperatives

In addition to the agricultural co-ops, the labor movement cooperatives also served an important function in twentieth-century business life. The community bakeries established by local trade unions were, like other ventures, a response to market injustice. When grain prices dropped in the 1880s, bread producers did not lower theirs, and so the community bakeries stepped in to provide the rye bread that was an essential part of the working-class diet more cheaply. Other early co-ops were formed after conflicts between trade unions and private companies, such as the cooperative dairy plant established in Copenhagen after struggles over wages and working conditions at the city's largest private producer.

But the worker co-op movement really took off after the great lockout of 1899, when tens of thousands of workers were plunged into poverty and hunger. This struggle made it clear that cooperative enterprises could provide jobs in times of conflict as well as contribute to strike funds from their surpluses. A carpenters' co-op was founded that year, followed by a bricklayers' co-op along with co-ops for many other building trades. The first cooperative brewery, Bryggeriet Stjernen, was founded in 1902, followed by co-ops for clothing and shoes, radios, building materials, machinists, printers, and even one for barbers, Figaro.

Workers' cooperatives experienced their greatest growth from the early to the mid-twentieth century. In the 1950s Stjernen had about 10 percent of the beer market, while the community bakeries accounted for 27 percent of rye bread sales.[15] As I will later discuss, it is important to understand that these worker cooperatives were not cooperatives in the original sense of the term, since they were owned and managed by trade unions rather than workers themselves.

A Democratic Finance Sector

Most people view the financial sector as the very incarnation of capitalism. Yet Denmark has a long tradition of financial institutions established according to democratic and nonprofit principles, with the aim of serving customers rather than boosting the earnings of shareholders. The first financial institutions in Denmark, the mutual savings banks, were in fact nonprofits, established not to make money but to encourage ordinary people to save for times of need. All the way into the 1980s the nonprofit savings banks constituted a significant part of the finance sector; SDS, for example, was Denmark's third largest financial institution until its conversion to a commercial bank in 1989.

With the growth of the cooperative movement came real democratic governance in the form of cooperative banks, in which each member possessed one vote regardless of how much one contributed. One reason the co-op banks were founded was to secure credit for the enterprises operated by the cooperative movement. As Niels H. Jessen, founder of the first co-op bank in Outrup in western Jutland, explained: "How silly it is that co-op members put their savings in private banks in the city, thereby increasing the power of those institutions. And then these same co-op members get together to form a new enterprise and go back to the same private banks to ask for their own money to be loaned back to them at a handsomely inflated interest rate, or sometimes are rejected outright."[16]

It was this same attitude that later motivated the Cooperative Council to found Andelsbanken in 1909—a co-op bank owned by the many cooperative enterprises. As Jørgensen put it, "Why should the farmers themselves not keep the profits they now, through their arrangements with the banks, turn over to the capitalists? It's surely no small sum they can save by taking this matter into their own hands."[17] By midcentury Andelsbanken was the fourth largest bank in the country.[18] The labor movement followed in 1919 by establishing the Arbejdernes Landsbank, owned by a group of trade unions. In the 1970s a new series of co-op banks were established, inspired by the new thinking of the time: Merkur Andelskasse, with roots in the Rudolf Steiner movement, and Fælleskassen, an outgrowth of the Georgist Land-Labor-Capital (JAK) movement.[19]

The same principal is behind the uniquely Danish model of mortgage lending. The first mortgage loan institutions were established in the mid-nineteenth century by borrowers acting collectively. The aim of these institutions was to secure cheap home loans for customers, without anyone else profiting from the transaction. All the way into the early 1990s the mortgage loan market was exclusively served by such nonprofits. Unlike in most other countries in the world, no one in Denmark earned money off the provision of home mortgage loans.

As with other aspects of the cooperative movement, the co-op banks were the collective response of ordinary people to the fickleness of the market and the greed of private capital. By the middle of the century these banks made up some 60 percent of the total activity in the financial sector, and thus it could be said that Danish finance was chiefly democratically managed and collectively owned.[20]

Housing and Utilities Without Profit

On March 12, 1912, a small group of union representatives met at the tavern Tømrerkro on Adelgade in Copenhagen, where they founded the Workers' Cooperative Building Association. The Danish financial sector was then in crisis, and building had come to a halt, just as a new wave of emigration from the countryside to the cities had further driven up rents. The representatives' idea was to apply the cooperative principle to the housing sector, making it possible to build solid, low-cost housing without lining the pockets of speculators.

The first cooperative housing units were built in 1913 on Nyelandsvej in Frederiksberg, and in the years following similar building co-ops appeared in Copenhagen and later in many other cities. Under the social democratic government in the 1920s and 1930s, the movement received political backing. The state offered low-interest loans and public financing for housing co-ops, ensuring that rent was determined not by market forces but by what was required for the management and upkeep of the buildings.

The cooperative housing movement began to take off in earnest after the Second World War; in the 1950s and 1960s roughly nine thousand units were built per year, rising to an average of ten thousand in the 1970s. Like its movement peers, the cooperative housing sector was focused on serving the needs of its members, but unlike other co-ops, it was not democratically managed. This began to change in the 1970s, when a powerful tenants' movement began to demand more of a voice and eventually secured a majority of seats in the leadership council for popularly elected representatives. Today some one million Danes live in 550,000 cooperative housing units, about 17 percent of the total population.

The utilities cooperative movement was likewise essential in ensuring that the remotest areas had access to clean drinking water, electricity, and heat. Today, consumer-owned utility cooperatives exist alongside publicly owned providers, and together they provide excellent service at low prices.

Although the cooperative movement did not make inroads to the same degree in other Nordic countries, at least a part of what I have described here applies across the region, especially with respect to agricultural and consumer cooperatives.

But it is not only as consumers, borrowers, tenants, or employees that we Nordics have become co-owners and co-managers of various enterprises within our economy. We have also done so as citizens of our welfare society.

The Democratic Public Sector

Today we tend to take our welfare benefits for granted. But we need not go back too many generations to find a time when we had to pay for health care or, lacking the means, we had to accept help from private charities, when education was only for a well-heeled elite, and when the ability to pay largely determined access to the basic necessities of life.

The development of the Nordic welfare society engendered a profound social transformation, weakening the influence of market forces and creating a new democratic sector within the economy.

The foundation stones of the Danish version of the Nordic welfare society were laid at the beginning of the twentieth century, when social democrats took power in a number of municipal constituencies. During the period of so-called municipal socialism, local governments engaged in a kind of socialist experiment that they hoped would prove that the idea of socialism could be realized. New public schools replaced the old private and religious institutions. Poor hospitals were replaced with modern municipal hospitals, and citizens received dental care free of charge.

Public libraries were constructed from Nakskov to Esbjerg, providing ordinary citizens with access to books and magazines; community and cultural centers, swimming pools and bathhouses, and elder- and childcare institutions proliferated. A new community-owned and democratically run economic sector took shape in the municipalities, securing for all citizens new rights and possibilities.

After the constitutional amendments of 1915, urban workers and rural smallholders became the majority of the electorate. Nine years later tobacco worker Thorvald Stauning became the first prime minister to hail from a working-class background. This popular seizure of power resulted in a foundational transformation of society and of the role of the state in the economy. Beginning in the 1920s but especially in the 1930s and the postwar decades, we in Denmark, along with our neighbors, developed what today is known across the world as the Nordic welfare society, that is, a society whose economy is governed in substantial part not by market forces but by a democratically run public sector.

Goods and services that in other countries are purchased on the private market have been transformed into public goods that we pay for through taxes and to which everyone, from the wealthiest to the poorest, has equal access. Many public sector goods are produced by the public sector itself, with the state serving as employer. This means that a growing part of the workforce does not work in order to enrich another person but in order to provide the best possible conditions of life for the people.

Universal access to health care and universal free education from primary school through university were instituted. Child- and eldercare facilities proliferated. But it was not just care, education, and health that were transformed into democratic and profit-free sectors. Rail and bus services joined industries connected to utilities, energy production, and telecom in being publicly managed, as did production facilities, such as mills, mines, and data centers, and the pan-Nordic publicly owned SAS was established for air travel. Even Bakken, the world's oldest amusement park located just north of Copenhagen, was for a time under public ownership.

The state also came to play an important role in the financial sector, supplying insurance (Statsanstalten for livsforsikring) and credit for mortgages (Realkreditfondene) and even for a time engaging in consumer banking (GiroBank, once the primary banker for tens of thousands of Danes).

The cooperative and democratic public sectors were not alone in creating alternatives to capitalism. A comprehensive social nonprofit sector also took root in Denmark and other Nordic countries in the twentieth century. We have a long tradition of free schools and folk high schools managed by civil society groups whose goal is not to make profit. We have charitable trusts such as OK-Fonden and Diakonissesstiftlesen that run nonprofit eldercare homes. And finally we have a number of so-called social enterprises, which are dedicated to providing employment for select groups. All told more than one million Danes volunteer in this sector, daily creating value for others with no expectation of monetary gain.

A Comprehensive Communal Economy

By now it should be clear that from the end of the nineteenth and up through the twentieth century a comprehensive noncapitalist sector was developed, which provided ordinary people with a degree of ownership and democratic influence on a significant portion of the larger economy.

For a period of around a hundred years, the proportion of the economy under democratic management steadily expanded. Sector after sector was taken out of the capitalist market economy and transformed into public goods to which all citizens had free access, regardless of purchasing power or wealth. Democratic power increased, while oligarchic power declined.

The development of a noncapitalist communal economy alongside the capitalist market was not only a Danish phenomenon, for it also took root in the other Nordic countries, but with significant differences. Sweden, for example, had more worker cooperatives than Denmark, while Norway and Finland were characterized by much greater state involvement in the form of state-owned enterprises that produce for the market. The market value of seventy Norwegian state-owned firms is equal to no less than 87.9 percent of GDP and includes such staples as the mobile telephone provider Telenor and the real estate firm Entra. In Finland, the market value of sixty-four state-owned firms is equivalent to 52 percent of GDP. Outside of the fully state-owned companies, both the Norwegian and Finnish governments own significant shares in private firms through their state investment funds.[21] In Norway, state and municipal funds control about one-third of the shares traded on the Oslo stock exchange.[22]

Here in Denmark, it needs to be conceded that the community-owned and democratically managed parts of the economy were far from perfect. While the agricultural co-ops were owned and democratically managed by the farmers themselves, for example, working conditions in their slaughterhouses and feed mills could be just as bad as conditions in those owned and run by capitalists. The pressures of big business eventually undermined the democratic principles of the cooperatives. As the co-ops expanded, the gap between the largest and smallest producers increased, and in certain places the democratic influence of the members was more formal than actual. In addition, democratic management proved to be no guarantee that decisions took into account social and sustainability concerns, as clearly shown by the poor environmental records of the big producer co-ops like Arla and Danish Crown.

The publicly owned portion of the economy was also not without its problems. All too often the public sector was burdened by top-down bureaucratic management and occasionally by cronyism and nepotism. The experience of the ordinary citizen was frequently the encounter with the petty official who knew best or who exhibited a one-size-fits-all mentality that did not account for individual needs and wants.

Yet aside from these difficulties, there existed a comprehensive sector within the economy in which citizens and cooperative members could exert some degree of influence according to the principal of one person, one vote, and in which ownership and management were not concentrated among a narrow elite. These experiences demonstrate that the democratic management of our business life, production, and finance is a wholly realizable possible.

The Antidemocratic Counteroffensive

In recent decades, however, we have witnessed the opposite development, the downsizing of democratically managed and community-owned parts of the economy in favor of the expansion of capitalism. This antidemocratic counteroffensive has impacted both the public sector and critical sections of the cooperative movement, reducing the influence of ordinary people on the economy and resulting in a greater concentration of wealth and income, thereby reasserting oligarchic power over democratic power.

The attack on the democratic public sector began at the end of the 1970s. Across the Western world, the Nordic region included, the right and economic elites launched a powerful campaign against public ownership, portraying state-owned firms as inefficient and old fashioned (unjustly, as we shall later see). The campaign had an impact, pushing successive Danish governments from those of Poul Schlüter to Poul Nyrup to Anders Fogh Rasmussen to Helle Thorning-Schmidt to privatize numerous sectors of the Danish economy.

The financial sector was hit first, beginning with the privatization of Statsanstalten for Livsforskring in 1990 and then the takeover of GiroBank by Danske Bank. A bit later it was the turn of vital infrastructure within the telecommunications network, which over loud protest was sold off in 1994 to private capital, which after just a few years, in 1998, sold it off again for a windfall profit of DKK 1 billion. In 1996 another crucial piece of infrastructure, Datacentralen, which managed the state health-care registry, was privatized, and the same fate later befell Kommunedata, the municipal data and software firm. Public transportation was also hit. By 2000, Copenhagen's airport had been converted to a publicly traded company with a majority of shares in private hands. In 2001, the municipal bus company Combus was dismantled, and bus routes are now managed by private companies. The ferry operator Scandlines, co-owned with Germany, was peddled away in 2007. While DSB and Banedanmark are still publicly owned, the management of parts of their networks has been subcontracted out to the private firm Arriva (which in fact until recently was owned by Germany).

The last organization to undergo large-scale privatization was the state-owned energy company DONG, which operates power plants, wind farms, and the greater part of the electric grid for Sjælland. In a highly contested process, a large block of shares was sold to Goldman Sachs in 2014, and two years later it was listed on the stock exchange. The state still owns 51 percent of the shares, but a majority in the parliament has agreed to dispose of its stake.

Concurrent with this wave of privatization, various governments have also subcontracted the management of public firms to private concerns. Under the slogans of free choice and free competition, the Fogh government changed Danish law to permit the subcontracting of the management of daycare centers and even the establishment of new private, for-profit institutions.

But it is not only the publicly owned sector of the economy that has lost ground. The cooperative movement has also suffered serious losses. Just as with the public sector, the cooperative principles of democratic management and profit sharing have in the neoliberal epoch come to be seen as old fashioned and a drag on efficiency and growth. Agriculture was steadily mechanized beginning in the 1960s, and the number of farmers fell year after year. Local dairies and slaughterhouses closed, and production ended up being concentrated in fewer and fewer facilities. This centralization concluded with the establishment of a large dairy firm, today Arla, and a corresponding meat producer, Danish Crown. Today both are global giants operating across the planet with subsidiaries and markets in many countries, which has led to debates about how member democracy can be maintained. Today many people find it hard to see the difference between large cooperatives and private firms. Yet Arla and Danish Crown are still democratically managed and profits are still distributed among the members as before.

While the agricultural cooperatives have managed to survive, the worker-owned cooperative enterprises have fared worse. By 1964, the cooperative brewery Stjernen had gone bankrupt after years of losing market share to Carlsberg and Tuborg. The textile cooperative Tilskærernes Aktieselskab closed in 1969, as did Como, the cooperative shoe factory, in 1971. A number of bakery co-ops also went under, while others were taken over by FDB, which thus kept them in the cooperative family. A new wave of closures and sell-offs began in the 1990s. Dansk Andelstrykkeri and the data cooperative KD with its 350 employees were swallowed up by Mærsk. In 2005 the last of the building cooperative giants, J&B Enterprise A/S, went into bankruptcy protection. Today only a few of the older worker co-ops remain, most of which are in the building trades.[23]

Public ownership of the financial sector has contracted most severely. Almost all the cooperative banks and mortgage lenders have been taken over by commercial concerns. After a new law was passed in 1988, the leadership of many of the cooperative banks persuaded their members to convert to publicly traded commercial firms, thus ending a century of democratic governance. Many of these failed on the stock exchange and have since gone under or been acquired by large financial concerns. Similarly, after the liberalization of mortgage regulations, commercial banks took over the old cooperative institutions one after the other, often in dubious ways that did not afford the members much say. The de-democratization of finance has cost homeowners, farmers, and businesses dearly, since the new owners demand annual returns and have thus driven up fees.

The cooperative housing sector is still strong, but few new units have been built in recent decades. From 2000 to 2015 fewer than ten thousand new units were constructed, compared to the hundred thousand during the 1970s. The center of gravity has shifted away from the co-ops, with the majority of new homes either owner-occupied or privately owned rental units.[24]

We have thus witnessed the marked weakening of the democratic, noncapitalist portion of our economy, both among the civil society cooperatives and the public sector. This means that we as citizens, employees, tenants, and consumers have less influence on the economy and our society, while the oligarchic power of elites has grown decisively in strength.

It is important that we learn from this weakening of the democratic sector. In an economy with both democratic and capitalist sectors there will be competition between the two modes of production. Capitalists have a powerful interest in colonizing and taking over those areas of production in the democratic sector, whether public or cooperative, since controlling them allows capitalists to expand the areas of the economy from which they can extract profit. As long as such competition exists, the democratic sector will face pressure from the nondemocratic.

But it is by no means inevitable that such competition will always result in less democracy. As noted, the tendency was in the opposite direction for long periods of the twentieth century, with the expansion of the democratic sector into formerly capitalist areas, which was driven by pressure from below and from civil society as well as through politics and favorable legislation.

The decline of the democratic sector in recent decades owes largely to the fact that the neoliberal ideological offensive has succeeded in convincing a majority that democratic forms of ownership are inefficient and old fashioned and that market forces and liberalization are modern, progressive, and emancipatory. It was this ideological victory that convinced so many cooperative banks and mortgage lenders to convert to publicly traded firms or fuse with large financial concerns and that persuaded so many politicians right and left to sell off publicly owned enterprises and introduce market reforms into the welfare state.

Political framing and power relations have therefore set the scene for competition between the democratic and nondemocratic sectors. Political decision-making can either set up barriers to or provide support for the one or the other. In the neoliberal era we have witnessed the transference of market power to large nondemocratic concerns, which has made it difficult for the democratic sector to grow and to develop, such as by limiting access to credit or investment.

But the success of the neoliberal offensive is also due to the lack of resistance from the political left, which should have risen up in defense of the democratic sector. But because both branches of the Western left misunderstood its nature and underestimated its value, they focused instead on "actually existing socialism" in China, Yugoslavia, and the Soviet Union, rather than protecting what had been built up just outside their doorsteps.

Finally, the de-democratization of the democratic sector was facilitated by the erosion of democratic participation and a declining sense of co-ownership in many areas. The democratic public sector did not afford enough of a voice for all employees and citizens. And as the cooperative enterprises became large, professionalization and top-down management undermined the influence and participation of ordinary members, leading to widespread indifference when the co-ops were either privatized or de-democratized. Altogether these are important lessons we must keep in mind as we move forward.

Democracy Reawakens

Despite these setbacks the Danish economy still has a strong democratic sector. A 2019 report found that more than eighteen thousand democratically managed enterprises are operating in Denmark. Democratically managed firms in our private sector account for just under 10 percent of total trade, and one in twenty private sector employees work for such companies.[25]

As of 2019, Coop, the cooperative provider of daily necessities, had 1.8 million members, which means that a majority of Danish households have the opportunity to vote and to run for the leadership councils that constitute its democratic management. Our utility sector is still dominated by consumer-owned cooperatives, and we have seen numerous privatized heat providers returned to cooperative ownership. Our largest mortgage lender is still the member-owned Nykredit. And both Arbejdernes Landsbank and Lån og Spar Bank are owned by the trade union movement and its pension funds. The democratically run co-op bank Merkur has nearly forty thousand customers, and Coop has recently established its own bank.

The level of democratic participation by the members is far from optimal in the large consumer-owned enterprises. For a long time Nykredit did not explicitly inform its members that they had voting rights, which meant that the leadership was generally made up of the economic elite. But after a member revolt in 2016, democratic procedures were streamlined, which has helped make members much more aware of the democratic nature of Nykredit.

The aftermath of the 2008 financial crisis has in general led Danes to rediscover the value of democratic ownership in many of the old consumer-owned enterprises. Coop has begun re-emphasizing the fact that it is a customer-owned operation that is not first and foremost concerned with turning a profit. And the general rediscovery of the advantages of democracy has led to the establishment of Tænketanken Demokratisk Erhverv, an institution that for the first time in Danish history has united the two branches of the democratic sector, resolving the old political divisions between the urban workers' cooperatives and the rural producers' co-ops.

The democratic public sector still remains strong in spite of privatization and marketization. Unlike in Norway and Sweden, privatization and outsourcing have largely not effected core welfare programs, which constitute the largest part of public sector enterprise. And even though as a result of the privatization of GiroBank the state no longer offers basic banking services, there are still numerous other public credit facilities, such as SU-lån for students, KommuneKredit, which provides cheap credit to municipalities, and Vækstfonden and Danmarks Grønne Investeringsfond, which provide capital to entrepreneurs and startups.

Much suggests that since the financial crisis public opinion has shifted toward the view that democratic ownership must be preserved in both the public and the cooperative sectors. Thorning-Schmidt's proposal to sell DONG shares to Goldman Sachs was met with a powerful wave of protest. In a matter of a few weeks more than two hundred thousand signatures were gathered in opposition to the sale, and public opinion polling revealed that 80 percent of the population was against privatization.[26]

Similarly, member protests forced Nykredit to scrap its plan to forego a century of union ownership by listing itself on the stock exchange. The decision of Kooperation's leadership to sell off ALKA, its venerable insurance firm, was severely criticized and resulted in demonstrations outside 3F's headquarters on Kampmannsgade in Copenhagen, while the decision of Ørsted (formerly DONG) to sell off Copenhagen's electric grid to a foreign capital fund unleashed a wave of protests and a tenfold increase in voter turnout to determine consumer representation on the company's board. The ensuing debate led parliament to mandate that critical infrastructure must be owned by either consumers or the state.[27]

Danes have in general rediscovered the cooperative idea, establishing new co-ops across the country. On Samsø in 2013 a group of citizens founded a community-owned organic land-use fund to which all citizens may contribute and that is used to purchase land and convert it to organic use by leasing it out to young organic farmers who lack the financial means to buy existing farmland.[28] The experience of Samsø quickly inspired the establishment of a new national organic land-use fund, Økojord A/S, to which citizens contribute a part of their pension funds in order to support the development of organic agriculture. In just three years the fund has grown to 730 members and has acquired seven holdings that are collectively owned and leased out to organic farmers.

Further examples of the renewed rural cooperative movement abound, such as Andelsgaarde, established by the sociologist Rasmus Willig. For dues of DKK 150 per month, members can help finance the purchase of agricultural land that will be farmed organically and in a way that takes into account climate change and biodiversity. In the little fishing village of Thorupstrand in northern Jutland, a producers' fishing cooperative has been established. Thorupstrands Kystfiskerlaug operates according to communal fishing rights, distributing them among its membership. The cooperative gives special consideration to young fishermen, providing them with better opportunities to establish themselves and challenging the concentration of fishing rights that marketization has engendered.

In the capital, an array of employee-owned enterprises has appeared. The largest is the contractor Logik & Co., whose seventy employees collectively make all decisions concerning the management of the company in weekly all-hands meetings. Furthermore, the firm has an equal pay policy, which means that all employees receive the same wages regardless of whether they are directors or workers. In a wholly different sector, a group of twenty academics established the data analytics bureau Analyse & Tal. Rabotnik is a graphic design cooperative, while KnowledgeWorker offers various consulting services on a cooperative basis.

Unlike in the previous era of union-owned workers' co-ops, the new generation is indeed owned and controlled by workers. Yet despite these good signs, Denmark is relatively behind in the establishment of new democratic enterprises. The latest figures from Cooperatives Europe show that in 2013 seventy-five hundred new co-ops were formed in Italy, 650 in Belgium, and 550 in Sweden. There are no precise numbers for Denmark, but the total is significantly lower.[29] It is remarkable that a country with such a long tradition of democratic enterprise has fallen behind. But this is largely due to the fact that other countries have consciously supported the growth of democratic firms with credit, consulting services, and tax advantages. It is therefore high time that we in Denmark also jump-start a democratic revolution in our business world and in our economy. More on that in the final part of the book.

What Can We Learn from 150 Years of Democratic Economy?

The story I have told in this chapter underlines my point that the capitalist mode of production has always faced competition in Denmark as well as in other Nordic countries. The establishment of collectively owned democratic enterprises, like the building up of the democratic welfare state, has always been the response of ordinary people to the injustice and inequality that is part and parcel of capitalism. And thus when in the coming decades we construct a new egalitarian and democratic economy, a Nordic socialism, we will hardly be starting from scratch. On the contrary we have much experience, knowledge, and praxis to build on.

Yet history also reveals that a democratic economy is subject to backsliding. The power relations between the capitalist and democratic sectors of our economy are not static; they can be changed, in one direction or the other. In recent years the capitalist part of the economy has expanded outward into more and more areas and market forces have been given leave to colonize new sectors of the economy. Our task now is to reverse this trend, to rediscover, to develop, to expand the democratic sector. And fortunately there appears to be a rising awareness of the value of collectively owned and democratically managed enterprise, in the form of both public ownership and the cooperative model. We as citizens have become increasingly aware of how the concentration of ownership negatively impacts our existence and hems in the space for democracy. It is encouraging to see so many rise to the defense of our common inheritance and to see so many new democratic enterprises established

But it is important that we learn from past experience and from the decline of the earlier communal economy. As long as the capitalist sector remains dominant, its democratic alternative will always be hard pressed, since private capital can expand its activities and earnings, crowding out more and more of the democratic areas of the economy. And capitalists will use their oligarchic power to bring about political change that favors their designs: privatization, outsourcing of public sector services, the de-democratization of cooperatives.

It is therefore necessary that we employ our democratic power to protect and to nourish the democratic sector. Just as in recent decades we have used legislation to promote the greening of our economy, so now we need to pass laws to support its democratization.

But it is equally important that the community-owned sector be grounded in democratic participation, in the public and private spheres. All kinds of institutions, including democratic enterprises, face the risk of democratic erosion and the rise of top-down bureaucratic management. This is an inherent risk in a modern economy based on labor specialization and large-scale operations. Yet we can still learn from past experiences to minimize this risk. We cannot escape the fact that the precondition of democratic economy is our own participation. If we do not embrace a sense of democratic responsibility, if we forget the advantages of collective ownership and democratic management, then we will squander what we have built and capitalists will be left to pick up the pieces.

In other words, the building up of a new democratic economy demands a combination of the political will to set up the proper political and economic structures, the development of sustainable democratic structures, and, just as importantly, an engaged populace ready to work together. We must emulate the poor laborers in Thisted who took the initiative to establish the first democratic consumer cooperative, the farmers who established the first dairy and slaughterhouse co-ops, the trade union activists who built cheap housing for their houseless comrades, and the citizens, employees, and politicians who built up a strong welfare society. This is the necessary foundation for the development of a Nordic democratic socialism that spreads out and democratizes ownership, thereby shifting the power over the development of our society from the few to the many.

In the following chapter I discuss how we can bring such an economy into being.

4

Nordic Democratic Socialism

In the first part of this book I have shown how a capitalist-dominated economy creates a self-reinforcing oligarchic power that makes it difficult or impossible for governments to pursue policies that benefit the interests of the majority and how the unplanned pursuit of profit margins prevents us from addressing the greatest challenges of our time: destructive global warming and the threat of extinction.

We have seen how the social democratic idea of regulated capitalism worked for a time but in the end proved fragile and temporary, since it did not alter economic power relations. The revolutionary left's solution to that problem, the seizure of power by extraparliamentary revolution, was hardly a realistic or attractive proposition in a democratic society with a highly developed and complex economy. Instead I have identified a third approach that combines the patience of social democratic reformism with the accurate assessment of the revolutionary left that sustainable change is contingent on a foundational democratization of ownership in the economy.

This road to change is based on a rejection of the traditional view of capitalism as an all-encompassing economic system that we either have to accept or reject entirely and on the recognition that as long as capitalism has existed ordinary human beings have created democratic alternatives. I have shown that Denmark and the other Nordic countries have always had an expansive democratic sector that has functioned either outside of or in opposition to the capitalist economy and that we can develop, deepen, strengthen, and reimagine it so that it might serve as the experiential foundation and the seed of a new Nordic socialism.

This brings us to the fourth and most important chapter of the book, which concerns the future and the precise nature of the democratic economy we seek to develop. *Where* do we want to go? And *how* shall we get there?

When we abandon the idea that capitalism is an all-encompassing system by recognizing that all societies are hybrids consisting of multiple economic logics and modes of production, we also forego the conception of socialism as an all-encompassing system. Instead we conceive of socialism as a society in which socialistic and democratic forms of ownership are dominant but not necessarily exclusive.

In this chapter, I attempt to identify a set of overriding principles for describing what a new democratically dominated economy, a Nordic socialism, would look like. I will try to address questions like how democracy might be extended into the economic sphere and our working lives, what democratic ownership means, how we can become owners, what role market mechanisms should play in a future economy, and how to create an economy that secures the greatest freedom and democratic influence for the individual while at the same time making optimal use of society's resources.

In chapter 5 I will transpose these core principles in a set of concrete reforms that constitute the first steps toward Nordic socialism.

Political Democracy Is Necessary but Insufficient

It is important to stress that Nordic socialism does not entail a transformation of our basic political structure: a parliamentary democracy with strong and inviolable individual rights.

No higher goal can justify the suspension of individual rights, and all social change must be anchored in democratic institutions and based on the will of the majority. It ought not be necessary to emphasize this. While today's left is generally at the forefront of the struggle to protect individual rights, democracy, and freedom, both in Denmark and abroad, it is important to acknowledge and learn from the instances in which the historical left has been guilty of curtailing democracy and individual rights, including cases of its more or less openly defending undemocratic and repressive regimes, flirting with the idea of the violent or extraparliamentary seizure of power, and espousing the idea of the permanent or temporary suspension of foundational individual rights.

There are many explanations for our previous failures, among them a lack of knowledge of conditions behind the iron curtain and the polarization of Cold War worldviews that led left and right alike to avert their eyes from the transgressions of "friendly" regimes.

But they also were the result of more fundamental ideological problems, first and foremost the idea that parliamentary democracy was "bourgeois democracy" and thus intimately linked to the capitalist mode of production. Socialism would thus require a new and higher form of governance like "council democracy," according to which workers' councils appointed political delegates to a national assembly.

In my view it is ironic to conceive of parliamentary democracy, individual rights, universal suffrage, and majority rule as bourgeois, given that it was largely the left that led the struggle for such ideals, while the right was typically highly critical of them. While it is correct that parliamentarianism triumphed during the same period as the rise of capitalism, it often faced powerful opposition from capitalist elites. And given the emergence of authoritarian, antidemocratic capitalist economies like China it is even more evident now that there is no organic connection between capitalism and parliamentary democracy. Capitalism can exist without parliaments, and parliaments can exist without capitalism.

For my part it is clear that the form of parliamentarianism in Denmark and the other Nordic countries has historically proven itself to be the best form of democratic governance, at least within the borders of the national state. It can and ought to be deepened and expanded, perhaps through more local control or through more referenda or more direct participation from the citizenry in the form of a citizens' parliament chosen by lot, as a number of Danish democratic theorists have proposed.[1] And as I will return to later, it is even more critical that democratic influence be extended into our working lives and the economy at large.

But the multiparty system itself, with its low barriers to parliamentary entry, a free and secret ballot, and protocols whereby the parliamentary majority determines who may form a government, does not need much tinkering, if only because no better alternative exists or at least none yet has been identified. The idea of council democracy, based on worker's councils in each place of employment, does not in my opinion provide any answer to the question of how retirees, the self-employed, or any other group outside the labor force is to be secured political influence.

Finally, and most importantly, the serious problems afflicting our current democracy are not the fault of the parliamentary system but the result of the oligarchic power wielded by the unelected economic elite. It is this undemocratic, *extra*parliamentary power that prevents fundamental change favoring the majority. Parliamentary democracy must therefore be liberated from oligarchic power, it must be renewed and fully realized through the democratization of the economy and of ownership.

Parliamentarianism and the protection of our individual rights are thus *necessary* preconditions for democratic governance, but they are not *sufficient*. As long as democracy is confined to the political sphere and does not encompass our working lives and the economy and as long as economic power relations are as they are today, our democracy will be incomplete and the freedom of the majority limited.

Capitalism and the Limits of Freedom

"Like everything around here, Ricky, it's your choice." So the boss informs his new delivery driver in the opening scene of British director Ken Loach's *Sorry We Missed You*.

The film portrays the miserable working conditions ushered in by the British gig economy in which permanent employment is increasingly replaced with "partnerships." Ricky is not actually employed by the delivery service but is an independent contractor responsible for his own hours, holidays, sick days, insurance. He works ten hours a day, often through the weekend. Calling in sick or making small mistakes are punished with fines, which hollow out his already meager income. His wife, Abby, works under similarly unreasonable conditions for a private in-home care provider. She must pay for her own breaks and transportation, and the workday rarely ends before 9:30 p.m. The family slowly falls apart because of the parents' inhumane working conditions and the lack of sufficient downtime for all the things life should be about: care, children, togetherness, love. Loach effectively sets the opening scene's insistence on Ricky's free choice up against the harsh reality of a labor market that is characterized by anything but freedom or independence.

The right has always sung the praises of capitalism as the domain of freedom that enables free human beings to enter into free contractual relations with other free human beings, as the pithy slogan has it. But the idea of free choice has always been a theoretical abstraction. Like most of the world's wage workers, Ricky and Abby rarely have much of a choice. They have rent that must be paid and children that must have clothing on their backs and food on the table. They are compelled to sell their labor power on a labor market over which they have no control or influence and that has steadily become more brutal and unforgiving.

In contrast to the liberal fairy tale, the capitalist economy is not a level playing field occupied by individuals with similar measures of power and possibility. Instead it divides us into a large majority that lives off the sale of its labor power and a small minority that owns businesses, banks, and other parts of the apparatus of production and purchase labor power from the majority. It is this latter class that unilaterally makes decisions regarding who is hired and how the time purchased from wage workers is utilized.

In a well-known lecture subsequently published in book form under the title *Private Government: How Employers Rule Our Lives (and Why We Don't Talk About It)*, philosopher Elizabeth Anderson, whose area of interest is the contrast between much celebrated democratic ideals and the reality of working lives, compares the absence of democracy in the workplace to a political system:

> Imagine a government that assigns almost everyone a superior whom they must obey. Although superiors give most inferiors a routine to follow, there is no rule of law. . . . Inferiors have no right to complain in court about how they are being treated, except in a few narrowly defined cases. . . . [This government] may prescribe a dress code and forbid certain hairstyles. Everyone lives under surveillance, to ensure that they are complying with orders. Superiors may snoop into inferiors' e-mail and record their phone conversations. . . . The form of the government is a dictatorship. In some cases, the dictator is appointed by an oligarchy. In other cases, the dictator is self-appointed. . . . Would people subject to such a government be free?[2]

She then proceeds to note that what she is describing is in fact the reality at most American workplaces.

Anderson supports her argument with a long series of examples of how American employers transgress the rights of their employees in ways we would never tolerate from the government. Amazon forbids its employees to speak to one another and calls such conversations "time theft." Employees of Apple stores must wait in line at the end of their shifts so their bags can be searched. Tyson Foods does not allow adequate bathroom breaks and instead encourages employees to wear diapers. So-called noncompete clauses limit the freedom of employees to work elsewhere, even after they have resigned. Anderson does not shy away from using the word "dictatorship" to describe relations between employees and employers. A dictatorship, as she explains, is precisely a form of government in which citizens (here the employees) are subjected to the authority of the dictator (here the employer) and in which the exertion of power is not vested in any democratic process.[3]

The liberal response to this is to cite the classical liberal idea of freedom of contract: that there can be no dictatorship when workers have the freedom to quit. But Anderson does not give much credence to this argument: "This is like saying that Mussolini was not a dictator, because Italians could emigrate."[4]

Furthermore, in most cases this freedom is limited to seeking employment at a different firm with the same kind of undemocratic authority or else abandoning the prospect of earning a living. Freedom of contract is, in other words, an abstraction that does not protect citizens from compulsion and subjection in the economic sphere.

In Denmark and Norway we are fortunate to have a workplace tradition that is less hierarchical and dictatorial than in other countries. Employees are often included in decision-making and have influence over workplace arrangements. Through the struggles of organized labor we have acquired rights that limit the power of employers. We cannot, for example, be fired because we wish to join a labor union. Yet even with our less hierarchical tradition and our hard-won rights, power relations are the same. It is the employer who unilaterally decides who to hire and who to fire. Employees who do not follow or who oppose the orders of the employers will sooner or later receive a pink slip. This is the juridical and practical nature of power relations in a capitalist labor market. To be able to take away a person's daily bread is an immensely strong card to play that regardless of culture or tradition sets the terms for the relationship between employee and employer under capitalism.

It is paradoxical that we silently assent to the idea that the place where we spend most if not many of our waking hours, our workplace, is a place where democratic ideals and principles do not apply.

As citizens we expect democratic influence over our political system. We view ourselves as competent enough to participate in debates on everything from the tax system to foreign policy. But when we set foot in the workplace, we assume the role of subject rather than sovereign citizen.

It is such contradictions—between the ideal of freedom and the reality of compulsion, between our roles as democratic citizens in the political sphere and as dependent subjects in the economic sphere—that a Nordic socialism must seek to resolve.

For a democracy that does not extend into a significant part of our social lives is wholly incomplete, unjust, and in the long run will not survive.

A commitment to democracy and individual rights thus necessarily entails the desire to change the economic system because our present system is based on an antiquated understanding of democratic participation, according to which many of the rights we enjoy as citizens are taken away the moment we enter the workplace, and further because of the concentration of capitalist ownership and the exertion of antidemocratic and oligarchic power.

A modern socialism must work toward the expansion of the democratic rights of the citizenry, such that we acquire far greater influence over our workplaces and the economy as a whole. The most important means of achieving these goals is the greater democratization and distribution of economic ownership. A broader and more democratic form of ownership of businesses, banks, land, and homes can provide ordinary citizens with much greater influence over the economy and secure a wider distribution of the wealth of society.

Ownership and Democratic Codetermination

Property relations constitute the beating heart of every society. Understanding how an economic system functions requires knowing who owns capital, the means of production, and the land. Those who own and manage firms determine labor arrangements, what is produced, and not of least significance, how surplus is distributed and employed. They decide if the firm will relocate to another country or if aspects of its production will be outsourced. Such decisions by ownership thus impact virtually every aspect of our lives, as workers, as consumers, as borrowers, and as citizens.

That most firms are currently owned either by a handful of wealthy families or by a majority group of investors and shareholders means that a very small group has great power, while the large majority are denied influence over decisions of importance. As employees we have very little say over our work arrangements. As local communities we are powerless if the capital fund that owns the local business decides to close it or to send our jobs elsewhere. As bank customers we can only shake our heads when the financial sector careens from one scandal to another or invests in fossil fuels despite the threat they pose to the survival of our planet. As citizens it is we who suffer the consequences when the conduct of banks or corporations plunges society into crisis, throwing people out of work and onto the streets.

This form of ownership also contributes to an ever-widening gap in wealth and power across society. We can of course redistribute wealth through a progressive tax system and thereby redress a measure of the inequality generated by this unjust system of property relations. But the most critical distribution of wealth occurs before the taxation phase, that is, what economists call predistribution. It is this skewed system that provides economic elites with extensive undemocratic and oligarchic influence.

The system of ownership wholly determines the way an economy functions, how it is rationalized, and which interests are protected. In an economy dominated by a narrow capitalist ownership class, short-term profit seeking determines investment and production decisions. Such short-term thinking exhibits little regard for workers or consumers and further constitutes one of the primary barriers to addressing the threats of climate change and the extinction of species.

In short, any strategy for democratic and sustainable social change must include a plan for the development of a new architecture of democratic ownership. As Swedish social democratic economist Rudolf Meidner puts it, "We cannot fundamentally change society without also changing the nature of ownership."[5]

The question of how ownership can be distributed and democratized has thus also been central to the socialist movement. For who indeed are the owners in a democratic economy? Who directs the enterprises and who decides how surpluses shall be employed? The state? The employees themselves? Consumers or local communities? And what about undemocratic firms? Do they still have a place in the future economy? And what can we learn from previous experiments with forms of social, democratic, and collective ownership? These questions are addressed in the following pages.

The Socialists and the State

"Damnit, Pelle!" Ejvind Larsen slammed his fist on the table, so that the coffee cups jumped. "No way are we going to replace the capitalists with bureaucrats in the finance ministry. It should be the people themselves!" This outburst from the former chief editor of the newspaper *Information* bears the kind of exasperation only known to those who for years have tried in vain to push the left into action. We're sitting in my office at Christiansborg, discussing something that has perplexed socialists throughout the last hundred years: the state, and even more so, what role the state should play in a socialist economy.

His point is clear enough: the state is no friend to the socialist. A socialist economy can never be built merely by replacing the capitalist whip crackers and power brokers with the state and its army of bureaucrats and public officials. Larsen has made this argument all his life. In his 1974 book *The Damn State*, he states that the left's fixation on the state amounts to a blind alley: "Society should take over the means of production, say the socialists. But what is society to the ordinary person? DSB, the postal and telephone services, city hall, bureaucratic departments. . . . As long as people associate socialism with petty officials, a right-wing fanatic like Mogens Glistrup will always appeal to their dissatisfaction."[6]

Many people still equate socialism with state control and state ownership of the economy, which makes sense given that in the so-called socialist countries of the former Eastern bloc, power was extremely centralized and that here at home both the social democratic and revolutionary wings of the socialist movement have maintained a firm faith in state solutions.

Yet the relationship between socialists and the state has always been more nuanced, for the founding fathers of socialism were themselves critical of the state. Karl Marx refers to it as a "parasite, feeding upon, and clogging the growth of, society" and argues that the first program of the German social democrats was plagued by a "submissive faith in the state."[7] According to Friedrich Engels, the development of a socialist society would send "the whole state machinery where it will then belong—into the museum of antiquities, by the side of the spinning-wheel and the bronze axe," while in *The State and Revolution*, Vladmir Lenin claims that "as long as there is a state, there is no freedom."[8]

But paradoxically, the very state that the founders of socialism wanted to consign to the dustbin of history also constituted a key element in the plans for socialist transformation they advocated. In *The Communist Manifesto*, Marx and Engels explain that the proletariat should "centralize all means of production in the hands of the state." Here and elsewhere they advocate for the nationalization of the economy that could be accomplished by the state taking over the private firms and banks. It goes without saying that a state power that owns and manages the whole of production would not be weaker but indeed much stronger. And when one simultaneously foresees the replacement of the market economy with central planning, in which production and prices are determined by the state, it is evident that the scope of the state shall be increased dramatically. It is therefore no surprise that an expansive and powerful state with a comprehensive bureaucracy took root in the countries that tried to develop a socialist economy on the Marxist-Leninist model. There was never any indication that the state was on course to *wither away*, as Marx and Engels had foreseen.

Well-informed socialists will surely object that the plan was incremental, that the stateless communist society envisioned by Marx, Engels, and Lenin was expected to follow a period of state socialism. But is it not paradoxical to expect that the overthrow of state power could be achieved through the development of an all-powerful centralized state power? State bureaucracies tend to increase their own power. A large and powerful state will create a powerful and influential bureaucratic class with its own interest in maintaining the scope of the state, as the emergence of the *nomenklatura* of the Soviet Union makes abundantly clear.

State power can of course be abused. An inherent problem of a socialism based on extensive state ownership is that there is only a single employer with a monopoly over the purchase of labor power. In the Eastern European regimes, the state used its monopoly to punish dissidents by denying them promotion or simply by banishing them from the labor market. In an economy with a large nonstate sector, the state will lack this monopoly power and thus its ability to suppress dissent and opposition.

The Soviet and East European regimes were of course not democracies but dictatorships. In a democratic socialist model with democratic governance and free elections, this kind of abuse of power might very well never happen, even with an expanded field of state ownership. But even in democracies it is, in my view, healthier to have more than one economic power center, which then forces the state power to balance itself against other power centers within civil society. In their 2019 book *The Narrow Corridor: States, Societies, and the Fate of Liberty*, economists Daron Acemoglu and James Robinson undertake a comparative analysis of states in an attempt to determine what makes for a successful society. Their conclusion is clear: successful democratic political systems that secure extensive freedoms for their citizens are rooted in a delicate balance between state and society. Using Thomas Hobbes as their starting point, they identify two opposing poles in the history of state theory. On the one side is the despotic Leviathan, that is, a powerful state, and on the other is the absent Leviathan, that is, a state that does too little. Between these two is a narrow corridor that the authors call "the chained Leviathan" where a good balance between state and civil society can be achieved.[9] In a *Financial Times* review of the book, economics commentator Martin Wolf identifies Denmark and the other Nordic welfare societies as examples of countries that have largely found the correct balance.[10]

The premises of the book may be debated, and it can be critiqued for overlooking the no less influential power centers located among the economic elite. But the idea that state power, regardless of how democratic it is and which economic model is adopted, must be balanced by a powerful and well-organized civil society seems to me to hit the mark. Therefore a Nordic democratic socialism must preserve and improve on this balance rather than erect a socialist despotic Leviathan.

Volkseigener Betrieb

Another reason to be skeptical of relying on extensive state ownership is that it does not in and of itself guarantee that the people will feel like they are the owners. Firms in East Germany were officially called "volkseigener Betrieb"—the people's companies. But those who worked at these firms had no real sense of ownership. In most cases, as Larsen notes, they saw the state as the employer, just as we see the private firm under capitalism as the employer, which is why the workers did not protest much when state ownership was abandoned after the fall of the regime. Had Soviet or East German workers felt that these were their companies or, rather, had they had a collective ownership right to them, then the story would likely have been different. Instead they learned that one employer had simply replaced another.

The same story repeated itself in the case of the West European social democratic nationalizations that took place in the years after the Second World War. The British Labor government of Clement Attlee, for example, nationalized coal mining, utilities, and railroads, but these entities were largely managed by the same leadership as before and run as if they were capitalist enterprises. Neither employees nor consumers experienced much in the way of change, which made it relatively easy for Margaret Thatcher, when she came to power decades later, to reprivatize all the state-owned industries and most of the utility sector. In other words, state ownership is fragile, at least in the form it has historically assumed in Europe. A single change of government can roll back decades of the development of democratic ownership.

What is interesting is that ownership by civil society, whether in the form of employee- or consumer-owned enterprises, has proven itself to be more resistant to political change. If we compare Denmark to Britain, we see that even after thirty years of neoliberal reforms in Denmark, market forces play a much smaller role in our infrastructure than in the United Kingdom, precisely because consumer cooperatives rather than the state largely own utilities, waterworks, and heating and electricity providers. Even though right-leaning governments have tried again and again to marketize our utility sector, it is still predominantly democratic.

Similarly, while the Thatcher government was able to privatize a significant portion of publicly owned rental units, Anders Fogh Rasmussen's attempt to one-up Thatcher by forcing the housing co-ops to sell off their units when he assumed power in Denmark in 2001 failed because unlike in Britain these units were owned by the cooperative associations themselves. If he had succeeded he would have undermined our democratic housing sector, thereby seriously reducing ordinary people's access to affordable housing.

While it might seem paradoxical to socialists, it has been the protection of private property rights and our tradition of direct democratic ownership by civil society that have put the brakes on every attempt to marketize the Danish democratic economic sector. In my view this is a powerful argument that a new wave of the democratization of our economy must to a large extent be based on the direct ownership of firms and infrastructure by civil society rather than the state.

A Nordic socialism should therefore dispense with the idea that a socialist economy must centralize all means of production in the state. As shall be discussed later, this does not mean that the state should not play a critical role, both as the direct owner of select enterprises and as regulator. It means only that a democratic society demands a balance between the state and civil society and the existence of more than one center of economic power.

How Can We Own in Common?

If the state shouldn't own enterprises in a democratic economy, then who should? In his brief but convincing *A Preface to Economic Democracy*, American political scientist Robert A. Dahl considers the advantages and disadvantages of various forms of democratic ownership.[11] One alternative to state ownership, prominent in socialist Yugoslavia, is so-called social ownership, or worker self-governance. But while the workers themselves run the firm on this model, they do not in fact own it. Social ownership can be compared to what we call self-ownership, according to which ownership rests in the enterprise itself, so that no single person can lay claim to its capital. This is already familiar to us from our civil society funds and institutions. Self-owned firms are typically goal driven, that is, run according to regulations that are very difficult or impossible to change.

Swedish social democratic minister and theorist Ernst Wigforss argued for an economy in which the dominant form of enterprise would be "social enterprises without owners," as an alternative to the Soviet model of state ownership. In this self-ownership model, the employees and other interested parties of a particular firm would possess democratic power over its operations but would have no rights to its capital.[12] But as Dahl notes, social ownership in reality is just another form of state ownership, since in the absence of other owners the state ends up with the power that private owners otherwise might have. Denmark's experience of the state-orchestrated privatization of self-owned community banks and mortgage lenders confirms this to an extent; no one could object because no one owned them.

Another form of democratic ownership is rooted in the idea of individual ownership: here each member owns an equal-sized share of the enterprise, such as in employee stock ownership. This configuration honors the democratic ideals of one person, one vote, and the equal distribution of surpluses. But the challenge is that when individual share owners leave the firm they must be compensated, just as when new members join they must purchase a share. If the firm is successful, it will become increasingly more expensive and more difficult for new members to join. And as shall later be discussed, experience has shown that de-democratization is also a threat, since future shareholders could easily be tempted to hand over the company to capitalist interests in order to secure a short-term windfall.

A third model is cooperative or collective ownership, according to which employees, consumers, or borrowers own the enterprise in common as a group and have full democratic control over its operations and the distribution of its surpluses. But ownership is not individual, so individual members cannot sell their shares on the market. Dahl compares this form of collective ownership with citizenship in a democratic state: "Just as citizenship in a democratic country entitles one to full and equal rights as a member of the polity, but does not entitle one to claim ownership of an individual share of a country's wealth, so too in a cooperatively owned enterprise members have full and equal rights but cannot lay claim to a share in the assets or net worth of the firm to dispose of as they choose."[13] Such an enterprise is thus democratically managed by the employees, who can further distribute its annual surpluses among themselves. But if they leave the firm, they cannot demand a part of it as compensation or sell off their shares to others.

Dahl views this form of decentralized yet collective ownership as the best possibility—a kind of golden mean that on the one hand prevents state centralization and provides strong autonomy but on the other avoids the problems that result from individual ownership: "cooperative ownership avoids the problems arising from the need to dispose of individually owned shares" and "like individual ownership provides more protection for the autonomy of the firm against bureaucratic control by the state than would state or, in all likelihood, 'social ownership.'"[14]

I share much of Dahl's conclusion that the most ideal forms of democratic ownership are those that involve decentralized economic democracy within individual firms, which prevent the state from acquiring excessive power and which are based on the cooperative model, in which enterprises are owned collectively by shareholders but in which the individual, just like the citizen of a state, cannot stake personal claim to its capital. And it is precisely this form of ownership that has been predominant in the Danish cooperative movement. But as I will later emphasize, I do not think that we should seek a universal form of ownership for our enterprises but instead develop a pluralistic landscape of multiple structures.

Theories and ideas are one thing, but concrete experience with democratic ownership is another. In what follows I look closely at our historical experience with three specific models: that of the cooperative owned by employees, consumers, or other democratic formations, that of fund socialism, and that of democratic public ownership. I conclude by discussing the role nondemocratic enterprises can and should play in a future economy.

The Cooperative: Democratic Private Enterprise

About seventy employees, including bricklayers, carpenters, apprentices, office workers, and the director of the contracting firm Logik & Co., have gathered at an office on Ryesgade in Copenhagen for the weekly assembly. But unlike at most other companies, the boss does not run the show. Instead all decisions regarding the running of the firm are made democratically by all employees. One of these decisions is that the firm has adopted the policy of equal pay. Everyone is paid the same, from trade workers to the director.

Leaving Logik & Co., driving down Ryesgade and turning right on Nørrebrogade, we see a Super Brugsen grocery store, one of the eleven hundred branches of Coop, a cooperative owned and managed by its 1.9 million members. Many of the individual stores have their own steering committee, and it is also through the local shop that members can vote for Coop's national council, the top layer of its leadership that selects the directors that manage the day-to-day operations of the organization. The employees also have the right to choose a number of the councilors.

Logik & Co. and Coop are two very different institutions. The first is small, governed by employees, and run through direct democracy, while the second is large, controlled by consumers, and run as a representative democracy. But they are both cooperatives, that is, private, but democratically managed enterprises. Other kinds of cooperatives, as noted, include the bank Merkur, whose membership is made up of depositors, producers' co-ops like the ecological dairy producer Thise, and multistakeholder cooperatives that both employees and consumers exert influence over.

Cooperatives have two defining traits. First and foremost, they are democratically managed, governed according to the principle of one person one vote, unlike in capitalist firms, where one's degree of influence is determined by the amount of capital one invests. The power of capital is replaced by the power of employees, consumers, or other interest groups.

Second, if there is any surplus, the members decide how it is to be used, and if the surplus is to be distributed, it is the members who benefit. Democracy and profit sharing are the core principles of the cooperative form of enterprise.

There are many reasons why cooperatives can constitute an important part of a new democratic economy. Although it ought not be necessary to mention it, a society with many democratically managed enterprises is of course a more democratic society. More people have a voice in important economic decisions than when capital funds, wealthy families, or private shareholders monopolize ownership. When cooperatives replace or challenge nondemocratic firms, we take power away from the economic elites and give it to ordinary people—workers, consumers, borrowers, and renters.

At the same time, worker cooperatives transform the workplace—the place we spend the majority of our working hours—into a democratic institution where employees collectively make decisions. Consumer cooperatives provide ordinary people with collective influence over which goods are available and how surpluses are invested.

Democratic ownership also encourages social responsibility. It is no accident that the consumer-owned Coop was the first to stop selling caged eggs, that the energy co-ops led the way in green energy, or that the democratic pension funds were the first to pull their investments out of fossil fuels. Democratically owned firms often have a different conception of social responsibility than those that must answer to their shareholders at the end of each quarter and that have no other connection to the enterprise or the local community than financial ownership.

Finally, cooperatives provide an important check on the rising economic inequality that plagues the capitalist economy. The surpluses of economic enterprises owned in common get distributed among many people instead of lining the pockets of a narrow capitalist elite at the top of society. In worker co-ops it is the employees themselves who harvest the surpluses rather than capitalists. By not turning over surpluses to external owners or shareowners, co-ops can also offer lower prices.

But perhaps the greatest argument for a democratic economy based on cooperative ownership is that co-ops have proved themselves successful for more than a century. The cooperative movement is a form of realized utopia, not just in Denmark but across the globe. Roughly one billion people in the world are members of cooperatives, and more than 10 percent of the world's workers are employed by a co-op. In Europe, more than 170,000 cooperatives across multiple sectors annually produce more than EUR 1 trillion in economic output, which corresponds to about 10 percent of the European economy. The sector employs nearly 5 million people and claims more than 140 million members.[15]

Worker Cooperatives

Worker co-ops are a particularly important form of cooperative because the people who work for them and thus create the value are granted a share in the profits and have influence. While in Denmark it is largely consumer and producer cooperatives that have always dominated, worker cooperatives are much more widespread in other parts of the world.

The most widely known and studied example is the Spanish cooperative Mondragon, the fourth largest employer in Spain. It has 270 subsidiaries, more than seventy-five thousand employees in thirty-five countries and annual net revenues of EUR 2 billion. Some of its associated firms are small, while others employ thousands. Mondragon has both production firms, such as its auto parts manufacturer, as well as distribution outlets, including Spain's second largest retail chain, Eroski, with a thousand outlets, and other businesses in sectors like optometry, gasoline, flowers, and perfume. Tænketanken Demokratisk Erhverv director Andreas Pinstrup Jørgensen describes a visit to one of the cooperative's factories:

> "I feel like I am an owner of all this," says Inaka as she extends her arms outward toward the production line many hundreds of meters long. I find myself at one of Mondragon's immense industrial facilities. . . . Inaka works at Ederlan, which produces brake blocks for the auto industry, and the factory is abuzz today. BMW has placed a large order, and the machines are humming. And yet production soon shuts down. It is time for the monthly all-hands meeting. We steal a glance into the meeting hall, where despite visible fatigue people follow along as three presenters report on the firm. At the monthly meeting the workers meet with the leadership, and all are informed of the firm's production, sales, finances, accidents, and the like. Here everyone has time to speak, and anyone can ask a question or suggest something new, Inaka tells me. A cooperative that is a part of the Mondragon

> concern also attends annual conventions at which strategy and candidates for the leadership council are put to the vote. In other words the employees, if they so choose, can fire their boss.[16]

Despite its immense size, Mondragon remains mindful of the democratic character of both individual subsidiaries and the concern as a whole. The highest authority is the "congress," which consists of 650 delegates chosen by the individual member firms. The congress chooses a hundred-person leadership council that meets regularly and appoints the day-to-day leaders, including the president, who serves as director of the whole concern. Mondragon's co-op bank, Caja Laboral, accounts in part for the cooperative's lasting success. This institution provides loans and investments for the individual firms so that they can develop and grow. In addition to the bank, Mondragon also has research and entrepreneurial departments that seek out new markets to expand the reach of democratic ownership.

Another well-known example of a large worker cooperative is the British department store chain John Lewis & Partners, the largest employee-owned firm in Britain with about eighty-four thousand workers. It was the founder of the firm who decided to turn over ownership to a fund that would run the company in the interest of the workers. The leadership consists of worker representatives and a director as well as a board of external directors. All profits not reinvested in operations are paid out in dividends to the employees. UK citizens across the political spectrum have developed a favorable opinion of the idea of worker ownership as a result of the success of John Lewis. In 2014, the UK parliament passed a law inspired by the John Lewis model that gives large tax breaks to private owners who choose to turn over or to sell their firms to an employee ownership trust. This has led to the establishment of many new worker-owned enterprises. Since 2014 the sector has grown 62 percent and now employs two hundred thousand workers in more than 370 firms.[17]

In Italy there a number of regions with strong traditions of worker ownership. In Emilia Romagna, whose capital is the lovely medieval city of Bologna, seventy-five hundred cooperatives account for one-third of GDP. Two of every three firms are worker co-ops. On the whole Italy is a leader in securing influence and ownership for its workers and is home to about twenty-five thousand worker cooperatives all told. This success is due not only to its strong cooperative associations and co-op banks but also to legislation that has consciously tried to encourage the growth of democratic enterprise. Employees can, for example, receive financial support to purchase the firms for which they work and have the right to be informed prior to the sale or closure of their employing firms. France has found similar success in this wave of democratic conversion. Between 2012 and 2017, 780 conventional French capitalist companies were transformed into worker cooperatives.[18]

Can Cooperatives Challenge Platform Monopolies?

One of the most exciting developments is a series of spirited attempts to challenge the large digital platform firms. Companies like Uber and Wolt are based on the "gig" or "partnership" model, which means that workers are not employees in the normal sense of the term. Instead they are classified as independent partners and therefore lack the rights typically associated with employment. They have no fixed hours, no holidays, no pension, no employee accident coverage, and no sick days. These large firms also use their market power and near-monopoly status to exert pressure on their contractors. Restaurants, for example, must pay a premium to companies like Wolt for the privilege of using their app. But just as the Nordic cooperative movement challenged global cartels in the past, so-called platform cooperatives that are collectively owned and managed by the employees, the customers, or both have formed that compete with the platform giants.

In New York the cooperative platform Up & Go provides cleaning services with a guarantee of fair pay. Since no global platform giant harvests a part of the transaction, the workers earn twice that of those who work for other companies. In Montreal the cooperative Eva has taken up the struggle against Uber. As of 2021, it had five hundred drivers who were paid fair wages and who had favorable working conditions and served twenty thousand customers.[19] Eva is an example of a multistakeholder cooperative; both the drivers and the customers are members and have the right to participate in the annual meeting and a right to a share in the profits.

Airbnb is also facing competition from a democratic alternative. In the summer of 2020, an international cooperative consortium launched Fairbnb, a pilot project offering holiday home rentals in five Southern European cities, whose profits are used to support local development projects chosen by the hosts and renters together so that the local community might benefit from the transaction. Denmark's first platform cooperative, Delebil's LetsGo, is 100 percent nonprofit and owned by a fund to which all members belong and for which they choose the leadership.

Radical ideas about transforming social media platforms into global consumer cooperatives have also been attempted. In 2017 a proposal to convert Twitter to a user-owned cooperative made it all the way to the annual shareholder's meeting, although it was voted down.[20] The idea of establishing new democratic alternatives to the platform giants or of converting existing concerns to cooperatives may become more and more appealing as dissatisfaction grows.

How Are Cooperatives Owned and Organized?

Cooperatives can be organized in various ways with respect to both management and ownership.

It goes without saying that the democratic processes of a small firm like Logik & Co. are different from those of a large company like Mondragon or Coop. The larger the enterprise, the more it must rely on representative democratic models. But this increases the risk of rank-and-file members losing influence, or even the possibility that ordinary members are unaware they belong to a co-op. In the worst case, the self-appointed leadership might abandon democracy and collective ownership regardless of objections from the membership, as happened with the Danish mortgage credit cooperatives. It is therefore critical that the rights of the members of large cooperatives are fully secured, such as when critical decisions are made subject to the approval of the entire membership. Combining voting for the central leadership with decentralized democracy in the individual firm, department, or retail outlet is another approach, which has been successfully adopted by Mondragon and Coop. Thinking through these issues of democratic structure when new cooperatives are established is critical.

A potentially more important question concerns the ownership form of cooperatives. Democratic ownership, as noted, can be either individual or collective. In the former case, individual members personally own a proportionate share of the capital. This means that members receive a payout when the they leave the firm or when it is sold off or dissolved.

Another form of organization, especially popular in Southern Europe, is collective ownership, in which each employee owns the enterprise but lacks the individual right to claim a share of the capital. Employees enjoy full democratic participation as well as a share of all surpluses not reinvested, but they cannot buy or sell individual stakes.

Whether a cooperative is individually or collectively owned largely determines its ability to maintain its cooperative and democratic identity. History is unfortunately littered with examples of cooperatives that abandoned their democratic character or were sold off to capitalist interests. That a new generation of members can sell off a decades-old enterprise, thereby appropriating the value built up by generations of previous members, poses a significant challenge to the cooperative movement.

In a number of Southern European countries, it is therefore mandated that a significant portion of the firm's capital be placed in a so-called indivisible reserve, that is, a fund to which no individual member may stake a claim and that serves as a form of social or self-owned capital. Research shows that cooperatives with an indivisible reserve are less at risk of de-democratization, since the employees do not receive as large a windfall as when a cooperative without such a reserve is sold off.[21]

Are Cooperatives a Fool's Errand?

As noted, cooperatives have long been criticized by the left on the grounds that they are mere small islands in a sea of capitalism and thus are subject to being outcompeted by capitalist firms or being compelled to operate more and more like them. Rosa Luxemburg made this observation very early on, arguing that it was bad strategy to establish worker-run cooperatives, since inevitably they face the necessity of "governing themselves with the utmost absolutism. They are obliged to take toward themselves the role of the capitalist entrepreneur."[22] American sociologist Sam Gindin, who has published widely on socialist strategy in recent years, agrees that "competition trumps everything. Despite isolated exceptions, competing on capital's terms while trying to hang on to values that don't enhance competitiveness means repeatedly facing a choice between jettisoning those values and accepting defeat in competitive terms."[23]

This critique was especially prevalent in Denmark after the defeat of the large worker-owned cooperatives, including the brewery Stjernen and the bread maker Rutana. Yet this says little about the durability of co-ops in general, since these enterprises were not real cooperatives but owned by the labor movement and managed by leaders appointed by union leadership. In fact, studies from the United States, France, Spain, Italy, and Germany show that true cooperatives are more productive and generally fare better than conventional firms. A 2016 comprehensive international review of cooperative enterprises demonstrates that average productivity was 4 percent higher in cooperatives than in conventional capitalist companies, an unsurprising result, since workers in capitalist firms see no benefit from increased productivity (indeed, productivity increases can even lead to layoffs).[24] In a worker cooperative the income of the employee is directly tied to the performance of the firm.

Cooperatives also appear to be more robust and resilient, especially during economic crises. In Italy in the years after 2008, cooperatives failed at a rate three times lower than their conventional competitors. And a 2012 study by the British organization Co-Operatives UK found that while 35 percent of all registered private concerns went under after 2008, the rate for cooperatives was only 10 percent and democratic firms were twelve times more likely to survive.[25] European co-op banks were also much less vulnerable to the crisis and thus provided a critical service in the form of stabile credit when private banks everywhere cut off access.

Cooperatives are also blessed with natural advantages in the competition against nondemocratic enterprises. Since they do not have external investors, at least to the same degree, they are not subject to external pressure for high returns on investment. Nor are they burdened by exorbitant pay packages for CEOs and board members. Both these factors significantly reduce costs. And because of the influence granted to workers and the promise of surplus distribution, they are able to attract the best talent. A recent U.S. study found that 72 percent of the fifteen hundred working Americans surveyed prefer working for a worker cooperative, while only 19 percent prefer working for a conventional firm.[26]

Cooperatives, however, don't merely need to survive but also need to be able to grow and take market share from capitalist enterprises rather than remaining a marginal element of the capitalist economy. Here the advantages are less clear. As noted, the cooperative democratic sector has grown in many countries. And yet it will surely be challenging to take the fight to the capitalist enterprises in a business climate at best characterized by an unfamiliarity with the cooperative idea and at worst by outright hostility. Many barriers, including here in Denmark, remain, since legislative and financial structures are slanted toward capitalist firms.

The future of the democratic economy thus requires securing favorable conditions for cooperatives and for worker ownership through political action. The development of a powerful cooperative movement from below must be accompanied by political struggle for conditions that encourage democracy and profit sharing. Experience confirms that countries with growing democratic sectors have all passed laws creating favorable conditions for the establishment of new cooperatives, for the conversion of conventional firms, and for the growth of existing co-ops. More on this later.

But even with the right political conditions, the expansion of the democratic sector is hardly enough to democratize ownership in general. Given the dominance of large publicly traded corporations in today's economy, there is need for other means. Here we take inspiration from the concept of funds socialism, an idea that took root in Scandinavia in the 1970s but has recently been revived by Bernie Sanders in the United States and the British Labour Party under Jeremy Corbyn.

Funds Socialism

Funds socialism encompasses several distinct ideas grounded in a desire to democratize the economy through the gradual transfer of ownership of large firms from narrow elites to democratically administered funds. The aims are to ensure that broader groups acquire a share of economic growth and further to widen influence and participation through the use of the voting rights that accompany ownership. The funds can function at the level of the individual enterprise, such that employees become owners and receive a share of the profits and influence over the management. Or they can be established at the national level, so that ownership and influence are distributed across the entire population.

Transforming power relations by using one of the core principles of capitalism, shareholding, might seem paradoxical. But the idea can in fact be traced back to Austrian socialist Rudolf Hilferding, who noted in 1910 that the impersonal, diffused, and distant mode of ownership that characterizes shareholding would make the democratization of the economy simpler and relatively painless, since at base this would involve replacing existing passive ownership with a democratically anchored form.

Funds socialism is attractive precisely because it does not propose a sudden and radical transformation of the existing system but only the reimagining and reengineering of its present structures. Simply transferring a rising measure of ownership from a small group of wealthy shareholders and wealth managers to a large democratic formation also doesn't affect the capital reserves of firms (as does taxation) or the day-to-day management of the business.

Denmark and Sweden on the Road to Funds Socialism

Denmark is known as the land that gave us handball and *hygge*. But the first proposal for funds socialism was also developed here. "The right to a share in the ownership of the value one creates. The right to a say in workplace decision-making. This is what we mean by economic democracy." Such was written on the back of the reddish black folders distributed by social democratic stewards to their coworkers during the 1970s.

Decades of near full employment and a historically strong labor movement that had already won many battles gave Danish workers the courage and tenacity to think radically, to question why a handful of individuals exert outsize control over the whole economic life of society, and why workers, on the other hand, enjoy so little influence over their working lives.

These questions were increasingly raised at workplaces and in the labor movement, as workers became aware that in order to acquire such control, they themselves had to have a share in the ownership of enterprises. Since no one was interested in emulating the Soviet model of the state command economy, alternatives were sought that could provide democratic influence and ownership stakes in existing private firms. It was this debate that led the Danish Trade Union Confederation (LO) to issue the proposal for what came to be called economic democracy (ØD), which took center stage in the debates and conflicts of the following decades.

"There is growing understanding that the issue of property rights is tied to the question of the distribution of power and influence," the LO explained in its first statement issued in 1970. "The labor movement sees democracy as incomplete as long as a small group of business leaders can decide the fate of thousands of workers and can influence the development of the whole society without any significant regard for the interests of society."[27]

The main author of this first draft of the ØD model, former social democratic finance minister Henry Grünbaum, did not attempt to conceal the ultimate aim: "Economic democracy, among other factors, hinges on transforming the power structures of Danish society. We want to change the distribution of wealth and ownership. And we will not beat around the bush here. We wish to change existing power structures. We wish that wealth distribution and property ownership could be changed. But we will also change the distribution of power. . . . There is no talk of half measures here. This is an attack on the currently dominant form of property relations."[28]

In order to redress unequal power and property relations, the LO proposed establishing a wage earners profit and investment fund under the leadership of a committee appointed by unions and the government. The fund was to be capitalized by requiring all firms to contribute an amount equivalent to 1 percent of total wages paid out to employees. This contribution would rise a half percent per year until reaching 5 percent annually. For publicly traded companies, contributions would be converted to shares in the firm, thereby establishing an employee ownership stake. Liquidity would thereby not be affected, since the capital would remain within the firm itself, albeit under different ownership, thus indicating the explicit goal of increasing savings and investment in the firm.

According to the plan, the capital of such funds would constitute the personal capital of the wage earners, and every worker would receive a certificate documenting the individual share. In order to secure a high degree of equality, the shares would be distributed equally among all employees, regardless of department or salary. Shares could not be sold but instead could only be redeemed after seven years or at retirement. The proposal would thus gradually provide employees with greater and greater influence over the management of the firm by granting them the voting rights associated with the ownership of shares. Employees at each individual workplace would appoint individuals to represent the worker-owned bloc of shares at the firm's annual shareholder meeting.

The ØD proposal thus constituted a two-pronged strategy for the democratization of the economy. First, the central fund, managed by the trade unions, provides workers as a group with greater influence over the economy as a whole by building up a democratically owned and managed fund of investment capital. Second, workers at each individual firm would gradually acquire more and more power, until they constituted the majority at the annual shareholder meeting. A study by Arbejderbevægelsens Erhvervsråd has shown that if the LO proposal had been adopted, more than half of Danish capital ownership would have been under the control of worker-managed funds by the early 1990s.[29]

The LO plan was then presented to the Social Democrats' party congress, and in 1973 the government of Jens Otto Krag submitted a formal proposal to parliament that would "secure worker co-ownership, co-determination and influence in the business world at large and in the particular firms, while at the same time insuring a more equal distribution of wealth and income."[30] But the Krag proposal differed from the original LO version in that the worker-owned stake would never be allowed to surpass 50 percent, thereby permanently securing majority ownership for capitalists.

The parliamentary proposal stirred up just as much debate as the original. The employers' side, unsurprisingly, raised the red flag, fearing that as the fund acquired more and more capital, the labor movement would gain far too much control over the economy and investments. They received support from the Danish bar association, especially from hard-knuckled lawyer Alf Ross, who published a series of polemics warning that the proposal would allow state socialism in through the back door: "The proposal has been articulated by brilliant minds who would that Marxist socialism come to Denmark, swabbed in sugary phrases about equality, property allocation, and workplace democracy."[31]

Predictably, the Venstre and the Conservatives shared the employers' position and refused to support the proposal. But today it might come as a surprise that the parties of the left also opposed ØD, especially the Left Socialists and the Communists. They did not believe that a central fund managed by "careerist union bosses" would represent the interests of workers. And they feared that ØD would weaken union sentiment, since the labor movement would in effect have to wear two hats, that is, that of both the owner of the fund as well as the workers' representative. Moreover, it was correctly viewed as a manner of keeping wages down through a form of compulsory savings taken out of the workers' own earnings. The communist rock band Røde Mor even wrote a song panning the proposal that ended with the line "An empty promise with nothing in it—that is economic democracy."

The Socialist People's Party responded more favorably but argued that the Social Democrats' proposal did not go far enough and thus declined to support it. Lacking support from the left, the Social Democrats could not achieve a majority and thus had to give up on the proposal, and subsequent versions of it met the same fate.[32] But the later establishment of labor market pension funds was in a certain sense an outgrowth of the ØD debates, since by virtue of these pension funds we now have large investment funds with growing capital that are under various forms of democratic control, ensuring that workers receive a greater share of society's capital gains. But the pension funds did not deliver on the full promise of economic democracy, namely, providing employees with co-ownership and influence over their workplaces.

On the other side of the Øresund, the labor movement had considerably more success establishing funds socialism. In 1971 the Swedish Landsorganisation set up a new leadership committee led by the prominent trade union economist Rudolf Meidner. This group presented an ambitious proposal that if implemented would have turned wage earner funds into the majority owners of most major Swedish companies over a period of only thirty-five years. The proposal was approved by an overwhelming majority at the 1976 LO congress, and after it was passed, the delegates arose as one to sing the "International." Although Olaf Palme, the social democratic party leader, had reservations about the Meidner proposal, it was included in the Social Democrats' party platform for the 1981 national elections.

Just as in Denmark, employers and their allies on the right launched a PR campaign of extensive print and television advertisements as well as direct mailings. The employer side even managed to assemble seventy-five thousand demonstrators to march through Stockholm holding signs that said, "The funds are the start—socialism is the conclusion," "They take power—you pay for it," and "Save jobs—stop the funds." The employers spent SEK 60 million on the stop-the-funds campaign, about the same amount all other parties spent on the election campaign.[33]

The Palme government was not intimidated and with the support of the left managed to pass the law. But it was a much watered-down version of the original Meidner plan. It did not contain a provision for the mandatory redistribution of ownership via a shareholder tax, instead calling for merely purchasing shares on the ordinary capitalist market, as is done with the Arbejdsmarkedets tillægspension, the Danish state pension fund. The main thrust of the plan concerning worker influence over the workplace was thus removed. Meidner was deeply disappointed, calling the watered-down version a "pathetic rat."[34] Even though the plan had been watered down, the wage earner funds did not survive the first change of government. When the right came to power in the early 1990s, one of prime minister Carl Bildt's first acts was to dismantle the funds.

A number of factors contributed to the crash and burn of the Scandinavian attempt at funds socialism. The proposal to have the funds run by the labor movement rendered it vulnerable to attacks from the right and from employers, both of which complained about careerist trade union officials and economic centralization. This critique was also effective in Denmark in alienating the left. Together with the powerful opposition campaign, this explains why public opinion polling in both Sweden and Denmark did not show strong support for the funds.[35] The movement had tried to do too much at once, according to Mogens Lykketoft, former Danish social democratic finance minister and one of ØD's leading spokespersons, in undertaking simultaneous efforts to increase savings, widen the distribution of capital gains, and secure workers a measure of influence over the workplace.[36]

Further, individual wage earners were hard pressed to see much advantage in the funds idea given that neither of the proposals suggested that the capital gains be disbursed as dividends to the workers, and in Denmark especially the proposal was associated with the expectation of wage restraint.

However, a new form of funds socialism has recently been proposed that may lead to more direct ownership and participation.

Bernie Sanders Revives Funds Socialism

Rudolf Meidner died in 2007 and thus did not live to see his plan for wage earner funds become the talk of the town among the American and British left some ten years later. Bernie Sanders's 2016 run for U.S. president gave a new generation of young socialists and social democrats hope that they could assume power and use it to institute transformational social reform. Searching for a realistic yet still radical reform slate, progressive think tanks brought the old Meidner plan back from the grave. In October 2019, Sanders announced a plan to establish what was termed a democratic employee ownership trust that would secure for workers a degree of democratic influence and a share in the profits: "We can move to an economy where workers feel that they are not just a cog in the machine—one where they have power over their jobs and can make decisions. Democracy isn't just the opportunity to vote. What democracy really means is having control over your life."[37]

Sanders's proposal is similar to Danish and Swedish plans from forty years earlier in stipulating that all large publicly traded firms transfer 2 percent of their shares to a fund managed by their employees until the workers' share reaches 20 percent. In practice this would make employee ownership trusts the dominant shareholder in many companies. The yearly contribution would not, however, remain in the fund, as was envisioned by Meidner and the proponents of ØD but would instead be paid out in dividends to the employees. Under Sanders's plan, some fifty-six million workers would benefit from increased influence over their workplaces and receive an average annual dividend of USD 5,000.[38] The proposal thus emphasizes the democratization of ownership and profit sharing at the level of the individual firm but does not include a central fund as in the Scandinavian model.

Under Jeremy Corbyn, the British Labour Party also introduced a proposal to establish employee funds that largely echoes the Sanders plan, although under this plan, the annual employee dividend would be capped at GBP 500 and the rest would go to the state to finance welfare programs and education.

Opinion polling has revealed surprisingly strong support on both sides of the Atlantic for these proposals. A 2018 poll in Britain showed that 54 percent support such an idea, while only 17 percent are opposed. Polling in the United States indicated that a majority support not just the idea of employee funds but further the idea of a fund in which the employee ownership stake could rise up to 50 percent.[39]

That the new proposals avoid many of the pitfalls of the Scandinavian originals may account for the strong support for them. On the one hand, the presence of a central fund managed by the labor movement is absent, and on the other there is the promise of annual dividend payments. This would provide millions of wage workers with an immediate boost, a benefit that would also make it more difficult to roll back the funds in the event of a change in government.

But by giving up on the idea of a central fund, the new Anglo-Saxon proposals have also abandoned the main goals of the original Nordic proposals, namely, that of securing democratic influence over societal investment and over the economy as a whole. This is one of the reasons that other socialist thinkers have preferred a more broad-based alternative.

Social Wealth Funds

As the name suggests, wage earner funds have the advantage of providing wage earners with a share of influence over and profits from their employing firms. But at the same time this can be turned into a critique of the idea. For why should only wage earners enjoy such influence and profit sharing? What about all the other social groups that constitute society—retirees, the disabled, the unemployed? Do they not have the same claim to influence over the economy and a share of its wealth?

This critique is the basis for the idea of social wealth funds, which are democratic, collectively owned funds that distribute a portion of profits across the whole population rather than only wage earners, thereby making wider democratic influence possible. It was the Nobel laureate economist James Meade who first proposed the idea of social wealth funds. In his 1964 book *Efficiency, Equality, and the Ownership of Capital*, he anticipates precisely what French economist Thomas Piketty argues in *Capital and Ideology*: that capital income will eventually increase faster than wage income, which will drive up inequality.[40] Meade concludes that curbing the extreme wealth inequality of the capitalist economy through taxation is not sufficient for the long term; rather, we must ensure that the distribution of earnings *before* taxation is not so skewed. His solution was to establish one or more wealth funds, financed by high taxes on inheritances, wealth, and capital gains, that would gradually purchase financial assets in a variety of sectors. This reallocation of ownership would provide citizens with both a say in the management of firms and a share of the profits.[41]

Social wealth funds manage financial assets the same way private equity funds do. But in sharp contrast to private funds they are democratically anchored, regardless of whether publicly owned, self-owned, or owned directly by all citizens. Profits from these financial assets can thus be used to finance either welfare programs or to pay out dividends to the citizenry. And at the same time, society gets a say in the management of the enterprises in which the funds are invested, a voice that can be used to support aims beneficial to society such as fossil-fuel-free production and workers' rights.

Meade's concept of social wealth funds has found new life in recent years. In 2018, the American think tank People's Policy Project, which advises the progressive wing of the Democratic Party, proposed that the United States should establish a social wealth fund in which citizens would own equal shares and whose leadership they would vote to elect. The fund would purchase assets such as corporate shares, bonds, or properties, and the profits would be distributed equally in the form of a universal citizen dividend. Startup capital could come from a number of sources, such as a one-time asset tax, a financial transaction tax, taxes on other forms of capital income, or from the state taking on low-interest debt. By borrowing at a rate near zero and investing the money in a broad portfolio with a higher rate of return than the interest, the fund would grow rapidly and over time would function as a significant part of the total capital assets of society.[42]

There are already many state-owned investment vehicles around the world, the so-called sovereign wealth funds. The largest is Norway's oil fund, which was established on the basis of Norwegian oil revenues in the mid-1990s. It is actually two separate funds, one of which invests outside Norway and the other of which invests in Norwegian and other Nordic stocks. The global fund has experienced explosive growth; by 2019, its value was estimated at NOK 10 trillion. It is a politically activist investment vehicle that avoids, for instance, the arms, tobacco, oil, and gas industries. It does not pay out citizen dividends, but the returns constitute about 20 percent of the state budget and therefore finance an important part of Norway's welfare society.

The U.S. state of Alaska, in contrast, pays out citizen dividends from its Alaska Permanent Fund, established in 1976 and financed by 25 percent of the profits from the use of the state's natural resources. The fund purchases corporate shares and other assets, and as of 2017 had reached a value of USD 60 billion. Every year it pays out a dividend to each citizen regardless of age; for 2019 the figure was a little over USD 1,000, thus more than USD 4,000 for a family of four. This constitutes a significant addition to family income, which has helped level off the distribution of wealth and has contributed to a 20 percent decrease in the state's poverty rate.[43]

Employee or Social Wealth Funds?

Both types of funds seek to spread democratic influence over private enterprise and to ensure a broader distribution of profits. The primary difference between them is who it is that receives these things.

The problem with employee funds is that they tend to produce greater financial disparities not just between wage earners and other groups but between different groups of wage earners. Under the Sanders model, for example, an Apple employee would receive a dividend twenty times that of a Walmart worker.[44]

There is nothing inherently just about this form of inequality, since it is based on where the individual is placed in the value chain, which is quite arbitrary.[45] Whether a given group of workers belongs to a fund with higher or lower dividends is also a matter of chance. If Google, for example, paid its cleaning staff directly, then they would receive a share in Google's employee fund, while those of Twitter, employed by a subcontractor, would instead belong to the much less profitable cleaning services contractor.

This arbitrary and distorted distribution of profits suggests that a social welfare fund encompassing all citizens would be a better means of securing a fair division of society's wealth. But a social welfare fund does not change the power relations at individual workplaces, since employees do not receive a say in management. In chapter 5 I will suggest a model that combines both types of funds. On the one hand, employee funds would be established at all larger firms, thus securing growing influence for employees as well as a share in the profits. But on the other hand, profits over a certain benchmark would go to a social wealth fund that pays out dividends to all citizens, given that the creation of value cannot be wholly attributed to enterprises, since all value creation is anchored in a long chain of value crisscrossing the entire economy.

Can Democratic Fund Ownership Function Effectively?

One of the advantages of the funds socialist model is that the funds intervene in the capitalist economy in a way already familiar to us. As I have noted, there are already many publicly owned funds with extensive investments in capitalist markets, the Norwegian oil fund being the largest. Here in Denmark we already have large democratic institutional investors like ATP and the pension funds. Capital ownership in general is now largely dominated by the index fund giants that invest in a broad portfolio of stocks across the market. The question is thus not whether or not we desire such funds, since they are already here, but whether we desire nondemocratic investment funds owned by a small group of wealthy individuals or democratic capital funds owned by the citizenry that can represent the broader interests of society and distribute profits among the whole population.

The same is true for employee funds, an example of which is the aforementioned department store chain John Lewis & Partners, which is among the most efficient and profitable firms in the sector. Several fund-owned large Danish firms, such as Velux and Dansk Supermarked, although they are not worker managed, demonstrate that fund ownership is just as effective as the broadly distributed passive ownership of conventional capitalist firms.

The durability or profitability of fund ownership is therefore not in question. The central challenge employee funds face is rather procuring the capital to set them up. Any plan to introduce obligatory taxation to establish employee funds would be met with fierce resistance from economic elites, just as happened in the 1970s. And since then capitalists have acquired a powerful new means of exerting pressure: the threat of taking investment—indeed even production itself—out of the country. An extensive set of funds socialist reforms would thus demand the substantial transformation of power relations within individual countries as well as a broader international movement in which multiple states adopt a similar form of distributed ownership.

Are Funds Socialist Reforms Really the Way Forward?

The concept of funds socialism, as discussed, has traditionally been contested by the Danish left. Some of the opposition to ØD was due to fears that it would give too much power to union leadership, while others objected to its coupling with wage restraint policies. But the resistance further turned on a fear of how it would impact class consciousness, for if workers were made co-owners of their workplaces, they would effectively function as both capitalist and laborer, which could in turn weaken the trade union movement and lead to a kind of solidarity with capitalists that would prevent more substantial change.

With respect to the trade union movement, I do not think there is reason for concern. Even with fully employee-owned funds, there would be a need to fight for collective agreements on wages and working conditions, since it is the only means we have to combat downward pressure on wages resulting from interfirm competition. And as wage earners we will always have an interest in securing wage increases.

The objection that class conflict would be watered down in the event of funds socialism is somewhat more interesting. The basic idea of socialism is after all to eliminate the distance between capital and labor by rendering the former superfluous, and this is precisely the aim of funds socialism: to work toward creating an economy in which capital ownership, at least in the larger firms, is fully democratized.

Funds socialism is no panacea, but in combination with other forms of democratic ownership, it could be an important element in a new pluralistic economic architecture. And in such a future economy, one of these other forms will surely be democratic public ownership.

Democratic Public Ownership

"Socialism with a sparkle" is the nickname for the city of Paris's takeover over its water utility, Eau de Paris, which twenty-five years after privatization was put back into the hands of the community. This has become an international story not only because one can now get free and fresh water—even with sparkles—from public fountains on the streets of the city. Nor is it because prices went down in a short time, service improved, and waste was reduced. First and foremost it is because the municipal government has rethought the idea of public ownership by abandoning the old top-down bureaucratic model in favor of democratic management that offers full transparency of the utility's operations and finances and whose leadership consists of popularly elected representatives, employees, consumers, and environmental organizations.[46]

Earlier in this chapter I dismissed the idea that a social economy be based on extensive state ownership. But this does not in any way mean that I oppose public ownership in general. On the contrary, I maintain that public ownership at the national, regional, and municipal levels should be a central pillar of a new more socialist economy.

There are many arguments in favor of significant public ownership. First, state-owned firms have the immense advantage of being self-financed, unlike their private sector equivalents, which must pay off surplus to owners. Second, public companies can provide vital services like internet, health care, or cell coverage in areas of no value to private firms. And most importantly, they are democratic. Public ownership is in its essence democratic ownership, and the public sector is a democratic sector. The elected officials who direct affairs must answer to the public, giving citizens the means to ensure that companies behave in socially and environmentally responsible ways. But this requires that the democratic nature of public firms be protected and nurtured.

What Will Be Publicly Owned?

Even the most vehement opponents of public ownership agree that certain areas of the economy, such as the military, police, and the courts, should be run by the state. The Nordic welfare society extends public ownership much further, to education, health care, and child- and eldercare, all of which are primarily run by the state on the grounds that the needs of the citizenry rather than the interests of private capital are paramount. When welfare services are privatized or subcontracted, a contradiction appears between the interests of society and of capitalists: we as taxpayers want the best school or the best eldercare for our money, but the private firm looks first and foremost to the greatest possible returns for its shareholders. And the money that goes to shareholders cannot be used to hire more teachers or purchase better instructional materials.

But public ownership need not be limited to welfare services. Many states also maintain publicly owned production facilities that sell their output on the market, what are called state owned enterprises (SOEs). A Danish example is Ørsted, which is traded on the stock exchange but is majority state owned. State ownership in other Nordic countries is, as I have noted, more extensive, and the range of SOEs is growing on the global level. Of the two thousand largest companies in the world, the percentage of those that are publicly owned rose from 10 to 20 percent over the past decade.[47]

In my view there are no serious arguments against the proposition that national, regional, and municipal governments should own or co-own a larger number of production facilities, especially in critical infrastructure, than they do today. The state, for example, needs to serve as co-owner of renewable energy facilities and of green technology as we overhaul the energy sector in the coming decades. This is simply far too important to leave to private, commercially motivated actors, and since immense capital investment will be required for this undertaking, cooperatives cannot do the work on their own.

Public Ownership Works

The privatization wave of recent decades has been justified by the stubborn belief that publicly owned firms must necessarily be less efficient than private, profit-motivated enterprises. But decades of studies have failed to find any real foundation for this claim, and it is regularly contested by its critics.

In his book *Our Common Wealth: The Return of Public Ownership in the United States*, Thomas Hanna catalogs a wealth of research demonstrating that public ownership can be just as effective as private. Among many others, one study compared British nationalized industries and energy production with their U.S. equivalents in the first three decades after the Second World War, finding that British productivity growth was higher than American.[48]

In Britain, which has extensively privatized critical infrastructure and utilities, research has shown that prices in the remaining publicly owned firms are 30 percent lower than in privatized enterprises.[49] In Denmark the think tank Cevea has demonstrated that cooperative and publicly owned heating providers have the lowest prices.[50] In a meta-analysis of more than four thousand Danish and international studies on the subcontracting of welfare service provision, the research institute VIVE concludes there is no evidence that private companies can deliver the same service for less than public providers without diminishing quality and working conditions.[51]

It should hardly be noteworthy that the public sector delivers services at lower cost, for when private interests enter the picture, they must turn over profits to their shareholders. And these profits are like an extra cost for which we as taxpayers must ultimately pay. Private firms furthermore all too often pawn off hidden costs onto society, such as poorer working conditions for workers that can lead to workforce deterioration or early retirement.

The many negative experiences of privatization and subcontracting have led numerous countries to bring various sectors back under public control. The Amsterdam-based think tank Transnational Institute identifies fourteen hundred examples of this in recent years, most in Europe, and concludes that the experience of returning services such as energy, water, internet, and welfare to the community has largely been positive: "These (re)municipalisations generally succeeded in bringing down costs and tariffs, improving conditions for workers and boosting service quality, while ensuring greater transparency and accountability."[52]

The privatization mania has as noted also impacted Denmark, where important natural monopolies such as fiber optics and cellphone networks have been sold off from community to private interests. This has resulted in large profits for capitalists that could have gone to society while also leaving large parts of the country without reliable access to the internet or cell service. The COVID pandemic revealed that privatizing vaccine production was a mistake and that the state needs to maintain its own capacity to produce vaccines through compulsory licensing if private pharmaceutical firms can or will not deliver the doses necessary for public health. As I will later argue, many areas like this should be returned to the community.

When We Own in Common, We Decide in Common

Yet despite its many advantages, public ownership in and of itself cannot guarantee that citizens, consumers, and employees have a sense of ownership and real influence. All too often public enterprises are run with the same kind of top-down management as private firms or even in a patronizing way that suggests that the state, the party, or the administrators know best and that it is better to turn authority over to them.

Over time, the sluggishness and paternalism of public institutions has made the right's case for privatization much easier. For if citizens and employees do not see any real difference or advantage in public services, then why resist privatization?

We must learn from this experience. In a future economy we must not settle for mere public ownership but demand *democratic* public ownership. Where we own in common, we make decisions in common. Employees must have much greater influence over public workplaces, which can be achieved through strengthening the power of employee codetermination representatives (MEDs), who ought to have much more influence over the hiring and firing of the leadership as well as representation on committees than currently. Worker participation, however, is not sufficient, since workers' interests will not always be the same as those of consumers or citizens. Therefore we must aim to promote greater direct participation by citizens in those areas of the public sector that serve the citizenry, such as education, health care, eldercare, and utilities. Here we can learn from the Paris water utility, whose steering committee is made up of elected officials, citizens, consumer organizations, and relevant NGOs. We could, for example, mandate that representatives of patients' rights groups sit on the boards of hospitals and that those of environmental organizations sit on the boards of energy companies.

Elected citizen representatives should be placed in the leadership of all public enterprises, or perhaps representatives could be chosen by lot, as Andreas Møller Mulvad, Anton Grau Larsen, and Christoph Ellersgaard suggest in their book *Tame the Elite*.[53]

The matter of citizen participation in public works raises the further question of how much we as citizens would be willing to engage in such affairs, since only a very few of us would have the energy necessary to run everything from water works to electricity to the local hospital. In order to simplify citizen democratic participation, the British NGO We Own It has proposed establishing a national consumer organization to secure civil society influence over all public enterprises. Anyone sixteen or older can join by indicating place of residence and which services are used. Members would be able to vote in elections for the leadership of both national public services as well as those local to them. Here in Denmark, Tænketanken Demokratisk Erhverv has proposed an annual democracy day on which all consumer-owned enterprises would simultaneously hold leadership elections. This is a fine idea and could also be applied to public institutions once we have secured citizen participation in their leaderships.

It must be emphasized that I am not arguing that the public sector should be run by roundtable discussions and direct democracy. The day-to-day management should be handled by professionals. But leaders must be made much more accountable to both citizens and employees and must use their knowledge to improve service quality.

The development of a more extensive democratic public sector at the local, regional, and national levels, along with cooperatives and funds socialism, constitute one of the building blocks of a new democratic Nordic socialism.

Ownership in Select Sectors: Finance, Land, Housing, and Information

When discussing the democratization of ownership, we must pay special attention to certain sectors, including finance, land, housing, and knowledge, information, and data resources. These differ from production enterprises, since their wealth is not primarily accumulated through the direct exploitation of labor power but through various forms of rent seeking. As earlier discussed, these sectors are increasingly significant in the distribution of wealth and the unequal power relations of our economy, and thus a democratization of them is no less important than the democratization of production. A proper discussion of the democratization of these four sectors could in itself fill up an entire book, but I will nonetheless attempt to outline the key points here.

Ownership of Banks and Money Creation

"Who should own the banks?" was the title of an editorial I wrote in 2009, shortly after the global financial house of cards collapsed, bringing the world economy to its knees. This question, needless to say, has hardly become less important in the years since.

Banks are an essential component of any economy. They ensure that the savings of some can be used by others who need money to invest, for example, in new production or in solar panels on the roof of the summer house. But banks do not just loan out funds that others have deposited, for they typically loan greater sums than they take in, effectively creating new money. This means that banks have immense influence on the money supply and thereby on which economic activities receive credit and investment. One of the principle sources of oligarchic power, indeed, is the ability to decide how much is invested and where.

This is why the socialist movement has always been critical of the private control of finance and money creation. Up through the 1970s the consensus view of the left was that the community should have authority over banks. The Danish Social Democrats' platform for 1977, for instance, called for the banking industry to be converted to self-owned institutions, with representatives of society constituting the majority of directors.[54] This idea was revived after the financial crisis of 2008, when private banks were only able to survive because the state came to their rescue with bailout packages. Then Goldman Sachs advisor Willem Buiter puts it this way: "Is the reality . . . that large private firms make enormous private profits when the going is good and get bailed out and taken into temporary public ownership when the going gets bad, with the taxpayer taking the risk and the losses? If so, then why not keep these activities in permanent public ownership? There is a long-standing argument that there is no real case for private ownership of deposit-taking banking institutions, because these cannot exist safely without a deposit guarantee and/or lender of last resort facilities, that are ultimately underwritten by the taxpayer."[55] The argument is easy to understand. Banks simply cannot function without a state and central bank to back them. Why then not just allow the state to take over management of the financial sector? Why absorb only the losses but not the gains as well?

While I certainly think the state should play a much larger role in lending, I remain skeptical of the idea of a state monopoly. I can see no reason why the state should take over well-run co-op banks or mutual funds such as Merkur Andelskasse or Fælleskassen or the equally efficient democratic pension funds that manage wage earners' pension savings. I also think that so long as taxpayers do not pay for the speculative losses of nondemocratic banks and that they are strictly regulated and have state representation on their boards, they can have a place in the future economy. A total nationalization of the finance sector would make the state the only provider of credit, thereby giving it all too much power.

The solution is to combine the establishment of state-owned banks with the expansion of our tradition of democratic cooperative banks, mortgage lenders, and pension funds, owned and managed by the customers. Co-op banks are already powerful in other European countries. Data from the European Association of Cooperative Banks reveals that the share of cooperative, nonprofit banks amounts to 20 percent of total deposits. And history shows that these co-ops are much less likely to engage in risky behavior than their publicly traded counterparts. After the 2008 financial crisis the International Monetary Fund concluded that cooperative banks were "generally able to avoid many of the mistakes made by larger private sector institutions."[56]

In Denmark today, legislation hinders the formation of new cooperative banks, and regulations kneecap the financial model of existing institutions. This should be turned on its head, as the state ought to be supporting and encouraging the cooperative movement.

If we are to have more democratic influence over investment and lending, then we must also build a strong public banking sector, in the form of both a public retail banking option for ordinary customers and a much stronger public investment bank, which at the very least would ensure investment in the green conversion and would also support a growing democratic sector in the larger economy through lending and investment.

It is critical that a public banking sector be managed professionally and at an arm's length from politicians. The lending regulations should be democratically determined, but the evaluation of individual credit worthiness should be insulated from politics. As shall later be discussed, earlier experience from Yugoslavian market socialism reveals that public lending to firms risks the artificial propping up of inefficient companies because local or national politicians fear that voters will punish them if they are responsible for closures and job losses.

Many effective and professional democratic public banks have already been established in Europe. In Germany, 413 publicly managed but self-owned banks count 50 million customers and constitute about 40 percent of total financial sector activities. The French state-owned Banque Postale has more than eleven million customers.[57] The United States has also seen the development of a powerful movement to establish public banking alternatives in recent years. In 2019 the governor of California signed a law that made it possible for regional authorities to own and operate public banks, and New Jersey has taken steps toward establishing a statewide public bank.[58] Denmark should follow suit.

The relationship between central banks and individual financial institutions, whether cooperative or private, must also be rethought. Today banks have far too much power over the money supply, especially because the physical currency created by central banks is increasingly being replaced by the digital currencies created by private banks. The central banks of many countries are considering the establishment of a central bank digital currency, in Denmark the e-krone. This would provide new ways to influence money circulation rather than leaving the matter to private banks.[59]

The goal must therefore be to develop a pluralistic, collectively owned finance sector that ensures that lending and money creation are democratically anchored, affording voters and shareholders extensive influence over the critical decisions regarding investment in society that today are left to a narrow unelected elite. In chapter 5 I suggest a slate of reforms that could help us achieve this goal.

Ownership of Land and Homes

How can someone own a piece of a country's territory, that is, something that is provided by nature? And why should increases in land value resulting from the rising wealth of society go only to the owner rather than the whole of society? Ownership of land and the right to profit from its increasing value have always been highly contested economic issues.

The labor movement has traditionally held that land should be owned by society. But even bourgeois economists like Adam Smith and John Stuart Mill have been critical of the idea that private interests should be able to earn from their ownership and leasing of land.[60]

In Denmark, land is primarily privately owned. Since the eighteenth-century land reforms, territory is divided up into thousands of private parcels. Approximately 9 percent of these are owned by the state and another small percentage are owned by democratic associations (such as those in the cooperative housing sector), but the majority are privately owned either by those who live on them or by investors who rent the land (and the properties on them) to others.

Land owners pay land taxes as well as taxes on commercial and residential properties, which brought in DKK 47 billion in 2020. But monetary returns from increasing property values accrue largely to privately owned properties, which tends to increase inequality between owners and non-owners. In the past, land and property ownership were distributed in such a way that their associated earnings were spread over a significant part of the population, but today, ownership has been concentrated and an increasing amount of land and property has become financial assets traded on global capital markets. In just the years between 2012 and 2017, foreign purchase of Danish properties increased tenfold, constituting 54 percent of total investment capital by 2018. In Copenhagen, the notorious American firm Blackstone purchased 160 properties in just a few years.[61]

At the same time, the Danish government has sold off state and municipal property, including buildings along Kalvebod Brygge in Copenhagen that have been turned into sterile corporate headquarters and buildings on Sluseholmen and Teglhomen that have been transformed into tightly congested luxury apartments. Meanwhile, construction of new cooperative housing is at an all-time low and with the passing of the "ghetto law" by the Løkke government in 2018, many cooperative housing associations were forced to either tear down properties or sell them to private investors.[62]

This concentration of ownership means that an ever increasing portion of gains from property value increases goes to a narrow economic elite, further reducing the number of units whose rent is not determined by the market and thus making it more and more difficult for people with modest incomes to afford housing. A democratization of the economy would reverse this by ensuring that housing is treated as a public good rather than as a means for economic elites to further enrich themselves.

As social democratic prime minister Jens Otto Krag put it in a speech before the party congress of 1970, "Our fundamental view is that housing should be a social good in which prices should not be set by supply and demand but according to the needs of society."[63]

It is fortunate that we have a long tradition to build upon here, that of our cooperative housing sector, in which rents are not determined by the market but only must cover building and management costs, and further in which all surpluses are reinvested in either maintenance and improvements or in the construction of new co-op units. But we can also find inspiration from improvement from abroad.

In Amsterdam, no less than 80 percent of the land is publicly owned because the municipal government views public land ownership as "a method of curbing undesirable outcomes like speculation."[64] Rather than selling off the land, the city rents it out on long-term leases. Residents either rent or own only the buildings standing on the land. Buildings can be bought and sold, but the land remains public.[65] Land rent incomes are placed in a fund that is used either to purchase new land or for development.

Another good example is Vienna, in which more than 60 percent of homes are cooperatively or publicly owned, waiting times to secure one are only a couple months, and rents are affordable for ordinary people—around DKK 5,000 for a large three-room apartment.[66] Rents are kept down through public support for construction and a mandate that the city has first right to the purchase of new developments.[67]

In the majority of countries that like Denmark have suffered from the financialization and privatization of the housing market, new efforts to bring the housing stock back under community control are underway. In 2019, after widespread protest over rising rents, Berlin's public housing association, Gewobag, purchased more than six thousand formerly privatized apartments, the largest renationalization operation in German history.[68] A group of British Labour Party experts have proposed the establishment of a land fund that would gradually and voluntarily separate ownership of land and buildings. The plan is simple: an independent and publicly supported fund would purchase the land on which a house stands that a family wants to buy and lease it back to the family for the duration of its residence. The family would then only need to purchase the home itself, which would decrease the amount of debt taken on, since houses themselves typically only constitute 30 percent of the total price. If implemented, this plan could result in a significant amount of land being transferred to communal ownership, reduce speculation, and ensure that increases in land value benefit the whole of society.[69] These are all models from which we can learn and take inspiration.

Private capital and speculators have also made inroads in recent decades in the purchase of rural land. Until a few years ago it was illegal to own Danish farmland if one did not farm the land oneself. But in 2014, the government of the Social Democratic, Socialist People's, and Social Liberal parties removed the only remaining regulations, opening the door for foreign private capital to purchase unlimited agricultural land.[70] Martin Merrild, the head of the agricultural association Landbrug og Fødevarer, warned at the time that the new law would make farmland into an object of speculation: "In practice it means that we have placed signs on all Danish fields that say 'Come and invest in our farmland. . . . Danish farmers can drive the tractors for foreign capital funds.'"[71] A February 2020 analysis by Danmarks Statistik revealed that in just the first four years after the new law was passed, foreign capital had purchased 66,500 hectares of Danish agricultural land, a figure constituting 2.5 percent of total land area. But in reality the percentage is much greater, since foreign capital typically buys land through Danish shell companies.[72]

This intrusion of foreign capital is likely a response to the long-term trend of steady growth in the size of individual Danish farms that has not only made it harder for young farmers to purchase farmland but also resulted in immense debt for those who manage to do. Agricultural land in Denmark is de facto owned either by the financial sector or by capital funds that use it as a speculative asset. The principal of self-ownership that has defined Danish agriculture for centuries is on the way out. This forces farmers into ever more intensive industrial and monocultural production, which puts pressure on the natural environment and water resources. The concentration of ownership also increases oligarchic power, making it more difficult to pass legislation at odds with the interests of the big landlords. Just as in the cities, it is as critical to put a stop to the concentration of agricultural land ownership. And we Danes can learn from our own past experiences.

This is not the first time Danish farmland has been concentrated in a few hands. Until the eighteenth-century land reforms only some seven hundred families controlled a large majority of Danish agricultural land. The reforms made possible the creation of a growing class of independent farmers, but the rural gentry still owned a significant portion of the land. In the early twentieth century, the Social Liberals and the Social Democrats began to demand new land reforms that would transfer the gentry's land to landless farmers and farmworkers. On October 4, 1919, the so-called Abolition of the Fiefs was instituted, which gave the state the right to expropriate a third of the land of large estates with compensation financed by a one-time tax of 25 percent on the total value of the property of the estate owners themselves. The landlords vehemently resisted, but the Danish supreme court ruled against them. The expropriated land was placed under public control and then either sold or leased to small farmers. As the historians John Erichsen and Ditlev Tamm write, "Land that for centuries had made up the great estates of noble families with names like Ahlefedt, Bertouch-Lehn, Brahe, Danneskiold-Samsøe, Holstein, Lerche, Lehn, and Reventlow was now taken over by newly minted farmers with names such as Andersen, Hansen, Jensen, Nielsen, Olsen, Pedersen, and Sørensen."[73]

Today these small farmers are all gone, usurped by a new nobility of capital funds and investors or by the bankers of heavily indebted small farmers. This calls for a new land reform that can secure broader ownership of agricultural land and free farmers from their dependence on private capitalist interests, enabling the development of an agricultural sector that does not damage the climate, the environment, and biodiversity. The current situation, in which the old model of self-ownership is being replaced by leasing, raises an urgent question: why should land be owned by private capital funds when we ourselves could own democratically and in common, which would ensure that increases in value do not vanish into the pockets of a new landed nobility and that the land is used sustainably? Initiatives such as Danmark Økologiske Jordbrugsfund and Andelsgaarde that purchase farmland and lease it out for organic use only are a step in the right direction.[74] But such citizen initiatives are not enough. If we are to reverse this trend, the larger society must get involved. One possible solution often discussed in the parliament is the establishment of a state land fund that would purchase land and lease it to farmers. In 2001 a committee appointed by the Social Democratic Nyrup government to study the idea concluded that such a fund, with a DKK 100 million contribution from the state, could purchase fifteen to twenty-five properties per year and that over time, the leasing income would make the fund self-sustaining. Agricultural organizations were supportive, but the election of the right-wing Fogh government killed the proposal.[75]

But the idea is hardly less relevant today. Democratically managed agricultural funds, backed by the economic muscle of the national or municipal governments, could very well put a stop to the financialization of farmland. Instead of being essentially modern serfs, bonded to international capital funds and wealth managers, Danish farmers could lease their land from a democratic fund of which they themselves are members and whose management they have a say over. The necessity of the rapid greening of agriculture is another good reason for establishing a democratic agricultural fund, since it could be used to pressure lessees to adopt organic and carbon neutral production.

Ownership of Information Resources

Knowledge, information, and data are essentially social phenomena. New discoveries and technologies are most often a part of larger social processes and always stand on the shoulders of thousands of years of accumulated knowledge. And data in particular only acquires value when it is collected from thousands of human beings. Despite this, the control of these resources now constitutes an important factor in the concentration of wealth. Tech giants like Apple, Google, and Facebook have amassed enormous power, power that is only likely to grow in the coming years as automation and artificial intelligence come into play. Democratizing the economy thus also demands that we gain ownership of our information resources.

Given that these resources are immaterial assets anchored in so-called intellectual property rights such as patents that secure for the owners the exclusive right to the use of the technology or knowledge, democratizing ownership of them can be accomplished only by either changing these property rights or by developing alternative models. But we do not have to start from scratch. Since immaterial assets are in their very nature more difficult to fence in and capitalize than physical products, new movements challenging the narrow control of information resources have formed as the information economy has grown. Wikipedia, created and edited by thousands of users who share their knowledge freely, is a good example. Initiatives like Creative Commons, Copyleft, and Open Source Software provide creators with the opportunity to share their products through open or partially open licensing, so that others can further develop them.

Medical and pharmaceutical patents have also faced new opposition. When the COVID pandemic erupted, the World Health Organization called for the establishment of a "corona pool." Member countries should "voluntarily pool knowledge, intellectual property and data necessary for

COVID-19," it argued, because "shared knowledge, intellectual property and data will leverage our collective efforts to advance scientific discovery, technology development and broad sharing of the benefits of scientific advancement and its applications based on the right to health."[76]

But the program was voluntary, and the major industry players, predictably enough, were dismissive. Albert Bourla, CEO of pharma giant Pfizer, called the initiative "nonsense" and even "dangerous."[77] In other words, voluntary solutions are clearly not sufficient; what we need is foundational reform of the entire intellectual property regime. While patents should not be eliminated, we do need serious reforms that limit their duration and that prevent firms from making minor alterations to prolong them. States must also have more leeway to circumvent patents in the interest of public health. Both EU and WHO international agreements would have to be renegotiated, which would of course provoke intense resistance from the interests of private capital.

And yet even working within the current system we can institute reforms that would broaden control over the ownership of information resources, such as mandating that private interests cannot lay claim to any knowledge or information that was produced with the help of public funds. In her book *The Entrepreneurial State*, British economist Mariana Mazzucato demonstrates how virtually all the major technological innovations of recent decades were initially supported by public research funding.[78] The twelve technologies that make the smartphone smart, including the touchscreen, Siri, and microprocessors, were all, for example, developed at U.S. public research institutes. More recently, COVID vaccines were largely financed by public funds. Moderna's vaccine, by its own admission, was 100 percent state financed, while others benefited from massive state funding.[79]

Despite such state support, however, it is typically private firms that enjoy the windfalls. In order to remedy this, the British think tank Common Wealth has proposed establishing a public intellectual property fund that would administer patent rights held in common. Concretely, this would mean that the results of all publicly financed researched would go to the IP fund rather than private firms. And just like private patent holders, the IP fund would license patents associated with publicly financed research to third parties in exchange for payment, which would be reinvested in new research, the results of which would create new public patents. A rising proportion of intellectual property rights would thus gradually come under the control of the community.

A public IP fund would not just provide income but would also give us democratic control over how we apply patent rights. We could, for example, choose to grant free licensing, as the WHO proposed for the corona pool, which would prevent trade secrets from hindering vaccine development and give poor countries rapid access to them.[80] Under current Danish law, patents developed using research conducted in public universities go to the university rather than the individual employees, but there is good reason to expand the scope of the law so that the results of all publicly financed research come under control of the community.

Any effort to democratize the economy must pay special heed to the control of mass data, not just for the sake of protecting of our private lives but further because the democratization of mass data access provides new possibilities for solving a whole series of long-standing social problems, from the climate to public health. But today most data are harvested by a handful of tech giants that primarily use this information for profit, such as for advertising purposes. We must return our data to the community, so that together through democratic means we can decide how data technologies are to be employed.

A first step here would be to ensure that all data produced by our public institutions, such as that concerning public health, the weather, the economy, or population growth, are used for the benefit of society. Since these data sets can be useful and valuable in developing new solutions to social problems and new technologies, much has been done in recent years to make as much public data as possible freely accessible. Yet international studies reveal that most information is still primarily used by private concerns, such as those that use meteorological data to provide services to agriculture or those like Uber, which uses traffic data to refine its algorithm.

As British-Danish researcher Rosie Collington notes, our present open access to public data resembles the old concept of the commons, that is, public lands that anyone could farm but that now only a few have the means and the technologies to harvest.[81] As a solution, she suggests establishing a public data fund to house all public sector digital assets. These would not be freely given away to private concerns, as they are today. Instead any firm that profited from these assets would have to pay a licensing fee, which would have the effect of preventing public data from being used for purposes that do not benefit society.

Barcelona has gone a step further. When the city was renegotiating its contract with Vodaphone, which provides the Catalonian capital with cell service, it demanded that all data produced be returned to the community. The same terms now apply to the private bicycle rental firms in the city.[82] The EU's GDPR regulations provide citizens with the right to the data they produce using Google, Facebook, or Instagram, all of whom profit by harvesting it. But it is a precondition for using Google Maps, Facebook, or Twitter that we give them access to our data, so our right to our data does not mean much in practice. Further, there is no real possibility of securing a share of the profits we ourselves generate through usage.

The most far-reaching solution, suggested by tech activist and *Logic* founder Ben Tarnoff, is a kind of data nationalization: "The solution is to take up the template of resource nationalism, and nationalize our data reserves. This isn't as abstract as it sounds. It would begin with the recognition that all of the data extracted within a country is the common property of everyone who lives in that country."[83]

But other activists and scholars are skeptical of state ownership and instead propose a cooperative solution. British think tank Nesta, for example, suggests that citizens receive the right to control all the data they produce on digital platforms. This data could be pooled in data banks administrated by a cooperative council in which all who contribute have voting rights. Members would get both control over their data as well as a share in the eventual proceeds from their sale.[84] Swiss-based MIDATA is an example of this model. Its members can upload their health and medical records and their personal genomic information, which is then securely shared with researchers.

A modern Nordic socialism must reject the narrow and exploitative model of ownership that defines today's information economy, thereby ensuring that control of our collective knowledge and data resources is democratized and distributed. In chapter 5 I offer concrete proposals for such.

Is There a Place for Nondemocratic Enterprises in a Future Economy?

The precondition for building a sustainable and just economy is reversing the present dominance of concentrated ownership. We must develop the various alternative ownership forms previously discussed to ensure that the democratic sector becomes as dominant as the nondemocratic sector is today. But does this require eliminating private, nondemocratically managed firms? I do not think so.

As has been argued, I believe we must reject the conception of certain modes of production as totalizing and all-encompassing and instead understand economies as hybrids, as a mix of coexisting systems. This means that we need not aim for the complete subjection of society to one specific production mode. As such, there is no reason to think that small- and medium-sized nondemocratic enterprises should not exist alongside their democratic counterparts. Just as today we have a smaller democratic sector within a primarily nondemocratic capitalist economy, so can we imagine a smaller nondemocratic sector within a future economy dominated by democratic ownership. The key point here is that we must seek to make the democratic sector large enough that it is democratic and not oligarchic power that sets the societal agenda. The democratic sector must be dominant but not necessarily *all* dominant.

I see no reason that in such an economy it should not be possible for single individuals to start new companies or to develop and sell new technologies and services. Society needs this form of entrepreneurship, to provide space for new ideas and innovation and because existing firms must be constantly challenged to avoid monopolization.

As we have seen, the collective form of ownership is by no means an obstacle to innovation or entrepreneurship. And yet individual entrepreneurs who work toward the establishment of new enterprises can also surely be a part of a future Nordic socialism. It is hardly the small entrepreneur who undermines democracy but rather the excessive concentration of ownership among economic elites, which is not primarily the result of successful entrepreneurship but of the excessive rewards of passive private capital. A future democratic economy must therefore distinguish between the creativity of the entrepreneur and the passivity—or perhaps parasiticalness—of capitalist investors, as exemplified by Nets earning billions from its ownership of the Danish payment infrastructure or Blackstone pushing up residential rents. We have need of the first, creative role, but not the latter, extractive one.

We must in other words seek to find a balance, which on one side secures the best possible conditions for entrepreneurs, inventors, and other go-getters, be they collective or individual, while on the other side preventing active, creative ownership degenerating into passive, exploitative ownership, which increases inequality and permits the nondemocratic sector to spread outward, furthering oligarchic power.

In sum: a Nordic socialism can and should have a place for a nondemocratic sector. Our task is to use legislation, credit, and favorable conditions to support, grow, and nourish the democratic sector, such that it can become as dominant as the capitalist sector is today.

The Right to Private Property Is Not Absolute

To suggest that a future democratic socialist economy could permit private capitalist ownership even on a limited basis will sound like heresy to many socialists. One of the central themes of socialist thought, after all, has been the question of the right to private ownership of the means of production. Socialists have correctly objected that the right to private property is not determined by natural law. Instead private property rights are in essence a guarantee that the state will use its power and, in the last resort, its monopoly over violence to ensure that the existing distribution of property, here understood as the ownership of the means of production, is maintained. In a democracy it is ultimately the citizenry who decide how private property rights shall be employed and protected.

Marx emphasizes how the origins of capitalist ownership involved outright theft, in which economic elites used violence to claim ownership of the land that previously constituted the commons, both within Europe and in the colonies. The emergence of modern capitalism is thus based on the historic injustice of the private seizure of public property. His solution is not only a redistribution of ownership but also a complete overturning of the private control of the means of production, what he calls "the expropriation of the expropriators." The necessity of the abolition of private ownership of the means of production has long constituted a kind of socialist Ave Maria.

Nonetheless I still believe that it is an error to maintain that a socialist economy must entail abolishing every form of private ownership of the means of production. A total break with private property would for practical purposes mean state ownership of all enterprise, which would lead to the centralization of all too much power in the state, since there would be no alternative economic centers of power anchored in civil society. If we seek a pluralism of democratic ownership forms, then the protection of private property rights is a precondition. Otherwise the state would be able to stake a claim on the property of cooperatives or other democratically managed and owned enterprises.

The demand for the total annulment of private property rights is also rooted in a crude understanding of property rights as a black-and-white matter, according to which we must either concede to the protection of all existing private property in all its forms or abolish it altogether. But property rights are not black and white, for the absolutist conception fails to grasp that such rights are already limited. Most constitutions, including Denmark's, provide for substantial interference with private property, if the democratic majority decides that such action is necessary for society as a whole. Paragraph 73 of the Danish constitution thus states that the right to private property is "inviolable." But immediately thereafter this is qualified with the injunction "except where required in the public interest."

Danish history provides many examples of how this clause has been employed. The most famous is the 1919 law that provided for the expropriation of one-third of the property of the Danish landed gentry and its redistribution to small farmers. More recently, the state has taken over financial institutions that either grossly violated the law or were facing collapse, such as Københavns Andelskasse, which had violated a series of money laundering regulations.[85]

A democratic majority can thus under present law make decisions contrary to the right to private ownership of the means of production, if the matter is of great concern to the common good. This is not the least relevant in the case of the climate question, for private property rights must not be invoked to prevent reforms necessary for halting the destruction of our planet. It is critical that such interventions be anchored in the law rather than in claims to exclusive state ownership of the economy or, worse, the arbitrary exertion of state power.

The democratic majority not only has the prerogative to override private property rights through expropriation but also to determine what rights follow from the right to the private ownership of the means of production. Here it is useful to revisit our previous experience with *functional socialism*.

The premise of functional socialism is that conceiving of property rights as absolute and indivisible is too crude. The important question is which rights and privileges society grants to private property owners. In order to understand this, we must look to the distinction between the *right* to property and the manner in which one may *use* that right. The power and control that follow from private ownership of the means of production can thus be more or less limited. Gunnar Adler-Karlsson puts it like this: "The concept of private property rights is not indivisible, but . . . involves many different functions that can be distinguished from one another. The idea of ownership, O, does not mean ownership in general, but refers to the functions a, b, c and so forth. . . . The consequences of this distinction are that it is not necessary to execute a full socialization of production to achieve socialism. It can be sufficient and more so economically advantageous to socialize only select functions of private property, for example b, but not c."[86]

Examples of how the functions of private property have been limited by democratic decisions include the Swedish "right to roam," which limits the rights of private owners of forests and fields to ensure that all citizens have a right to enjoy nature, Nordic rent regulations that protect tenants from eviction without cause and from unreasonable rent increases, and extensive corporate and capital gains taxes.

Adler-Karlsson goes so far as to conclude that thoroughgoing functional socialist reforms can ultimately transform private ownership of the means of production into an empty husk, comparing it to the wholly formal but not real power the Danish constitution grants to the regent: "Let us instead deprive our present capitalists of the ownership functions one by one, such that in a few decades they will be like today's kings, that is, more or less powerless symbols of a bygone age."[87]

As noted, I do not share wholly this optimism. Like Rudolf Meidner, I do not think that functional socialist reforms alone are sufficient to secure a sustainable democratic economy and that a real redistribution of ownership is critical. But I do agree that the right to private property is not indivisible and thus need not be rejected or accepted in its entirety. Functional socialist reforms can thus supplement the more foundational redistribution and democratization of ownership that constitute the principal theme of this book, especially in the transitional phase during which the large majority of the economy is still dominated by capitalism.

Functional Socialist Reforms

An important set of functional socialist reforms involves the matter of redistribution. So long as the concentration of ownership results in income inequality—predistributive inequality—redistribution through the tax system is both a necessary and useful means to ensure that inequality does not further concentrate wealth and economic power. Compared to peer countries, Denmark already has a high degree of redistribution through taxation. Yet this has not prevented steep rises in both income and wealth inequality.

In *Capital and Ideology*, Piketty argues for changes to our approach to taxation that would effectively render capital ownership temporary. Piketty wants to preserve the dynamism of private entrepreneurship and is thus not opposed to the founders of successful firms earning a great deal of money, but he also wants to counteract the inequality generated by actually existing capitalism. He proposes an ongoing and extensive redistribution through taxation that can ensure a *permanent circulation of wealth*, so that riches do not remain in the hands of the few who then pass it on to future generations. He suggests a series of capital gains, wealth, and inheritance taxes at much higher marginal rates. Tax receipts would then be redistributed among the population through, among other means, a one-time citizen dividend of EUR 20,000 at the age of twenty-five.[88]

American philosopher David Schweickart takes the concept of temporary ownership a step further, arguing that ownership of the means of production should not be heritable. Entrepreneurs and founders, he suggests, may enjoy the full fruits of their successful enterprises as long as they live, but when they retire or die, the enterprise should not be left to relatives or sold off to private capitalists but instead sold to the employees or to the public sector.[89]

Another means of curbing wealth concentration in the nondemocratic sector is to pass legislation mandating profit sharing, that is, making it obligatory for privately owned firms to distribute profits among the employees. France mandated this for all firms with more than fifty employees in the decades after the Second World War.

Functional socialist reforms can also be implemented to change the way firms are managed. For the right to the private ownership of the means of production does not give owners—even under the current regime—the power of absolute monarchs.

In the most common form of ownership for the largest firms, that is the publicly traded corporation, ultimate decision-making power lies with the shareholders. The annual shareholders' meeting, at which the largest shareholders dominate, constitutes the final authority. Here the board of directors is chosen, which then sets the direction of the firm. In most cases employees have little or no say in the running of the company because the mandate of the leadership is to serve the interests of the shareholders, first and foremost by providing maximal returns. And all too often this comes at the expense of employees, the local community, and the environment.

Does any of this actually make sense? It can rightfully be argued that those who invest capital in an enterprise should have influence over that enterprise. But why shouldn't the employees who invest their labor power and devote their physical and mental health to the enterprise enjoy the same? Their investment of labor power is no less vital to the firm than capital investment. Without labor power no firm can exist.

A typical argument for the present distribution of power is that it is the shareholders who take the risk, while the workers lose nothing if the firm goes under. But the reality is that most shareholders—be they individuals or institutions—maintain a broadly diversified portfolio, and so their risk is diffused and limited. The employees' risk, on the other hand, is highly concentrated. When a firm goes under, its employees not only lose their income but also the precise knowledge of company operations they have acquired over time, not to mention colleagues and even their personal identity. Why not then change the current corporation law to secure for employees the same influence the investors enjoy?

But is it possible to use the law to intervene in the management of private firms to recalibrate power and influence? The answer is yes. The way corporations are currently organized is generally presented in public debate as in accordance with some kind of natural law, and any interference from the state is dismissed as undesirable. But corporations are not prepolitical entities that the state may regulate only after the fact. They are in and of themselves political, defined by the laws of human beings rather than of nature. It is the current corporation law that provides shareholders with near absolute power.[90]

And we Danes have already used the law to secure influence for employees. In 1973 the corporation law was altered to mandate that in firms with fifty or more workers, the employees would have the right to elect two board members, and in 1979 the law was amended again to allow employees the right to elect fully one-third of all board members. Similar laws are found elsewhere in the Nordic region, and in Germany, where especially in heavy industry firms have operated since the 1950s according to the principle of *Mitbestimmung*, which requires worker representation equal to that of shareholders. But shareholders also elect a president with voting rights, ensuring that ownership has majority power.

Debates over workplace democracy have been revived in recent years. Piketty has proposed changes to corporation law that would limit owner representation to 50 percent of boards.[91] Belgian labor market researcher Isabelle Ferreras goes a step further, proposing that decisions that are today made unilaterally at large firms by a board chosen by investors should instead be approved by two separate chambers, one elected by investors of capital and the other by investors of labor power, both of whom would have the right to veto all critical decisions, on the model of the bicameral system common to many legislatures. Day-to-day affairs would still be handled by professionals who would be accountable to both the investor and employee chambers.[92]

In addition to providing employees with a well-earned say in the management of their firms, a new and more democratic distribution of corporate ownership would surely have other positive effects. The current concentration of power in investors generally leads to a short-term focus on returns rather than a broader and longer-term vision for the development of the firm. Greater employee influence would also result in greater social responsibility, since labor power investors, unlike many capital investors, are typically anchored in the locality in which the firm operates. Finally, a redistribution of power would no doubt facilitate the fair proportioning of wages to profits.

Democratic and Pluralistic Ownership

To summarize this section, a new conception of the organization of ownership must be at the center of any progressive vision of the future. Without such democratization the concentration of wealth will increase and oligarchic power will continue to exert influence on our democracy, thus obstructing solutions to the immense challenges our society faces. But democratization is not the same as nationalization. Nor is it animated by an exclusive commitment to one single form of ownership. For too long socialists have been preoccupied with one-size-fits-all solutions, with the idea that one kind of ownership must define the entire economy.

But economies are complex, consisting of many types of enterprises and activities, so that one distinct form of ownership cannot apply across the board. There is not much sense, for example, in permitting a small handful of finance workers to have power over society's investments; here public ownership and consumer cooperatives are much more appropriate than worker ownership. At the same time the goal of the democratization of ownership is multifaceted. We seek more democracy at the workplace but also more democratic influence for the whole of society. We want wage earners to receive a greater share in the value they create but also that this value is more broadly distributed across society. And the different forms of democratic ownership have different strengths and advantages when it comes to achieving these goals.

Public ownership ensures that the proceeds from production are used for the benefit of the whole population and allows for decisions to be made according to a broad societal perspective. But it does not give employees a share of the profits from their production and does not necessarily give them democratic influence over their working lives.

Consumer cooperatives give members direct ownership and influence, particularly with respect to the distribution and use of surpluses. But these democratic enterprises may be trained on the narrower interests of the membership and therefore not reflect the concerns of society at large.

Worker cooperatives provide direct democracy for the employees as well as a share in the proceeds. But they also tend to lead to sectoral inequality and do not benefit those outside the labor market.

Funds socialist models can take the form of both employee funds, which give employees influence and a share of the profits, and social wealth funds, which distribute surpluses not just to workers but to the unemployed, students, and retirees. Their scale, however, makes it difficult for employees and citizens to exert influence over them.

The various forms of democratic ownership can thus serve varying purposes, and therefore a new democratic economy should not be based on an ownership monoculture but instead on *a pluralistic landscape of democratic ownership forms* in which cooperatives and other democratic enterprises, fund socialist models, and new forms of public ownership combine to distribute wealth and influence.

A democratic sector within the larger economy would, at least for a long period, coexist with a nondemocratic sector. And individual founders and entrepreneurs can and should continue to play an important and positive role in a democratic economy. In both the democratic and nondemocratic sectors a new wave of functional socialist reforms can democratize certain functions of ownership, such as changing the power relations between employees and investors at private firms and redistributing wealth across various groups and generations at both the pre- and postdistributive phases.

Such a mix of ownership forms and functional socialist reforms would provide ordinary citizens with much greater influence over society, the economy, and their own everyday lives and would further undermine oligarchic power. This program would at the same time move the economy away from the short-term profit seeking of capitalists and toward broader concerns like the climate and working conditions.

But how we own and manage our enterprises is one thing, while how we organize the production and distribution of goods and services in a democratic and effective manner is entirely another. We now turn to another classic theme of economic debates: the conflict between market forces and democratic planning.

The Market Economy or Democratic Planning?

"You are against the market. You want socialism instead!" former finance minister Bjarne Corydon utters with spitting contempt. I am standing in the Danske Bank tent at the Citizen's Assembly on Bornholm, participating in a debate on the future of capitalism. Corydon's statement reflects the popular understanding of the relationship between socialism and the market, namely, that the one excludes the other, that the market is synonymous with capitalism, and that socialism entails replacing the market with economic planning in which production and prices are determined politically. But this binary opposition has as little to do with modern socialism as it does with actual economic reality. In the real world, the contention that capitalism and markets are synonymous holds up about as well the idea that socialism and markets are necessarily opposed to one another.

First, markets, which are mediums of voluntary exchange employing the price mechanism, have existed far longer than capitalism. Goods and services were exchanged and traded for thousands of years before the capitalist mode of production became dominant and market mechanisms expanded into new societal and economic domains. The most fundamental changes were the establishment of markets for labor power, capital, and investments. But the development of the market did not begin with capitalism.

Second, neither a planned nor market economy has ever existed in pure form. All the countries said to have market economies also engage in economic planning. Among the most successful capitalist economies at present are South Korea, Taiwan, and Singapore, all of which make extensive use of planning. Investment in these countries is largely directed by the state. Western economies, including those of Nordic countries, also use economic planning. Here in Denmark our health-care and education sectors are for the most part democratically planned and thus anchored in democratic governance. Market forces don't determine which courses of study are offered or which health-care services are available at hospitals, and we do not conduct a market transaction when we seek treatment for a broken leg or when we send our children to school. As we shall later see, the balance between planning and markets, including in the countries of the so-called socialist bloc, varies widely and changes over time. Nowhere has a fully planned economy ever existed.

Furthermore, there is much greater complexity and nuance in the relation between democratic planning and market forces than the typical binary opposition allows. It is more appropriate to conceive this relation as a matter of scale or as a continuum, or as former Social Democratic prime minister Krag put it in a 1943 editorial: "Economic planning is not a question of either/or, but of more or less."[93] And the degree of nuance deepens when we consider that the relation between markets and planning does not only concern which sectors are market determined and which are planned. To a large extent the relation is also a function of the social, political, and legislative frames to which the marketized areas are subjected. There are markets that function with a minimum of regulation and those that are strictly regulated and constrained by democratic planning that determines prices, supply, and demand.

The scope and nature of political regulation play an extensive role in shaping the concrete reality of our experience with the market as citizens, wage earners, and consumers. Think of the rental market. Here in Denmark rent prices have been strictly regulated in order to protect tenants from sudden increases. Rents are thus not set by the market but politically, and yet it is still a form of the market in which private investors own and lease properties. Market forces are still regulated, even though in recent years much has unfortunately been done to undermine this system. The market for labor power is another example. Many countries have minimum wage legislation, which effectively constitutes a kind of price control. Here we do not have such a law but instead employ collective bargaining to intervene in the labor market. And capital markets in all capitalist economies are regulated, although once again such regulations have been hollowed out in recent years, with disastrous consequences. An example is the capital reserve, that is, the amount of funds a bank must have on hand respective to the amount out on loan. Likewise there are rules to protect borrowers.

Finally, economic planning is evident at the macroeconomic level via central bank monetary policy, state budgeting, lending from public banks such as Vækstfonden, and a social safety net that in part determines the price of labor power. Democratic economic planning can thus take the form of direct public ownership or management of enterprises or entire sectors, direct or indirect regulation of prices, quotas and state supports, and macroeconomic direction through taxes, duties, and finance and monetary policy. Altogether, democratic planning is a means by which democratically elected decision makers either directly or indirectly intervene in the production and distribution of goods and services.

Not only has a pure market never existed, but as Polanyi observed as early as the mid-twentieth century, it is in fact impossible to institute a pure market in a democratic society because any attempt to carry out a complete marketization of labor power and capital would lead to opposition from wage earners and other social groups, which in a democratic society would result in demands for intervention to limit the scope of the market. This is precisely what happened in many countries in post–World War II Europe, where significant sectors were taken out of the market and transformed into public goods or were subjected to state influence through functional socialism. Health care, education, childcare, and housing were thus transformed from goods and services bought on the market to social rights.

Polanyi also rejects the neoliberal conception of the market as prepolitical and thus the insistence that there is a kind of pure *ur-market* beyond political interference, which would take shape in a pure and authentic form if only politicians would leave it be. The market itself, according to Polanyi, is inherently political, for it presumes the existence of the political. Without legislation on patent rights, for example, the market for medical goods would collapse, and without laws ensuring the right to land ownership, renting would be impossible. The state does not intervene from outside the market. The state itself creates the conditions and the limits of it.[94]

So when Bjarne Corydon and others describe the relation between markets and planning as a binary opposition, they are distorting reality, whether consciously or unconsciously. No society is or ever has been fully planned or fully market determined. All societies possess elements of both. Just as capitalism is not all-dominant when it comes to production, neither is the market when it comes to distribution.

And just like the relation between democratic and nondemocratic enterprise, that between markets and planning is not static but a constantly contested political field. There is nothing "natural" that dictates which sectors of our economy should be governed by market principles and which should be guided by democratic decision-making. Throughout history we have shaken up this balance, and there is no reason we cannot do so again today, either by setting limits on which sectors should or should not belong to the markets or by regulating those areas we have decided to leave to them.

The relationship between markets and planning is thus not binary but fluid. Throughout history, socialists have differed in their views on what role market forces should play in a socialist economy, and so before we proceed to outline the relationship between them in a future Nordic socialism, let us first take a look at earlier debates and prior experience with these differing views.

Socialist Pioneers and the Market

The earliest socialist thinkers did not view the market as the problem with capitalism but rather the concentration of ownership of the means of production. The so-called Ricardian socialists (whose name comes from the British economist David Ricardo) advocated an economy made up of firms owned and managed by workers that would exchange goods and services on a free market. Wage work would thus vanish, but the market would remain. The anarchist Pierre-Joseph Proudhon also proposed such a model while at the same time rejecting state planning in favor of a system in which worker-owned firms traded their goods and services on the market and in which prices would be determined by the amount of labor hours invested in the product. Similar ideas were pervasive among early socialist thinkers, all of whom Karl Marx subsumes under the single category of utopian socialist. It was Marx and Friedrich Engels who shifted the critique toward the market aspect of the capitalist system, identifying the development of the market itself as an obstacle to the development of a highly functioning and just society.

Their critique of the market is multifaceted. They first take aim at the anarchic character of the market system, emphasizing that rather than planning production with the aim of maximizing the fulfilment of human needs, the capitalist economy operates according to blind competition, sacrificing the needs of society for the eternal pursuit of profit. Production is not the result of democratic decision-making with an eye to the whole of society but instead a kind of unorganized byproduct of private profit seeking.

They then demonstrate how the anarchy of the market repeatedly plunges the capitalist economy into crisis. Suppressing wages in the interest of competitiveness naturally results in a growing gap between production and purchasing power, which then inevitably leads to overproduction. The subsequent closure of firms has immense costs for employees thrown out of work and results in the massive waste of their labor power. Marx and Engels emphasize the patent absurdity of the recurring crises of the capitalist market economy, noting that in contrast to crises of earlier ages, capitalist crises are due not to scarcity but to abundance, not too little production but too much, not too much with respect to human needs but too much with respect to consumer purchasing power.

Marx further argues that the act of producing for the market itself results in the *alienation* of labor, that is, that the market comes to stand in opposition to human beings as social beings, thus alienating workers both from the fruits of their labor as well as one another.[95]

Marx and Engels conclude that the alienation of workers from their labor and from each other means that worker takeover of capitalist firms is not in itself enough to put an end to capitalist immiseration. For as long as workers continue to compete against each other on the labor market they remain alienated and thus predisposed to greed, selfishness, and antisocial conduct, and the consequences of market anarchy—crises, unemployment, and inequality—would continue unabated. The radical vision of Marx and Engels thus calls for a rejection of the market itself. In a future socialist society, goods and services would not be exchanged on the market but be available to all citizens. Production would not be determined by anarchic market forces but planned collectively by the workers.

Regarding the specific details of how such a future economy without markets would function, however, Marx and Engels left very little for their ideological descendants, for they did not see it as within their remit to provide "recipes for the cook-shops of the future."

It is no understatement to say that Marx and Engels dramatically underestimate the challenges of completely replacing market mechanisms with politically determined production and prices. Russian revolutionary leader Vladimir Lenin was no less guilty of this, insofar as he argues that capitalism had simplified production and distribution to a "simple system of book-keeping, which any literate person can do."[96] The general absence of ideas on how a planned economy should function as well as the underestimation of the challenges of such a system became a serious problem in 1917, when for the first time a socialist party took power and set itself to implementing the ideas of Marx and Engels.

The Soviet Union and the Problems of Planned Economy

In the fall of 1917, the Bolshevik party took power in Russia in a bloodless revolution (or coup, depending on how one looks at it). The Bolsheviks immediately consolidated power by dissolving the constitutional convention that was to produce a new democratic constitution after the overthrow of the tsardom. This was the start of seventy years of authoritarian one-party rule that did not yield the kingdom of freedom dreamed of by Marx and Engels and many other nineteenth-century socialists.

From the start, Lenin and the Bolsheviks immediately began the attempt to realize the vision of Marx and Engels. By replacing the market with economic planning, Lenin argued, the entire country would become "one big factory." The new planned economy was not instituted all at once or according to a preexisting strategy but was rather effected piecemeal as a reaction to the civil war and the economic collapse that followed the revolution. Under the policy of so-called war communism, all larger firms were nationalized between 1917 and 1920, and the new constitution mandated that all market activities should be replaced with "planned, state-managed distribution of products."[97]

After Bolshevik victory in the civil war, the pendulum swung back in the other direction for a time. Under the so-called new economic policy of

1921 to 1928, a space was created for small business and industries and not least for peasants to sell their goods on the market. Although the state maintained control over heavy industry and raw materials, the party debated the idea of a mix of planning and markets.

Planning, however, became increasingly dominant after Stalin took power. A new comprehensive planning ministry, the so-called Gosplan, began to lay out the five-year plans that organized all production and set prices for both consumer goods and economic inputs. The Gosplan inventoried the whole of the country's resources and productive facilities, set priorities for how they should be employed, and determined a series of production targets for every enterprise, all the way down to the individual factory. At the same time the state banned or at least hindered the opportunity for small businesses and peasants to sell their goods. Instead they were given production quotas like the larger enterprises and were compelled to deliver their products at state-determined prices. The Soviet Union retained this comprehensive model of economic planning—adjusting it and, especially under Mikhail Gorbachev, considerably softening it—until its collapse.

If we only consider the economic data, Soviet planning was in fact successful for many years. Despite civil war and another German invasion, the Soviet Union managed in record time to achieve a comprehensive industrialization of a previously backward agrarian society. And in the decades after the Second World War the growth of the Soviet economy at least equaled that of the Western economies, so that by the 1960s it was generally believed it would eventually overtake those of the West.[98] The Soviets also succeeded in rooting out the principal malady of capitalism, unemployment, achieving full employment for most of the lifespan of the country.

But the impressive economic numbers hid a dark side. The rapid industrialization program and high growth rates were largely due to a much higher investment quota, that is, the percentage of GDP used for investment, than that of the West, where a greater part of the wealth created went to workers as rising wages. In other words, Soviet workers were *more* exploited than their Western counterparts, and their living standards significantly lower. Forced collectivization of agriculture and the violent exploitation of the peasantry, furthermore, resulted in a terrible famine that left millions dead.

It was also apparent from early on that while economic planning proved effective for heavy industry, arms production, and the extraction of raw materials, it was far less so for more diversified and specialized products. Throughout its existence, the Soviet Union was plagued by shortages of consumer goods; store shelves were often empty and when goods were available, long lines to buy them were the norm. Consumer choices were also strictly limited. Mostly, one had to take what one could get.

The problems of the planned economy intensified in the 1970s, as it became more and more difficult for the Soviet Union to keep up with the West. As consumer purchasing power increased with economic growth, the variety of goods and services also increased, thereby complicating the planning process. The first five-year plan encompassed three hundred products. By 1960 this has increased to fifteen thousand and by the 1980s the Gosplan was responsible for no less than twelve million different items.[99]

Starting in the 1970s, economic growth also became increasingly dependent on innovation, which proved to be an acute problem for economic planning, since in a state-planned economy there is little incentive for firms to innovate. They were expected to meet production goals set from above, but there were no real rewards for exceeding them by, for example, developing new methods or technologies. Greater production, on the contrary, usually meant higher quotas for the following year.

The seventy years of Soviet experience with economic planning, despite numerous successes, reveal several serious challenges. First, the centrally planned economy was never able to fulfill consumer needs or wants. Shortages and poor quality were frequent. And the more prosperous, complex, and information dependent the economy became, the more difficult it became to set production goals and prices from above. Second, the planned economy suffered from inherent inefficiencies. Firms were incentivized to overstate their input needs while understating their output capacities, leading to unnecessary overconsumption of resources. The absence of competition weakened the incentive to increase production through innovation. Finally, the centrally planned economy led to the strong concentration of power over production and distribution.

Whether the Soviet economy failed because of economic planning or the absence of democracy is an open question. Many socialists today argue that bureaucracy and excessive centralization were what dogged the Soviet economy and warn against rejecting economic planning merely because of its negative track record in Russia.[100] But the economist Alec Nove, who devoted most of his life to studying the Soviet economy, argues that this is to confuse the cause with the effect, that central planning itself must necessarily end in undemocratic bureaucracy:

> Those who choose to attribute the distortions of the planning system to bureaucracy and lack of democracy have put the cart before the horse. Given the aim of substituting planning for the market [and] administrative resource allocation for trade[,] . . . central control becomes an objective necessity. Given the immense complexities, one requires a complex bureaucratic structure to take a multitude of interconnected decisions which, of their nature, are not a matter for democratic voting. In no society can an elected assembly decide by 115 votes to 73 where to allocate ten tonnes of leather, or whether to produce another 100 tonnes of sulphuric acid.[101]

The many disadvantages of Soviet central planning inspired discussion and development of alternatives elsewhere that could avoid the negative impacts of the market economy while at the same time exploiting its advantages.[102] Such alternatives are broadly described as *market socialism*, the principal historical example being the fully market socialist economy of the former Yugoslavia.

Yugoslavia and Market Socialism

In 1945, after four years of terrible struggle, the army of communist partisan leader Tito pushed the last German occupying troops back over the Slovenian border. Unlike other eastern European countries, Yugoslavia was liberated not by Soviet tanks but by the armed resistance of the population. This quickly set the country on a collision course with Stalin and the Soviet Union, since Yugoslavs had no desire to turn over their newfound freedom to a newly dominant foreign superpower. The final break came in 1948, when Yugoslavia was expelled from Comecon, the Eastern bloc trade organization.

The break with the Soviet Union allowed Yugoslavian socialists the freedom to choose a different economic model than that of the centralized planning characteristic of the Eastern bloc. With Edvard Kardelj and Milovan Đilas taking the lead, Yugoslavian politicians and economists criticized the Soviet model on the grounds that it placed too much power in the hands of a central bureaucracy. They argued that private capitalism in the Soviet Union had merely been replaced with a state capitalism that did not give workers any more say than their counterparts in the West. In the years after 1948 they developed a new socialist model grounded in what was termed "self-management." Under this system, the employees themselves elected the leadership of their employing firms, which further were not subject to central planning but instead purchased their inputs and sold their outputs on a competitive free market.

The Yugoslavian model produced impressive results for years. In the late 1950s and into the 1960s, Yugoslavia boasted the second-highest growth rates in the world, eclipsed only by Japan. Living standards improved dramatically and all citizens had access to health care, education, and culture.[103] The socialist market economy did result in higher economic inequality than in the centrally planned socialist countries, both between and within firms. But income inequality was still significantly lower than in the West.

Beginning in the 1970s, however, the Yugoslavian economy began to face increasing difficulties. Rising inflation and foreign debt weakened performance. Productivity fell. Wages were hollowed out by inflation, which reached 150 percent per annum. A strike wave raised the question of how much control workers actually had.

The causes of the longer-term failures of Yugoslavian market socialism have been extensively debated. Advocates of economic planning have argued that it proves that the principles of socialism cannot be united with the means of the market. Others—especially the reform socialist economists of Eastern Europe—have noted that despite Yugoslavia's embrace of markets, its economy suffered from the same problems as the Soviet planned economy. The country's government was a one-party dictatorship, and in the end it was the state and the party that directed investment and the banking system. State banks thus tended to be too generous with loans, which meant that inefficient firms were kept alive and that wages rose faster than productivity gains could justify, which also led to inflation. Hungarian economist János Kornai uses the concept of *soft budget constraints* to describe how firms could always expect help from the state, whether in the form of loans, tax advantages, or lower input prices, since the authorities preferred to avoid closures and the consequent unemployment, which might result in protest and civil unrest.[104]

At the same time innovation suffered, since it was difficult to establish new firms in sectors that were already populated by inefficient companies. The Yugoslavian experience led many socialist reform economists to conclude that for a market socialist economy to function well firms had to have much greater autonomy, that the process of founding new firms had to be made easier, and that democratically managed but politically independent capital markets were a necessity.[105]

New Market Socialist Ideas

After the collapse of the Soviet Union and the Eastern bloc it became clear to many that the relationship of socialism to the market had to be reevaluated. A number of socialist economists thus began to develop new models for organizing a market socialist economy that would not produce the same problems Yugoslavia experienced.

One of the most well-known market socialist models is that of David Schweickart. In his book *After Capitalism*, he notes that a capitalist market economy consists of three separate types of markets. First there is the market for goods and services in which firms compete with each other. Next there is the market for labor power, in which wage earners sell their labor to the owners of firms. And lastly there is the market for capital, in which private financial institutions receive funds from depositors and then loan them out to firms.

Schweickart proposes keeping the market for goods and services to ensure that unlike in planned economies, firms have a clear incentive to produce what consumers want, do not waste natural resources, use the most cost-effective technologies, and keep up with the latest technological developments and innovations. But he also calls for eliminating the other two markets, arguing for replacing the labor market with a system of employee ownership and for democratizing capital markets by establishing a public fund financed by a tax on profits and the public financing of a network of independent local financial institutions that would provide loans not with an eye to maximal returns but based on an evaluation of how the enterprise would contribute to the broader society.

In Schweickart's model all investment must be carried out through the public banking network, so while founders can establish new firms and profit from them, they cannot use this wealth to purchase other companies. Thus no one can earn money by simply having money.[106]

Critics point out that even though Schweickart proposes a decentralized and independent democratic banking sector, power over investment in the end lies with the state, running the risk of encountering the soft budget constraints that troubled Yugoslavia. The public authorities who have ultimate control of the banks would tend to keep inefficient firms afloat to avoid the political fallout of letting them go under.

Economist John Roemer addresses this challenge with a market socialist model that has come to be called "coupon socialism." Unlike Schweickart, Roemer proposes keeping the market for capital, but in a new form that would avoid the concentration engendered by current capital markets. In this model, at the age of eighteen all citizens receive an equal share of coupons from the state, an alternative form of currency that can be used to purchase shares in the country's various companies. Citizens can invest their coupons as they wish, whether individually or as a member of a democratic investment fund. Enterprises can then exchange their coupons for central bank currency, thereby securing investment capital, and would like today continue to pay out dividends to shareholders. These dividends would be paid out in the national currency, which citizens could then either put into savings or use for consumption. Crucially, the fact that the citizen coupons cannot be exchanged for currency and currency cannot be exchanged for coupons thwarts the excessive concentration of capital ownership among a small number of elites. Competent investors who invest in the most effective firms will receive larger dividends, but these dividends cannot be used to purchase further shares, since they can only be had with coupons. Any coupons still in a person's possession upon death are returned to the state, which then distributes them to new citizens as they come of age.

If this model were implemented, it would yield a capital market that functions much like today's. Firms would still compete to attract investment, but surpluses would be much more broadly distributed across the population. The aim, according to Roemer, is to preserve the mechanism that present capital markets use to discipline the leadership of private enterprises. Everyone gets a share in the total surplus of society, but unlike Schweickart's model, Roemer's retains the decentralized allocation of investment characteristic of the shareholder model.

Roemer's model does not propose employee ownership of enterprises, since as today firms would remain in the hands of shareholders. But the shareholders would be citizens rather than a small handful of wealthy individuals, and thus he maintains that his model is indeed socialist because profit is socialized and because it breaks with the circularity of capitalism that sees money exchanged for capital and vice versa.[107] Other market socialists like sociologist Erik Olin Wright and economist Richard Wolff, drawing on the work of Eastern European socialist reform economists, go a step further, endorsing a more pluralistic capital market that would allow democratic financial institutions owned by customers or localities to play a role.[108]

Decentralized Planned Economy

There are also socialists who affirm the vision of economic planning but in a new decentralized and democratic form. The most well-known advocates are economists Michael Albert and Robin Hahnel, who have developed a model of decentralized economic planning they call "participatory economics." Instead of centralized state planning of production and distribution, they propose a comprehensive participatory process in which consumers and employees of enterprises democratically match demand with production.

In this model, at the beginning of the year, each citizen draws up a list of the products they plan to consume in the coming year. Lists may be based on the previous year's consumption, which would be fully recorded by a payment card. Citizen lists thus contribute to a price registry consisting of all available products, and planned consumption cannot exceed a person's budget, which is determined by how much that person works.[109] Prices in the catalog are only provisional, and after consumption lists are submitted, a data-driven analysis is implemented that attempts to bring supply and demand into agreement. If, for example, there is high demand for a product that requires scarce resources, then the price is raised. Citizens, now informed of the adjusted prices, are then given the opportunity to change their lists. This process is repeated several times until supply and demand are brought into full alignment. Such a planning process, argue Albert and Hahnel, can avoid many of the negative externalities of the market economy, most of all overproduction and unemployment.[110]

Critics note that while the model might in theory constitute an alternative to both markets and centralized planning, it could never work in practice because it is unrealistic to expect that citizens would be able to predict their future consumption, that is, which restaurants they will eat at or whether they will take a beach vacation and thus require a new snorkel.

The fact that modern economies offer millions of variations on individual products would further complicate the process of constructing a consumption list, since unless consumers were able to specify, say, what kind of shirt they wanted, producers would have no way of knowing if the shirt should be red or striped or made of cotton or wool.[111]

Advocates respond that such problems could be resolved through the use of modern data feedback, which large multinationals like Amazon and Google already use to suggest new products for consumers to buy, and that such methods could provide precise forecasts of future consumption patterns.[112] Amazon has in fact just patented so-called anticipatory shipping—software that can help make goods ready for delivery before we even know we are going to buy them.[113]

Market, Planning, and Nordic Socialism

Before we reach a conclusion on the role market mechanisms should or should not play in a new democratic economy, let us sum up.

First, the debate between markets and planning is not an either/or matter, a choice between pure planning or pure market allocation. There is a broad spectrum between these two poles, and all societies both past and present have existed somewhere in between. All have combined a degree of planning with a degree of market distribution.

Second, it is simply nonsense to speak of a single unitary market, for the markets for consumer goods, capital, and labor power are three separate things. And it is perfectly reasonable to maintain that market mechanisms are effective with respect to consumer goods, but less so with regard to capital, labor power, or critical natural resources.

Third, the marketized sectors of the economy can be subject to more or less regulation by political and social means, which intervene in the interest of the broader society. And the planned sectors of the economy, likewise, can be managed more or less according to market-like forms.

Fourth, and finally, socialists have historically differed widely on the question of whether and to what extent market mechanisms can be combined with a socialist economy. Altogether, these observations raise the question of where a modern Nordic socialism ought to be placed on the spectrum between market and planning.

That socialists reject a pure laissez-faire market economy goes without saying. But in my view it is also clear that the other pole—a comprehensive planned economy like that of the Soviet Union—is not desirable. In theory a democratically managed planned economy is a nice idea, that we as a society, with an eye to what is best for it, make democratic decisions on what shall be produced and how goods and services shall be distributed. But all previous experience suggests that in practice it is impossible to replace the information provided by market mechanisms with central planning—especially in a complex modern economy that requires extensive division of labor.

The problem is that complex production demands thousands, even millions, of decisions that must be coordinated with one another. Behind each of the products we consume is a long and complex chain of production. Just consider how many people were involved in the development of the laptop computer—not just those who worked on the assembly line but also those who provided the microprocessors, the touch screen, the hard disk, and the memory card. We are speaking of thousands of people here. And to this can be added all those who provided the necessary natural resources; oil, steel, lithium; and all the labor of processing them. Thousands more are involved in transporting the components from one link in the chain to the next. Thus it is hardly unreasonable to suggest that millions, in one way or another, were directly involved in the production of the various items in your living room. And each person has contributed only one small part.

But how do employees and firms know what products they are to produce? How do they know how much plastic should be made? And how do they know that the kind of plastic needed by the computer industry must be more durable and thus more expensive than typical plastics? And how do computer manufacturers know how many touchscreen machines should be produced or how many must have more powerful processing capacity? The number of such dilemmas and decisions are all but infinite in a modern complex economy with millions of different products and billions of workers and consumers. And these decisions have broad impact, for resources are not infinite and the mass production of one product means less inputs for others.[114]

The important question here is who should be making these decisions. While socialists have traditionally argued that society or rather "the people" should, it is simply not possible for large collectivities to make the hundreds of thousands, even millions, of microeconomic decisions required by our dynamic economy, in which access to needed resources is constantly in flux. In cases of fairly simple products for which demand is relatively inelastic, such as water or electricity or public transportation, production and distribution can be democratically planned without problems and without employing market mechanisms. But in a market economy more generally it is the price mechanism that does the heavy lifting of directing this process. Prices provide information as to how much people are prepared to pay for a particular good or service and as to how much value they place on one product in comparison to another. By collecting data on consumer preferences through the price mechanism, the great global network of producers can make rational decisions regarding their individual contributions to the production process.

Even if it were possible to replace the market's price signals with planning, citizens in such an economy would, like in the Soviet Union, have little influence on what was available for consumption. After many years of studying the Soviet economy, Nove concludes that "surely the most genuinely democratic way to give power to consumers" is to make it possible for them "to influence the pattern of production by their behavior as buyers. There is no direct 'political' alternative. There being hundreds of thousands of different kinds of goods and services in infinite permutations and combinations, a political voting process is impracticable, a ballot paper incorporating microeconomic consumer choice unthinkable."[115]

In his 2012 book *The Crisis and the Long Overdue Systemic Critique*, former Left Socialist parliament member Preben Wilhjlem comes to the same conclusion, arguing that market mechanisms "are an ingenious means of allocating investment and directing production at the microeconomic level, in which the consumer by choosing, so to speak, determines which cheeses and magazines and handbags and bumper stickers will continue to be produced and which will not, just as consumers choose whether they will spend their money on a new iPad or a more expensive red wine. The mechanism is not just ultrademocratic; it would in fact be impractical to make all these decisions with formalized democratic referenda, let alone by representative democracy. . . . Within its operational area, private consumption, markets are a good steering mechanism."[116]

It is not only to secure consumer input that a fully planned economy should be rejected. As noted, economic planning would centralize decision-making over the whole production process, which runs up against the very idea of democratizing enterprise and providing employees with extensive influence over production. Firms would instead be subjected to comprehensive central control from above and have little or no autonomy.

Market mechanisms, when properly defined, are an effective means of efficiently using the resources of society. Competition between firms, including those democratically managed, and the possibility of establishing new firms are able to prevent the propping up of inefficient companies.

I thus agree with Nove, Wilhjelm, and other market socialists: a fully planned economic system without market mechanisms is neither possible nor desirable. The employment of markets is unavoidable in a modern complex economy, if we want it to be efficient, to offer citizens real influence over their consumer choices and to prevent the growth of an enormous state bureaucracy that would manage our workplaces from above.

The Scope of the Market Will Be Contained and Limited

Rejecting the idea of a fully democratically planned economy does not amount to an embrace of the other extreme, a laissez-faire market economy, nor does it amount to claiming that the scope and the influence that market forces have in our present economy is desirable. Far from it.

Marx and Engels are correct in their critique of the downside of the market. Markets give consumers the freedom to choose, but this freedom is largely determined by purchasing power and thus unequally distributed. The rich have more freedom than the poor. They are also correct that the market economy—precisely because millions of microeconomic decisions are decentralized—is anarchistic and unable to take the broader interests of society into account and that the market economy thus has many negative consequences, not least of which are environmental destruction and climate change. Marx and Engels are also right that market competition leads to crisis and recession, which throw many out of work and thus are both damaging to the single individual as well as wasteful of society's productive resources.

All these negative effects are just as prominent today as they were in the nineteenth century, and indeed they have intensified during the past three decades, as more and more economic sectors have been marketized and regulation has been scaled back. The deregulation and privatization of capital markets in particular have generated more inequality and greater instability and thus deeper crises.

Given that a fully planned economy is not the way forward, our task is to find the optimal balance between the market's "ingenious" ability to coordinate production and distribution in defined sectors of the economy and the imperative of curbing and minimizing the negative consequences it invariably produces.[117] We must change the balance between markets and planning in favor of planning, and to achieve this we must limit both which areas of the economy are marketized and expand the scope of democratic regulation so that it can influence prices and minimize negative effects.

The Danish language lacks solid concepts for describing the movement toward a less market-dominated society. In the Anglophone world, the term "commodification" connotes the phenomenon of extending market forces into new economic sectors, such as through privatization of public services, while the opposite is referred to as "decommodification." Danish rough equivalents for commodification include "varegørelse" (consumerization) or "markedsgørelse" (marketization), but we have no equivalent for decommodification, no "afmarkedsgørelse," which is quite remarkable given that Danish society has long sought the decommodification of significant parts of the economy. The fact that Danish lacks such a word also suggests just how potent the binary opposition between markets and planning is here at home.

For lack of a better option, I employ the coinage "demarketization" to describe reforms and measures that can reduce the scope and influence of market forces on the economy. Demarketization can be used both for communalization (*fællesgørelse*), that is, for taking marketized sectors out of the market sphere and turning them into public goods, and for implementing democratic regulation, through which the state can mitigate capitalism's negative effects on society and the environment.

Communalization

Communalization describes reforms or changes that remove chunks of the economy from the marketized sphere by transforming them into tax-financed public goods and rights to which we as citizens all have access, without engaging in market transactions or, at the very least, in which society intervenes in price setting.

As I have noted, we in the Nordic region already have extensive experience with the communalization of extensive spheres of life. The fulfillment of many important needs from health care to education and leisure is not determined by wealth or purchasing power. We take many of our communalized sectors for granted, but a comparison with the United States demonstrates that there is nothing "natural" about which areas of the economy are marketized and which are communalized. And our communalized sectors have often been the result of long struggle to remove them from the marketized sphere.

Because nature does not determine which sectors are marketized and which are not, we can and should communalize new sectors. A good place to start would be the areas of our health-care system that are still marketized. That our teeth are not covered by the universal and free health care that covers the rest of our body is hardly rational. Marketized dental care creates unequal access, since low-income people cannot afford to pay. A communalization of the marketized aspects of health care would significantly reduce inequality of care and leave citizens less exposed to and dependent on the market.

Another area ripe for communalization is public transportation, which in many other countries and cities has already been transformed into a public good with free and equal access. Communalizing it would also help reduce pollution and carbon emissions, thereby improving public health. Access to broadband internet can and should be made a public good. The sharing economy we know from libraries can also be extended to new domains. Everyday items we rarely need to use such as lawnmowers or electric drills could be freely loaned out from tool banks across the country. This kind of communalization would also reduce our individual consumption, benefiting the climate and preserving natural resources.

Communalization can also be effected from the ground up. A good example of grassroots communalization is Wikipedia. Tens of thousands of volunteers contribute to its development, and it is freely available to anyone on the planet. An area that was once marketized is now communalized. Similarly, Creative Commons and Open License provide free access for noncommercial use of images, music, and scientific articles. This kind of communalization can, as noted, be supported by the state, such as by making publicly supported research results open access.

Democratic Regulation

As noted it is neither possible nor desirable to communalize the entire economy, since market mechanisms are the best available means to ensure that firms produce the goods consumers want. But the manner and extent to which economic planners set limits on the market vary widely.

Our existing economy is already characterized by many such interventions. During countercyclical periods, for example, the state can increase its investments to make up for the lack of private investment to fend off crises. But this form of democratically planned intervention has been handicapped in the neoliberal era because of fears of taking on excessive debt, particularly in the EU. In earlier times nearly every Western country engaged in industrial policy, in which democratic decisions determined how the state could support the development of select branches of industry. Another example of democratic planned intervention is our home heating system, which by virtue of its mandatory participation policy has increased the sustainability of the sector. The latest example is the climate law, which sets politically determined targets for carbon reduction, and the subsequent climate action plans, which compel individual sectors to reach these targets.

But the neoliberal era has generally been characterized by the refrain of "setting the market free" and by a widespread sense that democratic forces should interfere as little as possible. Our task now is to reverse this tendency. Democratic planning at all levels ought to play a much larger role than today in order to counteract the negative impacts of anarchic market forces.

Putting a stop to climate change and species extinction, both of which constitute mortal threats to life on the planet, is absolutely critical. A new model for democratic planning can take inspiration from British economist Kate Raworth's concept of the "doughnut economy." The inner circle of the doughnut constitutes the social needs we as human beings must have fulfilled in order to thrive: food, water, welfare, housing, social security. The outer circle consists of the planetary conditions necessary for us to live on the globe, such as biodiversity, a stable climate, fertile agricultural land, and a healthy ozone layer. Between these two boundaries is the doughnut, the space in which our economy can sustainably unfold.[118]

A democratically planned economy means that through political decisions we set the limits, the direction, and the goals of the economy to secure the well-being of all within the confines of our habitat. With such a frame, market mechanisms can function only insofar as they support such aims.

Implementing this model will require a new method of political economic governance. Today macroeconomic governance seeks to create the best possible conditions for growth as measured by GDP. In the future, economic planning and reform programs must seek to achieve a series of concrete democratically determined goals. Just as we have already set climate goals, so too can we set goals to bring down economic inequality, secure full employment, and put the brakes on species extinction. Goal setting must be followed by concrete reforms and action plans for all relevant sectors of the economy. Regarding the climate, for example, we need action plans to end North Sea oil production, ban the sale of gas- or diesel-powered vehicles, and limit the size of cattle herds.

Democratic planning furthermore seeks to minimize the negative impacts of market mechanisms on the labor market. It goes without saying that certain enterprises—whether democratic or capitalist—will prove themselves unable to compete on the competitive market and thus must go under. And people will lose their jobs. This is an inherent cost of achieving an efficient economy. But unemployment can be minimized, in part through a much more robust Keynesian offensive during countercyclical crises, in which the economy is restarted by public investment, and in part through a public jobs guarantee, according to which during periods of high unemployment the state offers work to anyone in need.

We must also be much more conscious of how we as a society make use of productivity gains. For years most of these gains have gone to increased consumption. But ever rising consumption levels make it impossible to keep production within the limits prescribed by the doughnut economy. It is therefore critical that economic planning must ensure that productivity gains are translated into more leisure time rather than consumption, whether in the form of a shorter workweek, more holidays, longer maternity and paternity leaves, or a lower retirement age. These are just a few of the examples of how we can use democratic planning and regulation to intervene in marketized sectors to mitigate the negative impacts of market forces. In chapter 5 I will recommend a series of concrete reforms that could expand the areas of the economy that are democratically planned and to which we as citizens have access regardless of our ability to pay.

Is It Good Enough?

Some socialists will be skeptical of the idea of that a complete break with the market economy is not required to effect significant change. Bertell Ollman, for example, argues that market mechanisms are far more to blame for the negative consequences of capitalism than the exploitation of labor power: "The market . . . is a more important feature of capitalism than is private ownership. Thus ownership can be transferred to the state . . . or to worker cooperatives, but if the market remains essentially intact so, too, will most of the problems associated with capitalism."[119]

Economist Robin Hahnel agrees, warning that the existence of even small pockets of market mechanisms in the economy would be dangerous, since competition promotes antisocial behavior driven by greed and fear, thereby undermining the solidarity and trust so critical to the development of a socialist economy. He compares market mechanisms to a terminal cancer that would rapidly spread.[120]

Such objections assume that markets possess certain inherent characteristics, regardless of the social context in which they are embedded. But markets are not all the same, since the particular social reality in which they are housed makes for significant differences, such as whether market actors are capital funds and profit-seeking corporations or democratic enterprises governed by citizens, employees, or consumers, or whether they are surrounded by weak institutions or by comprehensive political regulation. As Erik Olin Wright notes: "markets do indeed embody and foster greed and fear, but this is not because of something intrinsic to the sheer fact of market processes but to the social form of those markets in capitalism."[121]

The conception of the market as a cancer that automatically spreads is an example of the kind of thinking all too prevalent on the left, that is, the tendency to view capitalism and the market as a kind of organic living being with its own agency and power to act, a view that tends to be accompanied by a pessimistic understanding of human nature, according to which we are eminently prone to sleepwalking into the abyss of capitalism's siren song.

As this chapter has demonstrated, history shows the opposite. Markets have not always spread outward. Governments across the globe have been able to muster the necessary political will to keep markets out of significant economic sectors. That the market has expanded under neoliberalism owes not to some innate quality of markets themselves but to the well-orchestrated campaigns of economic elites seeking to further their own interests. Political struggle rather than an underlying natural mechanism drives the relationship between market forces and democratic decision-making.

To return to Jens Otto Krag, economic planning is not a matter of either/or but of more or less. We do not need to choose between a pure market economy and a pure planned economy. Experience has revealed that a fully planned economy like of that of the Soviet Union is not desirable. Market mechanisms are useful to transmit information between consumers and producers in a complex economy with extensive division of labor.

But market mechanisms are not useful in all parts of the economy. There is good reason to expand those sectors of our economy that operate outside the market, such that our access to critical social needs is much less dependent on ability to pay. And we must further seek to ensure that democratically anchored planning is employed to place limits on and set the direction of the economy, such that it functions to the benefit of the majority. And not least to ensure that we do not exceed the climactic and resource limitations of our planet.

Principles for Nordic Socialism

In this chapter I have discussed some of the most difficult and most important questions raised by the prospect of developing a more democratic economy. My overall conclusion is that the left has been all too fixated on totalities, such as a total break with the market or a total nationalization of production, and that this preoccupation is based on an erroneous theory of capitalism as an all-encompassing system that must be replaced by another all-encompassing system. But the reality is that societies and economies are hybrids.

A socialism for our time must be more nuanced, not the least with respect to attitudes toward the state, in which the left has placed too much faith, and toward the market, in which perhaps the left has had too little. Black-and-white solutions must be replaced with a desire to find the right balance. Less either/or, more both/and. The goal is not some prescribed ideal, not a total reimagining of society in accordance with what socialists envisioned 150 years ago. Instead our goal is a society that secures as much freedom, security, and well-being in as sustainable a manner as is possible for as many people as possible. This is our radical goal, and socialist ideas and reforms are just the means to achieve it.

The contours of a future Nordic socialism can thus be summarized in the following five principles:

1. Radical Democracy
   Political democracy and the unconditional protection of individual rights are a necessary precondition for any future Nordic socialism. But they are not sufficient. As long as our economy and working lives remain nondemocratic, the oligarchic power of economic elites will continue to undermine democratic governance, resulting in a growing gulf between democratic ideals and economic reality.
2. Skepticism Toward the State
   The present concentration of economic power among economic elites must not simply be replaced by a new concentration of economic power in the state. Instead the democratic self-organization of employees, consumers, and citizens must be strengthened. Political reforms will support such self-organization.
3. Pluralistic Ownership
   Rather than seeking a single model of ownership for the whole economy, a new Nordic socialism will develop a pluralistic architecture of democratic ownership forms that supplement and support one another and at the same time create an economy in which wealth, power, and influence are distributed among the many.
4. A Combination of Markets and Planning
   Neither a purely planned nor purely market economy is desirable. Instead we seek a balance in which market mechanisms are far less dominant than today, but still function in relevant sectors, and in which the framework and direction of the economy are determined by democratic decisions that ensure we do not exceed the limits of our habitat.
5. Curiosity and Based in Experience
   Development must be based on concrete experiences with democratic ownership and management rather than on pre-existing visions of an entirely new postrevolutionary society. Instead of working from detailed models of a future economy, curiosity, creative experimentation, and trial and error shall be the rule. Every step forward provides new experience on which to build further.

These are the principles on which a Nordic socialism must be erected.[122] We cannot know in advance how a new mixed socialist economy will take shape and develop, what forms of democratic ownership will emerge as predominant, or how much space we will need to allot to markets in those areas we cannot plan beforehand. These will all be determined by our experiences as a society.

But how do we get started? What are the first steps? Which changes and reforms can bring us closer to Nordic democratic socialism? This is the subject of the final chapter.

5

Ten Reforms Toward a Democratic Nordic Socialism

There is no easy fix that would allow us to build a future Nordic socialism. It will require a broad democratic process to roll back decades of capitalist colonization of our economy and society so that democratic ownership and decision-making once again afford the majority a greater share of the wealth and democratic influence.

Just as in the previous thirty years of capitalist colonization, this process will involve the interplay of various elements of civil society from below with political reforms from above, including at the international as well as national, regional, and local levels. But whereas it was elites who schemed to carry out every neoliberal colonization, socialist recolonization will mobilize broad layers of society: wage earners, consumers, and small-scale producers.

This process will gradually lead to labor power, investment, and consumption migrating away from the capitalist sector and toward the democratic, setting the stage for a time when oligarchic power no longer has a role in society. Citizens, rather than the anarchic logic of the market, will democratically set the framework and the goals for economic development. And the people acting in common shall decide how the wealth of society will be used, where it will be invested, and how working life will be organized.

In what follows I present a slate of ten reforms in broad outline that could move society and economy in this direction. This is not a comprehensive list, and many others could be proposed, but in my view implementing these ten reforms could constitute a first step toward a new democratic economy—a Nordic socialism.

The reform slate has two goals: to facilitate the democratization of the ownership and the management of our firms, banks, land, and information resources and to foster a broader movement toward more democratic planning and less market anarchy.

Reform 1: Expand the Democratic Sector

The fostering of a new wave of cooperatives owned by employees, consumers, and other civil society groups is an important element of building a democratic economy. Experience from other European countries demonstrates that it is critical to develop the correct institutional, legal, and political conditions for a cooperative economy to thrive. Here I outline a number of key initiatives for removing barriers and providing public support for democratic enterprises.

Give Cooperatives the Right of First Purchase and Tax Advantages

In Denmark and other Nordic countries, we are in the midst of an immense generational turnover of private firm ownership, as up to 60 percent of owners across twenty-three thousand different firms that employ more than a million people will retire in the next ten to fifteen years, providing a unique opportunity to democratically transform thousands of companies. Other European countries have successfully managed this process of generational turnover, facilitating a democratic transition. In Italy and France, workers can, with the support of a cooperative investment fund, purchase and take over their employing firms, and in Britain owners can avoid capital gains taxes if they choose to sell their firms to an employee fund.[1] Denmark should follow these examples by instituting favorable tax rules for owners to sell firms to employees. And receipt of such tax advantages should be conditioned on the democratic transition of the firm, with the establishment of an indivisible social fund to secure the best conditions for the long-term survival of the enterprise. The same tax advantages should apply to the conversion of infrastructure such as waterworks or heating to consumer ownership.

Employees and consumers must also be granted the right of first purchase when nondemocratic firms change hands, just as now tenants have the right of first purchase when landlords decide to sell their property. Such a measure would provide workers and consumers with the collective right to buy their employing firms or utilities at the same price it is offered in a transparent sales process.

Better Access to Capital

The largest barrier to the establishment and development of democratic enterprises is access to capital. One reason for this is a general lack of knowledge about cooperatives among bankers and investors, but another obvious reason is that democratic enterprises cannot take in capital from external investors the same way nondemocratic ones can, since they cannot permit outside parties to secure influence over the management of the firm. A powerful and growing democratic sector thus requires access to capital on its own terms. Experience from elsewhere in Europe suggests that the presence of both public and private democratic investment funds strengthens the cooperative sector. We must therefore establish a public cooperative investment fund that can lend to, underwrite, and invest in democratic enterprises. Access to credit should be conditioned by the maintenance of an indivisible self-owned capital reserve.

Clearly Define the Cooperative Enterprise

Existing Danish cooperatives are organized in several distinct forms. Some are registered as associations or producer co-ops, while others are owned by unions or funds. Elsewhere in Europe, however, specific forms of cooperatives have been more clearly defined in the law, with particular rules for things like member rights and responsibilities. This greater clarity makes it much simpler to distinguish democratic from nondemocratic firms, thereby ensuring that tax advantages are correctly applied and making it much easier to establish new co-ops. Denmark thus needs to pass a new cooperatives law that establishes clear regulations. While still retaining autonomy over basic functions, all co-ops established under such a law would have to meet the legal criteria as set out to ensure democratic governance. Especially important is that complete or partial collective ownership of the firm's capital be mandated, which could perhaps be accomplished by mandating that a part of the surplus be placed in an indivisible social fund that would support both the current functioning of the firm and its preservation for future generations. In exchange for this contribution to the reserve, the firm would be granted a tax deduction.

Democratization of Existing Cooperatives

If we are to base a future economy on democratic enterprise, it is critical that such democracy is in fact real. But as noted, democracy has not always been the rule in Denmark's older producer and union-owned cooperatives. There must of course be a certain degree of autonomy within the individual enterprise, such that the rules can be tailored to its particular needs. But on the other hand, the ordinary member must not be denied a measure of influence. Legislation is therefore needed to establish minimum standards for large democratic enterprises to ensure that rank-and-file members have real influence and that vital decisions are not made without their input, such as by requiring approval via referendum of all major changes to ownership or the distribution of surpluses.

Other initiatives that would both strengthen existing cooperatives as well as stimulate a new wave of democratic enterprise in Denmark include giving preferential treatment to co-ops for public contracts, expanding public support and consulting, and additional tax advantages. More targeted intervention toward specific goals, such as the development of platform cooperatives to challenge multinational giants like Wolt and Uber, is also essential. A pan-Nordic collaboration between states and labor unions to establish consumer- or worker-owned platform alternatives could be effective. Imagine a food delivery service like Wolt but owned by the drivers and restaurants themselves, all of whom would be members of a pan-Nordic association.[2]

Reform 2: A Modern Funds Socialism

Building the framework for a new wave of cooperative enterprise is an important step toward a more democratic communal economy, but it is not sufficient to change the distribution of wealth and power in our society. The ownership of large capitalist corporations, and thus the distribution of profits, is perversely skewed today. It is therefore time to revive the concept of funds socialism that so long animated the Nordic labor movement, that is, the gradual transfer of capitalist ownership to democratic funds managed either by the employees of the individual firm—so-called wage-earner funds—or by a national social fund, in which dividends are paid out to all citizens.

Each approach has pros and cons. Wage-earner funds provide employees with direct influence over their employing firms and a share of the profits they have created through their labor. But only the workers at private firms benefit; other groups like retirees or public employees do not. Workers at more profitable firms (e.g., pharmaceutical companies) also benefit much more than those at less profitable ones (e.g., retail shops), which contributes to inequality between sectors. And while wage-earner funds are compatible with concern for the interests of the larger society, there is no guarantee that the financial interests of the employees might win out in the end.

Social wealth funds function much better in this last aspect. Broad-based ownership ensures that they can use their ownership share in private firms to further societal aims. And the profit sharing, as with the Alaska Permanent Fund, applies not just to workers to but to all citizens. But they do not provide a measure of direct influence for employees of private firms. A new funds socialist model should therefore combine aspects of both, as described below.

Wage-Earner Funds

To establish wage-earner funds, firms with more than a hundred employees should be required to pay an annual "democracy tax" in the form of newly issued shares corresponding to 2 percent of total market capitalization. These shares should be placed in a wage-earner fund for each individual firm. The fund will be self-owned and its leadership elected by all employees at the annual shareholder meeting, in which all may participate and anyone may choose to run. The management of the fund should be transparent and guided by broad strategic goals determined at the annual meeting, in which all employees have equal voting rights. The individual workers cannot buy or sell shares, not even when they leave the company or retire, but the fund pays out an annual dividend to all employees, consisting of the fund's share of the firm's total dividend payout.

The newly issued shares will serve to thin out the ownership of existing shareholders, but only modestly. And such thinning out already occurs through the granting of stock options to the upper layers of management. Another possibility is to make the program voluntary, but refusal to take part would result in a tax penalty, which must be large enough to ensure that it is in the firm's financial interest to participate. It is also important to find ways to prevent corporations from avoiding democratization by such means as subcontracting or hiding profits in holding companies with few employees. And there must also be a solution to problems raised by foreign firms operating in Denmark and Danish firms in which a majority of shares are owned abroad. One possibility would be to make the democracy tax apply to all activities undertaken by such firms within the country.

The establishment of wage-earner funds must be extensively debated in civil society, in labor unions and in individual firms, and it is also essential that it be accompanied by extensive educational and informational campaigns to prepare workers for their much more active role.

In order to minimize inequality between sectors and between wage earners and non–wage earners, a cap of DKK 20,000 should be set on individual dividend payments. Any amounts over this figure would then be contributed to a social wealth fund.

The Social Wealth Fund

The goal of a Danish social wealth fund is to steadily increase the share of democratic ownership in Danish firms. The purchase of shares will be financed in part by surpluses from wage earner funds and in part by a series of new taxes on capital gains, profits, and financial transactions. The existing inheritance tax will be paid in the form of shares transferred to the social wealth fund, which would have the effect of preventing the liquidity crunch caused by the current system of cash tax payments.

Every year each Danish citizen will receive a nonredeemable certificate of ownership corresponding to their share in the fund. The portion of annual capital gains not reinvested will then be distributed via an annual citizen dividend regardless of age. If over time the social wealth fund grows sufficiently, the citizen dividend could then function as a kind of universal basic income.

The social wealth fund should be self-owned and regulated by law but independent in its day-to-day management, overseen by a representative council consisting of important actors from both civil society and government, including labor unions, consumer organizations, and environmental NGOs. The fund should engage in an active investment politics promoting sustainability, democracy, and jobs with good working conditions. The independence and by-laws of the fund would ensure that a parliamentary majority could not eliminate or privatize it without approval through a national referendum. The citizen dividend could be temporarily increased during periods of low demand and temporarily decreased to fight inflation, thereby mitigating the effects of cyclical impacts.

The establishment of wage-earner funds and a social wealth fund would have many positive effects on society and economy. The wider distribution of capital profits would markedly reduce economic inequality, and broader ownership would further undermine the present short-sighted profit seeking of economic elites and result in more attention being paid to firms' impact on employment, the climate, the environment, and local society as well as their long-term flourishing.

With significant democratic capital at our disposal, we can increasingly free ourselves from dependence on tax-evading foreign capital funds, thus guaranteeing that returns on investments in Danish enterprises remain in Denmark and are subject to Danish taxation.

The size and scope of both wage-earner funds and the social wealth fund must be the subject of ongoing political debate. Firms could be owned through a combination of a democratic fund and private capitalist investors, a form of hybrid ownership, or larger firms could be 100-percent owned either by employees or by a combination of employees and the social wealth fund, constituting a more comprehensive democratization.

The very first reform should be changing the pension law so that state pension funds with extensive investments in Danish enterprises would be required to transfer half of their voting rights to representatives elected by the employees of the firms in which they invest. Trade union pension funds should be encouraged to do the same.[3]

Reform 3: Back to the Community—New Democratic Public Ownership

Although direct citizen ownership in the form of cooperatives and funds socialism is often preferable, public ownership at the national, regional, and municipal levels is also an important part of a future architecture of democratic ownership. Public ownership permits broad social concerns to be taken into consideration, provides citizens with democratic influence, and ensures that surpluses go back to and are reinvested in the community. But new measures to reduce bureaucracy, foster a collective sense of ownership, and boost the influence of citizens, civil servants, and civil society at large are needed.

Renationalization of Critical Infrastructure

Unfortunately, over the past few decades our telecommunications network and harbors and airports, all of which should be under democratic control, have been either partially or wholly privatized, and the rollout of fiber optic and cellular networks was also a private affair. While a majority of utilities are still community owned, the marketization of the electricity sector in the 1990s and the later partial privatization of DONG, now Ørsted, has weakened democratic control over a critical element of the green transition.

Our goal should be to return critical infrastructure needs into the hands of the community within the next ten years, either as public works or as consumer cooperatives. Public and cooperative ownership can then be employed to ensure the transition to a green economy. Just as communal fossil resources were wholly or partially owned by public or cooperative institutions in the past, wind, solar, and other communal energy sources ought to be in the future.

Public ownership must also be expanded into a number of other areas. The privatization of vaccine production has rendered society vulnerable to pandemics, since private firms can subject us to shortages, and should therefore be returned to the state. More broadly, the monopoly or oligopoly status of private pharmaceutical firms must be challenged by developing public alternatives. Public ownership of the finance sector and payment infrastructure should also be widened significantly. Finally, law should require that any government that wishes to privatize a public enterprise over a certain value threshold must first receive approval in a referendum. It is the people, rather than any arbitrary and temporary government, who own public infrastructure, and thus governments should not be able to sell off public assets over the objection of the citizenry.

Municipal Socialism

Municipal governments are our smallest and most public-facing political entities and thus play a decisive role in our welfare society as the administrators of our public schools, eldercare homes, and large parts of our utility services. During the so-called municipal socialist period of the early twentieth century, Danish municipal governments were used as a laboratory for democratic community ownership, which resulted in the establishment of many new welfare institutions, housing cooperatives, and productive enterprises. But today the ability of municipalities to engage in marketized areas has been hampered by a combination of the so-called municipal statutory authority (*kommunalfuldmagt*) and selective interpretation of EU rules.[4] At the same time, municipal governments have been pressured or even compelled to outsource more and more of their functions to private profit-seeking subcontractors.

A comprehensive municipal socialist reform to restore the ability of municipalities to play an active role in the economy would include several measures. First, all obligatory outsourcing mandates should be abolished. Second, profit seeking within the welfare provision sector should be banned, just as is already the case in our free schools. Unions, funds, and other nonprofits could still engage in welfare provision, but commercial providers shall be excluded. Third, municipalities should again enjoy much greater opportunity to establish municipal enterprises, if a majority of residents desire such. If a local enterprise is threatened with closure, such as when generational turnover proves difficult, the municipality shall have the right to take over the firm.

At the same time, municipalities should use their purchasing and contracting functions to support local and sustainable democratic firms, thereby ensuring that municipal spending circulates among the local community and creates local jobs rather than vanishing into the pockets of large nondemocratic firms with no connection to the area.

Democratization of the Public Sector

"When we own in common, we decide in common" should be the slogan for a thorough democratization of the public sector. In a communal economy with a much larger public sector than today, it is all the more important that we demand democratic governance to provide citizens, consumers, and employees with much greater influence and sense of ownership. Unfortunately, however, the public sector over time has become associated with the opposite. And since the concept of "new public management" has gained currency in recent years, we have witnessed a further rolling back of democratic influence.

A new democratic model for public ownership should strengthen the direct influence of civil servants and citizens on public sector institutions, from eldercare to education to municipal utilities. First, the power of employee co-determination representatives (MEDs) should be increased, so that public employees have a greater say in the organization of work. Second, educational institutions must be democratized, so that students, teachers, and technical personnel regain decisive influence over schools. Third, employees, consumers, and relevant NGOs (particularly environmental groups) should be granted direct voting rights in the election of leadership for larger national, regional, or municipal enterprises. Finally, in order to make it easier to influence public enterprises such as utilities or public transportation, a democratic consumer organization should be established to facilitate participation in board elections, such that citizens and consumers can have a real say.

Reform 4: A Democratic Bicameral System in Large Firms

Even if all three of the reforms I have outlined were instituted, the democratic sector would, at least in the near future, still only constitute one part of the larger economy, as a significant portion of enterprises would remain investor owned and thus nondemocratic, while others would be owned by consumers or a social wealth fund. And thus further reforms are needed to ensure that all workers, that is, those who create the value, have much more of a voice than than they do today.

By no means is it a given that capital investors in a firm have the legal right to absolute power while workers who invest their labor power are denied any influence at all. This is not a matter of a division of power ordained by nature but a question of politically determined parameters, as evidenced by the fact that we Danes already took the first step to secure worker influence in the 1970s, when we changed corporation law by mandating that employees could elect one-third of board members in all firms with more than thirty-five employees. While this was a landmark achievement for democracy, the balance of power still lay with investors, who could overrule workers at any moment. This is not the kind of equality we normally associate with democracy.

A New Corporation Law

The present laws of incorporation that deny employees real codetermination should be replaced by a bicameral system. Under such a system, the members of one chamber would be elected by capital investors and the members of the other by labor investors. Decisions that today are made unilaterally by capital investors would require the approval of both chambers. The day-to-day management of the firm would still be handled by professionals, but unlike today they would be responsible to both capital and labor investors. This proposal would not eliminate the property rights or the influence of investors. It would only secure an equal measure of influence for employees.

Aside from bringing corporate leadership into the age of democracy, this new form of governance would very likely lead to more responsible corporate conduct. Enterprises would no doubt focus less on short-term profits and more on society and the local environment in which the workers live and work.[5]

Reform 5: Democratization of Finance and Investment

The financial sector is the nerve center of every society. But the current domination of this sector by private, nondemocratic financial institutions is not beneficial for the majority. A thorough reform of the finance sector requires both a serious expansion of democratic ownership and comprehensive regulation to remove the poisonous teeth of private capital from the system.

Rebuilding a Powerful and Community-Owned Democratic Finance Sector

Denmark has a long tradition of democratic community ownership in the financial sector. Mutual savings banks, co-op banks, cooperative mortgage lenders, and public financial institutions made up most of the financial landscape until just a few decades ago. It is time to reestablish, build up, and strengthen democratic and public alternatives in finance.

The first step is to establish a public nonprofit banking alternative. Only twenty-five years have passed since we had such an institution—GiroBank. And many other European countries still do have them. A public bank would allow citizens to reject private banks, giving the community much more influence over the direction of societal investments and more of the profits. Private banks should not be able to take all the earnings from the creation of money and debt when such earnings could go to the community.

A public bank should be established either from the ground up or through the breaking up of large private financial concerns as a regulated but self-owned independent institution, similar to ATP, the Danish pension fund. It would be operated according to politically determined guidelines that would ensure its investments and lending contribute to sustainability and full employment. A representative council chosen by its customers would be its highest authority. At the same time, a public payment infrastructure using cellular phones, debit cards, and a payment service should be set up. Critical financial infrastructure should not enrich Nets, Visa, or PayPal or any other global rentier capitalists as it does today.

At the same time, the state-owned growth fund and other public investment banks should play a much larger role, have much greater financial resources at their disposal, and be given a broader mandate to further societal goals, among them contributing to the green transition and the building up of democratic enterprise by providing capital.

It is critical that all public financial institutions be run by professionals and at an arm's length from politicians to avoid the consequences of soft budgetary constraints, which can keep inefficient and resource-wasting firms afloat.

At the same time as we build public financial infrastructure, we should support the development of a powerful sector of civil society co-op banks and mortgage lenders. Current legislation forbids the formation of new co-op banks and makes it difficult to establish new housing cooperative-owned mortgage lenders. This legislation should be turned on its head, as the state should actively support the building up of a democratic finance sector by creating favorable conditions and providing state guarantees.

Democratize Existing Democratic Capital

Up through the 1970s and 1980s, a series of public and labor market–based pension funds were established, which today invest hundreds of billions on behalf of wage earners. The degree of democratic influence afforded to workers has varied, and a number of investments such as in fossil fuels or companies that fight against union organizing or move Danish jobs overseas do not serve their interests. Providing wage earners and the population as a whole with a greater say over how their pension savings are invested is thus necessary. The publicly anchored pensions funds, Lønmodtagernes Dyrtidsfond and ATP, should be fully democratized. Their leadership is currently chosen by the government and other interests; in the future, a majority of representatives should be elected by the contributors, and candidates should be required to clearly lay out their investment priorities.

These national elections could be held in conjunction with those at the regional and municipal level.

Labor market pension funds are administered quite differently. The leadership is chosen through either direct elections or by trade union leaders. In recent years greater engagement among members has led to positive change. Legislation that, for example, requires democratic representation as a condition for receiving tax deductions on pension contributions or that taxes them at the lower capital gains rate should thus be enacted so as to encourage labor market pension funds to give their members as much democratic influence as possible.

Breaking Up Financial Conglomerates

The many scandals in recent years involving tax evasion, tax havens, money laundering, and recurrent financial crises caused by irresponsible behavior have raised the question of whether the reckless and short-sighted profit seeking of the private financial sector is indeed compatible with responsible banking. We must therefore begin to consider if the nondemocratic banking sector can eventually be entirely eliminated, while in the short term we must seek to insulate society from the negative consequences of private financial activities.

An important first step is to break up the big financial conglomerates. Denmark has larger banks than other countries with a similarly sized economy. While the balances of the largest U.S. banks correspond to less than 20 percent of the United States' GDP, Danske Bank's balance alone corresponds to 150 percent of Denmark's GDP, making it one of the countries most threatened by the "too big to fail" problem, whereby banks become so large that the state is forced to rescue them in times of crisis.

Breaking up the large banks would weaken them enough so that they no longer could threaten the economy with collapse. Reinstituting the sharp distinctions between commercial banks, investment banks, mortgage lenders, insurers, and pension funds should be the first step, and the second should be placing a cap on the total financial assets of individual banks.

Such an initiative would force a number of large financial concerns, not the least Danske Bank, to sell off significant parts of their operations and would also make it possible to establish new public or customer-owned financial institutions from those assets. Any bank that repeatedly engages in criminal behavior should be taken over by the state.[6]

Reform 6: Land and Housing as Use Value, Not Market Value

Our homes are central to our well-being. Treating housing as a speculative asset on financial markets leads to economic instability and makes it harder and harder for us to thrive. We must therefore ensure that good low-cost housing is available to all and that all future increases in land values are not concentrated among the few. This requires a series of initiatives involving changes to the nature of ownership, functional socialist intervention in private property rights, and reining in market forces.

Stop All Sales of Public Land

The selling of public land is fundamentally stupid. Land and buildings are among the only assets we have that do not depreciate but instead gain in value year after year. When we sell off public land to private investors we get a one-time infusion of cash, but all future increases in value go to private investors, even though the cause of rising land values is a result of the development of the whole society. All such sales should therefore be forbidden.

Public land can instead be used for new public construction projects like municipal housing cooperatives or be leased out following the Dutch model that keeps increases in land values in the hands of the community. In addition to the ban on the sale of public land, we should institute a municipal right of first purchase to any land that could be used for new city and housing developments. If a municipal government submits an offer, the private owner must sell the land to the government. The price will be set according to the value of the site before the decision to develop the area was made so that the municipality does not pay for the increased value created by its own investments.

More Housing Outside the Market

In our cooperative housing sector, rents are not determined by the market but instead must only cover the costs of construction and upkeep. This creates housing without profits that can be afforded by people with average incomes. New legislation to stimulate the extensive expansion of the cooperative housing sector should include several features.

First, a new law should mandate that at least 50 percent of new housing must be cooperative, which would correspond to the existing share already present in municipalities near Copenhagen, among them Herlev, Ballerup, and Rødovre. At the same time, the construction of private rental properties should be capped at 25 percent of all new construction. These initiatives would help bring down the price of building land.

Second, the rights of tenants to collectively purchase property must be extended. Today tenants of private properties already have the right to purchase the property before it can be sold to another party. This gives renters the first right of purchase, if they are able to persuade a majority of the tenants to form a cooperative housing association. But many renters do not have the resources to purchase ever more expensive properties. The obligation to offer property to tenants first shall therefore be strengthened by granting tenants the right to join an existing housing cooperative in the area.

Third, housing cooperatives should be granted the opportunity to finance their purchases with a one-hundred-year mortgage loan. This would provide a major advantage for co-ops over private investors, facilitating their expansion.

End Private Speculation in Rental Markets

Our long-term goal is to get a point where no one makes money from owning other people's homes. But the profit-seeking rental market cannot be eliminated all at once, so in the meantime we must improve conditions for tenants of private landlords, who can then contribute to developing a mixed housing sector.

First, renters should be fully protected. All deregulatory measures of recent decades should be rolled back so that private rentals, including newly built or renovated units, are subject to politically determined rents rather than those of the market, thereby putting a stop to the unreasonable rent increases of recent years. Rents for small businesses, which have also been subject to private speculation, will be determined the same way.

Second, a municipal right to allocate shall be instituted. Today municipalities have the right to allocate 25 percent of cooperative housing units to residents with special social needs. It is not fair that the cooperative housing sector bear all the responsibility for this, so municipalities should also have the right to 20 percent of the private rental stock for such purposes. The rent for these units should not exceed the cost of a similar unit in a housing cooperative.

Establishment of an Independent Land and Ground Fund

A regulated but independent and self-owned land and ground fund should be established, This fund would offer to purchase the ground under the house of any potential buyer and then rent it back to the buyer through an interminable lease, thereby significantly reducing the amount of debt most buyers today must take on and bringing down the cost of housing. If the homeowner decided to move, the house could be sold but not the ground, which would then be leased out to the new purchaser. The rent would be pegged to the value of the land but could not exceed current metrics of wage and price inflation. When the ground is to be leased anew, a new rent would be set based on its current value.

The same policy should apply to cooperative housing associations, both public and private, thereby reducing the cost of new construction. Current homeowners would have the option sell their ground to the fund if they so choose, which would be a good option for retirees who want access to their home equity. The land and ground fund would be democratically managed by a leadership elected by all borrowers covered by the law. Until the fund is self-sustaining it would be financed by a gradual reduction of the mortgage deduction and a tax on capital gains from real estate sales.

A Democratic and Sustainable Agricultural Reform

The Danish agricultural sector is in dire need of comprehensive reform to convert significant areas of current farmland to nature preserves and to reduce livestock production.

Years of concentrated ownership have trapped famers in a debt spiral, while at the same time foreign capital funds have been buying up agricultural land for speculative purposes, which has forced farmers into steadily more intensive industrial production that is bad for the climate, environment, and biodiversity. Reforms targeted at distributing and democratizing ownership can put an end to the debt spiral, contribute to sustainable development, and open a new chapter in Danish agricultural and cooperative history.

First, legislation should be introduced that bans the sale of agricultural land to private speculators, and changes in the law that made it possible for foreign and Danish capital funds to buy up Danish farmland should be annulled. Public funds and other democratic institutions like the Danmark

Økologiske Jordbrugsfond and Andelsgaarde should continuously purchase and lease out farmland. All state support for Danish equity fund purchases of foreign agricultural land should cease.

Second, a regulated but independent national organic farming fund with a leadership consisting of representatives of participating farmers, public authorities, and environmental NGOs should be created. The fund would purchase land on the market, at foreclosure auctions, and from debt-ridden farmers that would then be leased to organic farmers, whose rents will be determined by the profitability of organic and sustainable agriculture. Contracts should be interminable except in case of default and be heritable. Climate and environmental screening should be conducted prior to leasing. Low-lying land, which emits a high level of carbon, and other environmentally vulnerable areas would be excluded from leasing.[7]

Municipalities should also be permitted to purchase local agricultural land in a similar manner, and tax deductions should be granted for all investments in democratically managed land funds like the Danmark Økologiske Jordbrugsfond and Andelsgaarde.

Reform 7: Data Socialism

A democratization of the economy must also encompass our information, knowledge, and data resources, all of which are currently owned and controlled by large corporations. This concentration of ownership slows innovation and gives a handful of tech and pharma giants immense monopoly power, which they use to influence politicians and legislation the world over. Data harvesting by these firms further constitutes a threat to our private lives and to the free formation of public opinion.

Foundational changes to intellectual property laws that would place broad societal concerns over the profit seeking of the tech monopolies are thus needed. Since intellectual property rules are largely determined by the EU and the WTO, this conflict necessarily stretches beyond our borders. But there are reforms we can implement within our borders to increase democratic control over our knowledge and information resources.

Public Research Findings Cannot Be Privatized

Denmark is among the countries that most heavily invest public funds in research. In 2020 total investment came to DKK 25 billion.[8] Additionally, private firms receive generous tax deductions for research and development purposes. It is critical that all findings from publicly financed research are owned by the community. Already today Danish law, at least formally, mandates that all findings made at public research institutes belong to the host institution, but private firms still all too often make off with the lion's share of profits from the commercialization of publicly financed research.

We should therefore establish a self-owned institution to be called the Danske IP-Fond under the aegis of the Danish research ministry. The fund should either directly own patents resulting from publicly financed research or support the public research institutes who own them. Just like private patent holders, the fund would be able to license its properties to third parties in exchange for payment. It would be regulated by law, and it would seek to balance the need for earnings with the need to foster innovation by providing access to the technologies and products it controls. In the event of pandemics or other global threats, the fund would contribute its patents to global patent pools like that of the WHO or the UN-backed Medicines Patent Pool.

The Right to Our Own Data

Data, both that collected by our public sector and that we produce when we use apps and services on the internet, are a valuable resource. Mass data can help us find innovative solutions that can contribute to things like reducing energy consumption or food waste. But today most data are harvested by profit-seeking large corporations and are all too often used for dubious purposes that compromise our private lives and threaten the democratic public sphere.

Data are in their essence social, since their value is largely dependent on the participation of large numbers of people. We should therefore move toward a model that treats data as a common resource and that provides ordinary citizens with far more control and ownership over them.

First, a public data bank should be created to collect all data generated by the public sector. Both public and private entities would have access to the data stored in it, but commercial use would be conditional on payment. All public institutions that collect data—for example, the telephone service—would have to contribute their datasets to the data bank. The data bank would be independent and have a strict mandate to protect against the use of its data by the state or by private interests for purposes contrary to the public interest. A council selected by lot from all Danish citizens would ensure that the data bank fulfilled this function.

Second, a new law is needed to secure real ownership of data for each citizen, both that generated in the public sector and that harvested by the tech giants. Private corporations should be directed to disclose all the data they have collected in a standardized format. Citizens could then choose whether they want all or parts of their data transferred to the public data bank or to private democratic data cooperatives. Voluntarily transferred data could then be provided free of charge to researchers or sold for commercial use.

While the reforms proposed up to now have primarily concerned the democratization of ownership and the management of enterprises, banks, land, and information resources, the next two involve finding the correct balance between market mechanisms and democratic planning.

Reform 8: Communalization and New Public Goods

An important component of the Nordic welfare society we established after the Second World War was the transformation of previously marketized sectors such as health care and education into public goods. Accessible to all citizens, these goods were thus made independent from the unequal distribution engendered by the market. In order to further reduce the influence of market forces on critical aspects of our lives, we need a new wave of communalizing reforms that would provide citizens with free access to other important public goods.

New Public Goods

A good place to start would be those aspects of our health-care system that for arbitrary reasons have historically been excluded from free and universal access. Dental care, mental health treatment, and, most of all, prescription drugs should be transformed into public goods covered by our universal health insurance system. User fees for the public transportation we use to get to and from work should also be eliminated, as should charges associated with digital infrastructure, such as broadband and cellular services, that are now required to participate in a democratic society. Communalizing reforms financed by taxes on capital, inheritances, and wealth would further contribute to reducing inequality.

A Public Sharing Economy

We must begin to think more radically about our own private consumption. Each of us owning identical copies of the same tools and sundries we use only rarely is not a sustainable practice. Here we can build on our tradition of public libraries by establishing tool banks permitting citizens to borrow things like electric drills, lawnmowers, or hedge clippers. We can take inspiration from many such Libraries of Things around the world, such as the city of Toronto's sharing banks for tools and kitchen implements.[9] Bicycle and EV sharing should be run by the public authorities.

Rather than continue down the unsustainable path of rising *private* abundance, such a sharing economy for *communal* abundance would provide broader access for all but with less impact on the climate.

Reform 9: Democratic Doughnut Planning

Even after the institution of extensive communalizing reforms, significant parts of the economy would still be based on market exchange. But to a much greater extent than today the direction and goals of the economy will be determined by planning anchored in democratic, popularly elected institutions. The Danish climate plan of 2019 is an exciting example of a new kind of thinking. Here parliament passed a law whose dictate is to reduce carbon emissions 70 percent by 2030. Subsequent climate action plans for every sector of the economy ensure that everyone contributes to this goal.

Expanding on this form of goal-directed intervention can come to constitute a modern model of economic planning through which economic development is democratically directed. Taking inspiration from Kate Raworth, I call this model "doughnut economic planning," since its fundamental aim is to ensure that economic and market forces are contained within a space that provides for both human needs and those of the planet. This form of planning is not the same as the centralized microplanning of production characteristic of the old Eastern bloc, because it is democratic deliberation that sets the specific goals and the broader framework for the economy as a whole, in which market forces may operate as long as they contribute to those goals.

Democratic Goal Setting

In the future, overall economic development should be anchored in democratically determined plans that set concrete goals for the direction we wish the economy to take and the particular problems we wish it to solve. Such goals could be the reduction of economic inequality or putting a stop to species extinction. When democratic consensus has settled on a particular goal it should be mandated by law, which would require the government and the parliamentary majority to find the means of realizing it within all relevant sectors of the economy.

These means must be the subject of continuous democratic debate. The goal of increasing biodiversity, for example, could be followed up with an action plan dictating that significant parcels of land be returned to nature by 2040, while the goal of reducing economic inequality could be followed up with tax reforms or other initiatives that secure a better distribution of the resources of society. Such action plans must be legislated by the government and the parliament but must also be subject to democratic debate with the participation of the public. The evaluation of the success of action plans should also be subject to a similar democratic process.

Reform 10: Full Employment and a Public Jobs Guarantee

As long as sectors of the economy are still based on market competition, firms will fail and thus people will lose their jobs, with all the associated negative consequences for individuals and society as a whole. Efforts to combat unemployment and to achieve full employment must therefore constitute an element of future democratic planning.

A New Mandate for the Central Bank

The neoliberal breakthrough of the 1980s resulted in dramatic changes to the role of central banks across the world. They were insulated from democratic control, and their mandate was narrowed to merely fighting inflation, which had a number of negative consequences, including making cyclical crises worse than they used to be, most visibly after 2008.[10]

Central bank reform should ensure that the mandate includes not only keeping inflation down but other critical social concerns and goals. First, the goal of full employment should be emphasized, so that it is much more evenly balanced against that of inflation reduction. And perhaps even more important, monetary policy should contribute to solving the climate problem. Finally, the central bank must take back control of money creation by establishing a central bank digital currency and by tightening control over private bank lending.

Farewell to Neoliberal Budget Priorities

The period following the 2008 crisis clearly demonstrated that austerity and wage cuts only deepen and prolong crises. State budgets are not the same as household budgets. Taking on debt and increasing the money supply during downturns is both wise and economically sensible. We must therefore reject the balanced budget law, the EU's budgetary restrictions, and any other law or rule that limits the possibility of conducting an aggressive Keynesian budgetary politics that props up employment during periods of declining private demand. Direct payments to citizens—so-called helicopter money—will be an important tool during crises.

A Public Jobs Guarantee

If such a financial and monetary politics cannot deliver full employment, then a public jobs guarantee with the state as employer of last resort must ensure that no one is unemployed for long periods. Allowing people to remain unproductive simply because private employers have no use for them is damaging to them and a waste of resources. With a public jobs guarantee, anyone who has lost their job should be offered either a public sector job or retraining in a vocation for which there is demand.

The jobs provided by the program should be considered temporary, enabling all those impacted to reenter the general labor market when demand returns. Specific jobs might include construction or assisting in welfare provision. In the coming years, publicly guaranteed jobs could be used to support the green transition. A public jobs guarantee would ensure that we make use of all the resources at our disposal for the betterment of society and would help curb the impacts of economic crises by propping up consumer purchasing power.[11]

A More Socialist Society

How will our society and our everyday lives change if we implement this slate of reforms? Much will remain the same. We will still have a modern, efficient, and prosperous economy. But the economic gaps between us will be lessened, and we will enjoy much greater democratic influence over our private and working lives. When we ourselves have a say in our workplaces, others cannot decide to move our jobs abroad or replace us with low-wage workers from elsewhere. When we ourselves own our banks, we will not be powerless when bankers invest billions in drilling up that last of the world's oil supply. When we constrain the market and transform marketized sectors such as pharmaceuticals, dental, and mental health care into tax-financed public goods, we are less vulnerable and more secure.

And most important of all, the oligarchic power of elites is proportionately reduced as more and more parts of our economy come to be democratically owned and managed. Just as oligarchic power is self-reinforcing, so democratic power can be. Every step we take toward distributing and democratizing ownership further limits the power of oligarchy. And when the ability of economic elites to influence politics is weakened, we discover new and better democratic reforms that further tip the balance away from oligarchy. When we have expansive democratically managed investment capital in public banks and investment funds, our society becomes much less vulnerable to pressures from financial markets, and when we have democratic enterprise, the threat of investment strikes from elites is less effective.

This new and growing democratic power will provide us with much more effective ways to address the challenges we as a society now confront, not least of which are the climate and biodiversity crises that threaten future life on the planet.

Epilogue
Questions and Answers for Nordic Socialism

While I am hardly able to anticipate every question and objection my ideas and proposals might raise, I will nonetheless attempt to address some of the issues to which I think readers deserve answers.

Is it Socialism?

Does what I suggest really amount to socialism? If by socialism one means that all private ownership of the means of production has been abolished, that ownership of all enterprises and banks is in the hands of the state, and that market mechanisms have been entirely replaced by centralized state planning of production and distribution, then no, this is not socialism.

But I do not believe that such a version of socialism is either possible or desirable. Nor do I think that its conception of society and economy as constituting a totality with a single mode of production is in touch with reality. Societies and economies are always hybrids with many coexisting and competing modes of production. What I describe is a society and economy that is much *more* socialist and much *less* capitalist than today, in which socialist and democratic production modes are just as dominant as capitalist modes are today, but without the goal of achieving a *purely* socialist economy, which I believe to be illusory.

Is it possible to imagine still more comprehensive changes that move us closer to a future stateless society of general abundance, as earlier socialists envisioned? Perhaps, since we cannot foresee what possibilities technological and human progress will bring. But nothing in my program for the development of a democratic communal economy stands in the way of further advances. On the contrary it would provide us with a wealth of new knowledge in how to conduct democratic enterprise and how to move away from market anarchy and toward democratic planning.

Socialism in One Country?

Is it really possible to institute Nordic socialism in a single country embedded in a globalized economy that makes it relatively easy for economic elites to move investments, capital, production, and jobs from one country to another? There is no doubt that there is much more space for change within the single national state than we have been led to believe, for individual states are not powerless in the face of globalization. The development of a democratic sector need not necessarily threaten the interests of global economic elites. But at the same time, it is clear that certain reforms will be met with powerful resistance, in the worst case with investment strikes or capital flight.

International anchoring, cooperation, and strategy are thus necessary preconditions for the realization of a democratic economy at home. A full discussion of this remains outside the scope of this book, but in broad outlines such a strategy must combine several elements.

First, we must build up a powerful international alliance of parties and movements capable of coordinating plans for economic democratization across national borders and continents. The recent cooperation between American and British progressive forces gives grounds for optimism here, as their coordination has helped influence progressive policy platforms.

Second, we must make use of existing international organizations to encourage democratic reforms across borders. This applies not only to the EU but also to the Nordic bloc, with our long traditions of solidarism and democratic enterprise. We would benefit from much greater pan-Nordic political collaboration than we have today. Democratizing reforms such as the establishment of funds socialist models or the expansion of employee influence at the workplace will be made all the easier if they occur simultaneously across countries, since the risk of capital flight would be reduced.

Third, one of our chief tasks should be returning control of the economy back to national democratic states. Neoliberal oriented globalization and free trade agreements have been and remain a proven method of reducing national democratic autonomy to curb working-class power. By turning over critical decisions to institutions like the WTO and the EU, in which power relations favor capital, and by binding individual states to common trade and budget rules, economic elites have reduced the autonomy of democratic national governments. The complete liberalization of the movement of capital, for instance, has markedly tipped the balance of power toward capital. It is vitally important that we reverse this development by restoring to the national state the means to protect itself from threats and pressures from economic elites.

These last two points would seem to be in conflict. Is it possible to work simultaneously for more international cooperation and for greater power at the level of the national state? My sense is that it is. With regard to the EU, it is certainly possible to push for reforms such as those that increase the influence of employees of private firms or that support cooperatives or other democratic enterprises, while at the same time opposing the rules permitting the free movement of capital. It does not have to be an either/or. Denmark's relationship to the EU in the future shall therefore be determined by the direction such cooperation takes, with respect to both progressive common rules and the autonomy of individual states.

But an international strategy is also critically important because even if Denmark and the other Nordic countries develop a democratic communal economy, it will be embedded within a world economy dominated by global capitalism. Because of historically unequal and unjust trade relations, this system has led to a constant transfer of wealth from poor developing countries to rich countries, including to Denmark. A fully democratized Danish economy would still be integrated into this unjust system, would still be party to the exploitation of the labor power and resources of the Global South. The development of a socialist-dominated economy in Denmark must therefore go hand in hand with a global struggle to change the rules of the global economy—not least an effort to overturn the liberal free trade agreements that keep the South in poverty and engender an anti-solidaristic race to the bottom, which is to the benefit of neither the working classes of the South nor their Northern comrades.

New global trade agreements should thus demonstrate a commitment to greater international cooperation to fight climate change, tax evasion, and the abuse of labor power and natural resources and to ensure a return of autonomy to national states—most of all to those of the South.

A Denmark with a more democratic and socialist economy would be able to play a much larger and more solidaristic role in global institutions and negotiations, since the narrow interests of capital that now set the agenda for our foreign policy would have much less influence.

Will Nordic Socialism Be Economically Efficient?

A concern for economic efficiency has rarely been paramount in the left's discussion of socialist reforms. Democratic influence, fairness, and the distribution of wealth have instead been main concerns. But economic efficiency is important. When an economy is operating efficiently, it makes optimal use of societal resources—both labor power and natural resources. When, for example, we keep a firm that uses more natural resources than necessary afloat, it is at the expense of the environment and climate. And if we do not incentivize the pursuit of innovation in labor processes, we end up using more labor power than necessary.

Developing new solutions or technologies that increase productivity means we are able to produce the same amount with less resources and labor power, which in turn means that we as a people can work less and enjoy more free time (or what ought to be called free time). There is thus good reason to keep in mind how democratizing reforms affect productivity.

Extensive research, as I have pointed out, supports the conclusion that worker-owned or partly worker-owned firms perform better in all important metrics. They are more productive and more innovative. They last longer and are better able to weather crises and downturns.[1] It should hardly be surprising that the motivation to improve performance and to innovate is stronger when we ourselves receive a share of the gains.

Gallup International periodically produces a global workplace report that among other things tracks worker engagement in workplaces around world. Its 2017 report finds that 85 percent of employees report being either "not engaged" or flat-out "unengaged." It might be expected that the figures would be lower in Denmark, given our relatively nonhierarchical workplace structures. But 84 percent of Danish workers described themselves as not engaged.[2] Gallup estimates that this lack of engagement accounts for an annual loss of—get ready—USD 7 trillion in productivity. According to Gallup, workers are unengaged because they are willing to give "their time, but not their best effort nor their best ideas."[3] I do not think it unreasonable to suggest that a democratization of working life would address this waste of resources.

Regarding democratic fund ownership, we already have extensive experience with wholly or partially fund-owned Danish firms. That such firms should somehow be less efficient because the professional directorate is backed by a democratic mandate is difficult to argue. With respect to banks or other financial institutions, research also shows that democratic cooperative and publicly owned banks not only are more efficient but are further much more able to provide stabile credit flows for the whole country during financial crisis periods.

Nor would an increase in democratic planning at the expense of market forces lead to decreased efficiency. Several of the fastest growing economies in the world today use extensive economic planning, just as Denmark did in the decades after the Second World War, during which productivity growth was higher than at present. Finally, we must also recall that oligarchic and market-dominated capitalism are not especially efficient, as capitalist economies have experienced falling productivity growth rates for decades. Many economists argue that the focus on short-term profits means less long-term investment in technology and capital goods, since profits are either paid out as dividends or spent on stock buybacks to attract new investors.[4] More democratic control and less dependence on short-sighted, profit-seeking investors would likely lead to more far-sighted investments in the real economy, which in turn would yield productivity gains.

Will Nordic Socialism Solve the Climate Crisis?

Is a book about democratizing the economy really appropriate for the times, given that by far the greatest threat we face is climate change? It could, after all, be asked how much use a more democratic and just economy would be if our planet were no longer habitable.

In my view, however, the solution to the climate crisis is intimately connected to the democratization of the economy. First, an effective and rapid green transition will require extensive investment in the coming years. Recent decades have made it clear that we cannot rely on private market-driven investors to do the job. My contention is that the more capital that is directed through democratic decision-making, the broader the societal concerns taken into consideration will be. This is evidenced by how the democratic influence of members of pension funds and co-op banks resulted in divestment from fossil fuels and increases in investment in green alternatives and by how the members of the grocery chain Coop and of consumer-owned energy cooperatives have taken the lead in green solutions. More democratic capital, in the form of both state investment banks and increased member influence at pension funds, would mean less short-sighted profit seeking and more investment in socially beneficial enterprises.

Industries with interests in the fossil fuel economy have been able to use their economic power to frighten governments and international institutions away from making critical decisions, but by fostering democratic power at the expense of oligarchic, we can empower our democratically elected governments to make the many difficult decisions necessary to change the means by which we produce, distribute, and consume.

Lastly, the struggle for economic justice and for the climate are inseparable insofar as both demand broad popular buy-in. Movements like the Yellow Vests in France or trends like the protest votes of American Midwest workers for Trump, reveal in all clarity that if the bill for climate change mitigation is sent to people already financially distressed and if there is no guarantee that a job in the old economy is going to be replaced with a secure and well-paying job in the new, then people will turn their backs. This is why the Green New Deal is so promising. Climate activists and the labor left are working hand in hand in order, just as I have suggested in this book, to combine a radical environmental politics with social reforms, democratic planning, and the creation of new secure jobs.

Social justice is all the more important, since we face a future without exponential growth and thus a future where the members of a small elite cannot be permitted to hoard as much of the wealth of society as they do today. The slogan of young climate activists that "climate struggle is class struggle and class struggle is climate struggle" is not wrong.

Who Will Be the Agent of Change?

Both bold vision and concrete reform slates are necessary to engender the faith, hope, and enthusiasm needed to change our society. But ideas and visions are not enough. Real change demands that ordinary people be persuaded to engage in movements, organizations, and parties, especially when change threatens the interests of privileged groups.

The cooperative movement in Denmark was not built on ideas alone; it was actualized by farmers who organized at the grass roots. Our welfare society and labor relations model were established through the efforts of a powerful labor movement organized into trade unions and parties. More recently a movement of young people has managed to force politicians to take the climate threat seriously, and other movements such as #MeToo and Black Lives Matter have provoked debate and resulted in concrete changes.

So who shall fight for a new wave of economic democratization—for a Nordic socialism? Who shall constitute *the collective subject*? We must ask two questions: Who has an interest in change? And who is best able to fight for it?

Historically, socialists have identified the working class as the social group with the greatest interest in freeing itself from the capitalist exploitation of its labor power. And there is no doubt that wage earners will have a strong interest here, not the least in the democratization of working life. But it is hardly only as workers that we find ourselves in conflict with the capitalist economy. We also do so as borrowers who must rely on a financial sector that constantly drives up fees and other hidden charges, as tenants whose rents rise steadily as capital funds buy up housing, as consumers whose data is harvested by tech giants, and as small proprietors who are undercut by tax-evading multinationals. Furthermore, climate change is something wholly new, insofar as all of us, whether wage earner, retiree, student, or small proprietor, must face up to the consequences of global warming. In other words, it is an overwhelming majority of the population that has an interest in a new democratic economy.

But the existence of a community of interest is no guarantee that there is consciousness of such interest; that consciousness is created by common experiences and often by social movements that bring people together to work for concrete political goals.

Many social struggles in recent years have been focused on narrow identitarian interests, such as ethnicity, gender, and sexuality, that is, all those that have come to be called identity politics.[5] Such struggles are not necessarily anticapitalist, and the oppression they decry does not necessarily result from the capitalist economy. But the negative consequences of such oppression are no less destructive than those brought on by a capitalist economy, and minority struggles are often based on the same egalitarian ideas of emancipation from subjection that animate the struggle for a democratic economy. A movement for change must therefore acknowledge that despite our immense common interests we are indeed different from one another and that not all of us enjoy the same privileges and possibilities. This demands solidarity and the will to stand up for one another—particularly against forms of oppression that do not affect one personally.

On the other hand, it is equally important to insist that despite the particularities of identity, we must seek to define a broader community of interest among the majority that suffer the negative consequences of the capitalist economy and the exertion of oligarchic power. It is this community of interest, if it is well articulated in political movements and election campaigns, that is able to work for change. Therefore it is critical that the trade union, housing cooperative, and climate movements, together with political parties, unite our common interests for the coming conflict with oligarchic power.

Regarding the question of which groups have the greatest capacity to work for change, socialists have as noted historically pointed to the working class. This is because it is this group—especially employees of private firms—that has the power stop or slow down production, thereby interrupting the flow of capital. In this way, the working class possesses a means of power similar to that of capitalists when they withhold investment or move production abroad.

This means of power projection is still relevant, and there is no doubt that the kind of reforms I have proposed will require the backing of a strong, organized, and aggressive labor movement, particularly in those instances in which economic elites attempt to oppose democratic change through economic sabotage or threats of offshoring or disinvestment. But on the other hand, we must not rely too much on this form of power projection in today's conditions. In a political democracy with universal suffrage it is possible to exert influence, even when threatening the interests of elites, if a parliamentary majority can be had. To achieve such a majority it is necessary to look beyond the employees of private firms, who no longer today constitute a majority, to build a much broader alliance with public employees, small proprietors, freelancers, students, the unemployed, and retirees. The task of building what Antonio Gramsci calls a *historic bloc* is the most important task of the left today, although not one to which this book has provided a clear solution.

My (perhaps naive) hope is that the divisions that for a century have separated the labor movement into reformist and revolutionary wings can be bridged by a focus on achieving a democratic and pluralistic economy that unites the radical revolutionary vision of fundamental change to property relations with the gradualist strategy of the reformists. For if there is one lesson we can take from the twentieth century, it is that sustainable social change demands both the patience and pragmatism of the reformists and the idealism and persistence of the revolutionaries.

Outro

Refshaleholmen
Monday, August 28, 2042

You are sitting up on the communal rooftop terrace of your co-op housing building, looking out over the Øresund. Sweden is still visible in the late summer twilight. Down on the sand below, the last of the beachgoers are packing up their things and heading toward the metro.

You gaze out over the rooftops of the newly built homes on Refshaleholmen, pondering the immense changes of recent decades. Much remains as it always has been, and yet society has undergone fundamental changes since the process of economic democratization began in the 2020s.

Refshaleholmen itself is an example of the new and growing democratic economy. When construction of the artificial island was first approved, the plan had been to sell parcels to private investors—just as had been done with former development areas like Nordhavn and Ørsted. But after the political fallout from a financial crisis in the mid-2020s, the plans were changed. Instead of selling off the land and the buildings, the government put them in a democratic, communally owned development fund.

It was not so long ago that you took part in the elections for the leadership of the development fund, which also has representatives from the state and from the Copenhagen municipal government. Various environmental organizations also have seats on the council, ensuring that the interests of nature are represented. Early on the fund decided that 60 percent of the land on the new island would be leased out to cooperative housing associations. This is why with your modest income you were able to exchange your apartment in Nordvest for your current one here, where you can enjoy the evening sunlight and the view over the blue sea.

The building you live in is carbon neutral, built by one of the many new cooperatives specializing in sustainable building. A central plank of the fund's development plan was that democratic enterprises should play a key role in the economic life of the new island. The hotel just down the road is managed by its employees, as are many of the restaurants and small businesses on the island. The era in which service sector jobs were insecure, degrading, and poorly paid is over, now that a large part of the service sector has been converted to worker cooperatives.

You stand up and look down at the parking lot. It is not particularly full, since after debate the fund decided that only EV sharing will be permitted on the island. Today this seems wholly natural, since after the EV-sharing fund received state support it has become the most common form of private transportation. All parking facilities in the country must reserve 25 percent of spaces for them, but in housing co-ops the figure is 75 percent. But most people, of course, still rely on public transportation and even more so now since it was transformed into a free public good.

Refshaleholmen is special because it was democratic and communally owned from the start. But the entire country is also in the midst of great changes. The democratic transition picked up speed after the second large-scale financial crisis, which constituted the formal conclusion of the era of neoliberal finance capitalism. A few difficult years followed, with rising unemployment and steep declines in land and property values, which led many citizens, farmers, and businesses into insolvency. But these years made it clear to all that we had to rethink the nature of our economy.

Unlike during the 2008 financial crisis, most people around the world refused to cover the losses of the banks and the large corporations, agreeing that it would be stupid to bail out a system that did not serve the interests of the broad majority. Instead the biggest banks were taken over by the community. Here in Denmark, Danske Bank was the first of many to be broken up into smaller, democratically managed institutions. Realkredit Danmark was also taken over, and a state-guaranteed rescue package required that the institution be returned to its it former status as a nonprofit, borrower-owned mortgage lender. These initiatives formed the foundation for the establishment of a new democratic public bank with branches across the country that was able to secure cheap credit for founders of green and democratic enterprises. The many insolvent homeowners and farmers received support from a new land fund, which paid off existing debts and took over the land, renting it back to them through interminable leases. Since then, land value gains have gone to the fund and therefore to the whole society, while homeowners and farmers have gotten out from under the thumb of private bankers.

Another outcome of the financial crisis was the election of a Red-Green majority to parliament, which set in motion what it called the "decade of economic democracy." In the years following, hundreds of small- and medium-sized business were converted to democratic cooperatives, most often as a result of generational turnover in ownership, which provided a financial incentive for the former owners to sell to a worker cooperative. But the government's institution of a public jobs guarantee was also important, as it eased the fears of wage earners. This made it nearly impossible for Amazon, Wolt, and other low-wage employers to hire labor power. And when Coop and the other old cooperatives decided to make capital and consulting available, a new wave of co-ops spread across the country, among the most exciting of which are the new platform and data cooperatives. Today it is hard to believe that global tech giants were once able to harvest our data for profit.

Most controversial was the introduction of an obligatory wage-earner fund. In the pharmaceutical factory where you work, the wage-earner fund now owns about 30 percent of the shares in the company. The day of the annual dividend payout is always a special day. You see it as a yearly reminder that it is in fact you and your coworkers who create value for the firm. And it cannot be denied that you probably put in a little extra effort at work, since you know that the success of the firm is reflected in your dividend payment. But perhaps it is the new democratic influence you enjoy at work that makes the difference.

After the changes to the corporation law and the introduction of the bicameral system, you and your colleagues have a completely new role at the firm. You yourself have served in the employee chamber. It was exciting but also challenging to learn about and participate in the workings of the company. Yet it was only after the new leadership was installed that the extent of the changes became truly evident, for now management must answer not only to the investors but also to you and your coworkers. You feel much more secure now, since you now know that investors you have never met can no longer move production to a low-wage country. But all this did not come without a fight. The employers' federation threatened holy war, and it was only after the pan-European strike wave following the financial crisis that capital across the continent began to accept the new division of power.

Your thoughts wander further as the last rays of sunlight touch the arches of the Øresundsbro. The democratic transition has not just changed the nature of ownership. It has also decidedly shifted the balance between market forces and democracy. It was the "climate election" that kick-started the move toward a new kind of democratic planning. It came to be called that because the climate became the main issue of the election, as young climate activists nearly shut down the country with colorful protests against government hesitance, and because it took place at the same time as a number of natural disasters, most prominently the cloudburst that flooded most of Denmark's large cities.

You can still remember election night and the days after the electoral earthquake, before a coalition climate government was formed, which declared that all other political disagreements would be set aside until a climate plan honoring the Paris Agreements was adopted. Many at the time thought it would be impossible, but Denmark is in fact now on course to be carbon neutral by 2045 principally because the new government quickly and aggressively implemented a series of democratic action plans that directly intervened in the market economy, such as limiting the size of cattle herds, forbidding the sale of new gas- or diesel-powered vehicles, and instituting a new high but socially just tax on carbon emissions.

The business community was skeptical, but the new mixed leadership councils proved to be eager to develop green solutions, which were later exported to the rest of the world. And it has also been helpful that so much of the business world has been democratized. Since employees, consumers, and borrowers now have more influence, corporate conduct has come to reflect their concerns.

Denmark has since become a model for climate policy, and you would be hard pressed to find a head of state who has not visited to learn about its successes. Scholars and researchers around the world have likewise praised the Nordic form of doughnut economic planning that allows market mechanisms to operate but only within a strict democratic framework that determines the direction of economic development. The immense success of democratic planning in addressing the climate crisis has led to a fundamental paradigm shift in political economy. In the years following, a series of further action plans were adopted after extensive public debate. As a wage earner you were especially grateful for the equality plan, which over the course of ten years reduced economic inequality to the lowest levels ever recorded. Comprehensive reforms shifted the tax burden upward. But the communalization of several additional sectors also played an important role. Today it is strange to recall that only a couple decades ago you needed to have your debit card in your pocket when you went to the dentist or to the psychologist.

After a decade of economic planning, it also seems strange that we once allowed anarchic market forces to direct so much of societal development. Even the parties of the right no longer insist that planning is inherently bad.

There is still a great deal of political disagreement. The new party of the left, the Real Socialists, still contend that private capital has too much power. They oppose the bicameral chamber system because they do not think investors should have the same degree of power as the workers who create the wealth. They also think that market forces play too large a role and that economic planning should be more extensive. On the other side, Aske Ellemann-Jensen, the newly elected leader of the Liberal Center party, argues that society has become too socialistic and that market forces must be expanded to stimulate more competition and initiative.

The debate over the correct balance for the economy will never end. And perhaps this is good, you think, as you empty your glass and shake the many thoughts out of your mind. Tomorrow, after all, is another day . . .

Nordic Socialism: The Road to a Democratic Economy

My journey to a future Refshaleholmen is, of course, speculative and, yes, rather optimistic. But I hope it underlines the main point of this book: socialism is not a utopia. On the contrary it is an imminent and reachable alternative to the ever-more oligarchic and undemocratic capitalist economy that dominates our society today. It exists not just up in the airy world of ideas but is anchored in and builds on our previous experience of efforts to create democratically managed enterprises, markets, trade, and production. And it is an alternative that we can begin to develop in the here and now that does not require the dramatic overturning of the present system.

The goals are the same as they always have been for socialists: to democratize ownership and the economy so that the economic sphere does not continue to operate without democracy but is directed as much as is possible by the foundational principles of democratic governance. This is precisely the precondition of a truly democratic society, where the interests of the majority guide the development of a society, where the wealth is shared among all, and where we will find the democratic agency to confront the climate crisis.

But the new society will be realized without relying on binary distinctions between forms of property relations, markets, and societies. And rather than proposing an all-encompassing and uniform model of socialism, I advocate a pluralistic socialism, in which we employ market forces wherever appropriate but constrain them where economic planning functions better, and in which we do not start from the assumption that a single form of ownership is the right form across the board but instead develop a pluralism of ownership forms that assures we as citizens, employees, and consumers achieve maximal influence over the course of our own lives and the society we inhabit.

It is this form of pluralistic democratic socialism I have, with a debt to Donald Trump, chosen to call "Nordic socialism" because it is anchored in the specific Nordic experience of the well-organized and solidaristic welfare society that Trump and the rest of the American right so fear. But we could just as well call it a communal economy, a cooperative economy, or just plain economic democracy. The name is not important.

The Nordic prefix should not be understood to suggest a kind of cultural essentialism, according to which such a socialism could only be developed here in the Nordic countries. On the contrary it is my hope that the ideas discussed in this book can serve as inspiration elsewhere in the world, just as I have taken so much inspiration from socialists in other parts of the world who have tried to develop concrete ideas and proposals for a more democratic economy.

As socialists our most pressing task is to provide an alternative for the many people across the globe who have justly lost faith in a system that does not serve their interests. We must show that change is possible. And if we fail in this the antidemocratic forces of authoritarianism will be ready to pounce. This is why it is incumbent on we socialists to move beyond our utopian visions and begin to develop a pragmatic and concrete socialist alternative.

Let us proudly reclaim Trump's slur as our own by building a Nordic socialism, a new society rooted in our experiences that would be a real alternative to oligarchic capitalism.

We have talked enough about socialism. Now let's build it.

Notes

Foreword

1. "Sanders Calls USSR and Cuba Authoritarian, Not Socialist, Pivots to Finland," Grabien, March 9, 2020, https://grabien.com/story.php?id=277983.

2. Cover, *The Economist*, February 2, 2013, https://www.economist.com/cdn-cgi/image/width=1424,quality=80,format=auto/sites/default/files/print-covers/20130202_cna400.jpg.

3. "Remarks by President Obama, President Niinistö of Finland, and Prime Minister Solberg of Norway at the Nordic Leaders' Summit Arrival Ceremony," White House, Office of the Press Secretary, May 13, 2016, https://obamawhitehouse.archives.gov/the-press-office/2016/05/13/remarks-president-obama-president-niinist%C3%B6-finland-and-prime-minister.

4. Lane Kenworthy, *Would Democratic Socialism Be Better?* (Oxford University Press, 2022), 169; Jonathan Chait, "Reminder: Liberalism Is Working, and Marxism Has Always Failed," Intelligencer, *New York*, March 23, 2016, https://nymag.com/intelligencer/2016/03/reminder-liberalism-is-working-marxism-failed.html.

5. Kenworthy, *Would Democratic Socialism Be Better?*, 1.

Introduction

1. United States Council of Economic Advisors, "The Opportunity Costs of Socialism," October 2018.

2. Both Bernie Sanders and Alexandria Ocasio-Cortez have suggested that Denmark and the Nordic countries generally are a model for democratic socialism. See, for example, Chris Moody, "Bernie Sanders' American Dream Is in Denmark," CNN, February 17, 2016, https://www.cnn.com/2016/02/17/politics/bernie-sanders-2016-denmark-democratic-socialism/index.html.

3. Trish Regan, "Everyone in Denmark Is Working for the Government," Fox Business Network, August 14, 2018, https://www.youtube.com/watch?v=pSFfTG42Jl8.

4. For a Danish leftist analysis of the Regan controversy, see Andreas Møller Mulvad and Rune Møller Stahl, "The Real Denmark," *Jacobin*, October 14, 2018, https://jacobin.com/2018/10/denmark-welfare-state-socialism-nordic-model-regan.

5. "Kapitalisme," *Den Store Danske*, https://denstoredanske.lex.dk/kapitalisme.

6. The American left, however, identifies the Nordic economy and society as socialist or at least partially so on the grounds, for example, of the extent of democratic ownership in the Nordic countries. See, for example, Matt Bruenig, "Nordic Socialism Is Realer Than You Think," August 5, 2017, "Public Wealth in the U.S. and Nordic Countries," November 8, 2018, and "Nordic Governments Own 33% of the Region's Wealth," August 8, 2019, https://www.peoplespolicyproject.org.

7. Jason Hickel and Martin Kirk, "Are you Ready to Consider That Capitalism Is the Real Problem?," *Fast Company*, July 11, 2017, https://www.fastcompany.com/40439316/are-you-ready-to-consider-that-capitalism-is-the-real-problem.

8. Mark Fisher, *Capitalist Realism: Is There No Alternative?* (Zero, 2009), 2.

9. Frederik Borgbjerg was a prominent early twentieth-century Danish socialist and editor of *Socialdemokraten*. Hjalmar Branting was the founder of the Swedish social democratic party and the first popularly elected prime minister of Sweden.

Chapter 1. Diagnosis

1. Fiona Harvey, "Atmospheric CO2 Levels Rise Sharply Despite Covid-19 Lockdowns," *The Guardian*, June 4, 2020.

2. AFP, "How Labour Reform Has Left Germany's Working Poor Desperate for Change," *The Local DE*, May 11, 2017, https://www.thelocal.de/20170511/how-labour-reforms-minimum-wage; Angel Ross, "An Overview of America's Working Poor," PolicyLink, accessed January 24, 2025, https://www.policylink.org/data-in-action/overview-america-working-poor.

3. Philip Inman, "Number of People in Poverty in Working Families Hits Record High," *The Guardian*, February 21, 2020.

4. Peter Kelding, "3F'erne: Politikerne forstår ikke vores problemer," *Fagbladet 3F*, January 10, 2017.

5. Grace Blakeley, *Stolen—How to Save the World From Financialization* (Repeater, 2019), 80.

6. Blakeley, *Stolen*, 80. Danish data is not available.

7. Gerald A. Epstein, "Financialization and the World Economy," in *Financialization and the World Economy*, ed. Gerald A. Epstein (Edward Elgar, 2005), 3.

8. Anders Lundkvist, *Dansk kapitalisme: Gennembrud, storhed og stagnation* (Gyldendal, 2009).

9. Duncan McCann, "Commoning Intellectual Property: Public Funding and the Creation of a Knowledge Commons," Common Wealth, July 29, 2020, https://www.common-wealth.org/publications/commoning-intellectual-property.

10. McCann, "Commoning Intellectual Property."

11. Shoshana Zuboff, *The Age of Surveillance Capitalism: The Fight for a Human Future at the New Frontier of Power* (Profile, 2019).

12. Steve Pizzigati, *The Case for a Maximum Wage* (Polity, 2018).

13. Bernie Sanders, "Corporate Accountability and Democracy," July 2019, https://berniesanders.com/issues/corporate-accountability-and-democracy/.

14. OECD, "Decoupling of Wages from Productivity: What Implications for Public Policies?," *OECD Economic Outlook*, vol. 2, 2018, https://www.oecd-ilibrary.org/fr/economics/oecd-economic-outlook-volume-2018-issue-2/decoupling-of-wages-from-productivity-what-implications-for-public-policies_eco_outlook-v2018-2-3-en.

15. Niels Storm Knigge, "Uligheden er steget i Danmark," Kraka, April 4, 2019, https://kraka.dk/analyse/uligheden_er_steget_i_danmark.

16. Arbejderbevægelsens Erhvervsråd, "Stigende indkomstuligheden i Danmark," September 2019, https://legacy.altinget.dk/misc/AE_Indkomstudvikling-deciler%20sept19.pdf.

17. Arbejderbevægelsens Erhvervsråd, "Siden 2010 er indkomsten stagneret for de 40 pct. Fattigste," September 2018, https://ae.dk/files/dokumenter/analyse/ae_siden-2010-er-indkomsten-stagneret-for-de-40-pct-fattigste_0.pdf.

18. OECD, "Inequalities in Household Wealth Across OECD Countries: Evidence from the OECD Wealth Distribution Database," working paper no. 88, June 2018, https://www.oecd.org/en/publications/inequalities-in-household-wealth-across-oecd-countries_7e1bf673-en.html. The OECD's accounting does not, however, include labor market pensions. Including these means that the wealthiest 2 percent have nearly half the wealth. See Arbejderbevægelsens Erhvervsråd, "Halvdelen af befolkning sidder på 5 pct. Af formuerne I Danmark," September 2017, https://www.ae.dk/analyse/2017-09-halvdelen-af-befolkningen-sidder-paa-5-pct-af-formuerne-i-danmark.

19. OECD, "OECD Income Inequality Data Update: Sweden, 2015," https://www.oecd.org/en/countries/sweden.html.

20. In their book *The Spirit Level: Why Greater Equality Makes Societies Stronger* (Bloomsbury USA, 2019), Richard Wilkinson and Kate Pickett show through extensive comparative analyses that societies with greater economic equality fare better on virtually every metric of human well-being from health to social trust to child welfare to substance abuse.

21. Allan Christensen, "Millionregn over Løkke: Venstres valgkamp fik rekordbidrag fra erhvervslivet," Avisen.dk, November 19, 2016, https://www.avisen.dk/venstre-hoestede-rekordbidrag-fra-erhvervslivet-20-m_416273.aspx.

22. Henrik Dannemand, "Valget 2019 ventes at sætte økonomisk rekord," *Berlingske*, February 25, 2019, https://www.berlingske.dk/politik/valget-2019-ventes-at-saette-oekonomisk-rekord.

23. Morten Frich, "Mærsk gav fire mio. kroner til partier, som forhandler ny Nordsø-aftale," *Information*, February 16, 2017, https://www.information.dk/indland/2017/02/maersk-gav-fire-mio-kroner-partier-forhandler-ny-nordsoe-aftale.

24. Hans Jørgen Whitta-Jacobsen, "Staten kan få langt mere ud af nordsøolien," Berlingske, April 16, 2012, https://dors.dk/oevrige-publikationer/kronikker-artikler/staten-kan-faa-langt-mere-nordsoeolien.

25. Frederik Bjerre Andersen, "Banker støtte bankpakke-politikere," *Ekstra Bladet*, July 1, 2009, https://ekstrabladet.dk/forbrug/dinepenge/article4296470.ece.

26. The tax rebate was rolled back by the social democratic government that took power in 2019.

27. Cecilie Agertoft, "Rige familie i fælles lobby-arbejde: Nu tjener de fedt på ny lov," *Avisen*, April 12, 2017, https://www.avisen.dk/rige-familier-i-faelles-lobby-arbejde-nu-tjener-de-f_438978.aspx.

28. Corporate Europe Observatory, "The Financial Industry Employs 1700 Lobbyists and Spends €120 Million a Year to Influence the EU," April 9, 2014, https://corporateeurope.org/en/pressreleases/2014/04/financial-industry-employs-1700-lobbyists-and-spends-120-million-year.

29. Lasse Jensen, "De største britiske aviser propaganderer entydigt for Boris Johnson," *Information*, December 11, 2019, https://www.information.dk/debat/2019/12/stoerste-britiske-aviser-propaganderer-entydigt-boris-johnson.

30. CEPOS, "Trend mod lavere selskabsskat siden 80'erne i bade Danmark og OECD," May 22, 2020. While the base Danish corporate tax rate has been lowered, a number of tax deductions have been withdrawn so that the overall tax base has widened.

31. Andreas Baumann, "Nyt lys over skattely: 9000 milliarder dollar er gemt af vejen," *Mandag Morgen*, October 29, 2017, https://www.mm.dk/artikel/nyt-lys-over-skattely-9000-milliarder-dollar-er-gemt-af-vejen.

32. M. Hernandez, "El Ibex 35 se da la vuelta tras la investidura y pierde el nivel de los 9600 puntos," El Mundo, January 7, 2000, https://www.elmundo.es/economia/macroeconomia/2020/01/07/5e146e13fc6c83114f8bf82c.html.

33. FT Editorial Board, "Mexico's President Risks Undermining Himself," *Financial Times*, May 5, 2019, https://www.ft.com/content/0d5a119c-6856-11e9-9adc-98bf1d35a056.

34. Aristotle, *Politics*, translated by Benjamin Jowett (Clarendon, 1885), 81.

35. Jeffrey Winters, "Oligarchy and Democracy," *The American Interest* 7, no. 2 (September 2011), https://www.the-american-interest.com/2011/09/28/oligarchy-and-democracy/.

36. OECD, "The Role and Design of Net Wealth Taxes in the OECD," April 12, 2018, https://www.oecd.org/en/publications/the-role-and-design-of-net-wealth-taxes-in-the-oecd_9789264290303-en.html.

37. Jørgen Steen, *Som gjaldt det livet* (Information, 2020), 164.

38. Alan Greenspan, interviewed in *Tages-Anzeiger*, September 9, 2007.

39. MP Pension and P + Pension are two pension funds that have undertaken such divestment.

40. Gar Alperovitz and Thomas M. Hanna, "Beyond Corporate Capitalism: Not so Wild a Dream," *The Nation*, September 11, 2012.

41. Robert J. Brulle, "The Climate Lobby: A Sectoral Analysis of Lobbying Spending on Climate Change in the USA, 2000 to 2016," *Climactic Change* 149, July 2018, 289–303; Sandra Laville, "Fossil Fuel Big Five Spent €251m Lobbying EU," *The Guardian*, October 24, 2019.

42. Jason Hickel and Giorgos Kallis, "Is Green Growth Possible?," *New Political Economy* 25, no. 4 (2019): 469–86.

43. European Environmental Bureau, "Decoupling Debunked: Evidence and Arguments Against Green Growth as a Sole Strategy for Sustainability," 2019, quoted in Steen Nielsen, *Som gjaldt det livet*, 27–28.

44. While it is often claimed that Denmark has successfully decoupled emissions from growth, many goods Danes consume are produced overseas and thus cannot be counted. Furthermore, partial decoupling is hardly sufficient. If global warming is to be halted, a complete decoupling that significantly reduces carbon emissions below current levels is necessary. Climate scientists argue that such an absolute decoupling is not compatible with continued growth.

45. NOAH, "Den grænseløs vækst—Er eksponentiel vækst mulig?," May 2015, https://www.noah.dk/sites/default/files/2017-01/Den%20gr%C3%A6nsel%C3%B8se%20v%C3%A6kst_0.pdf.

46. Tim Jackson and Peter A. Victor, "Unraveling the Claims for (and Against) Green Growth," *Science*, November 22, 2019, 950–51.

47. Herman E. Daly, *Steady State Economics*, 2nd. ed. (Island, 1991).

48. Wall Street investor John Fullerton and his partner Tim McDonald have suggested an alternative investment model that would compensate investors by providing them with a continuous share in the profits of the firms that they invest over a longer period. Such an approach would ensure that sustainable, profitable firms that are not growing are able to attract investment and could thus serve as mechanism for a steady-state economy. For a full discussion, see Kate Raworth, *Doughnut Economics: Seven Ways to Think Like a 21st-Century Economist* (Random House, 2017).

49. Karl Polanyi, "The Essence of Fascism," in *Christianity and the Social Revolution*, ed. Karl Polanyi, John Lewis, and Donald K. Kitchin (Scribner, 1935), 359–94.

Chapter 2. Change

1. This division into two competing blocks was always loosely defined. In the course of the past century there have been numerous attempts to build bridges between reformism and revolution, among them the so-called Third Way socialism of Karl Kautsky and the Austro-Marxism of the interwar period. The populist socialism of the Danish Socialist People's Party and Southern Eurocommunism of the 1970s also occupied a middle position, simultaneously critiquing social democratic regulated capitalism as well as the revolutionary insistence on radical

rupture in favor of the gradual transformation toward socialism. See, for example, Geert Petersen, *Socialismens Nødvendighed* (Lindhardt and Ringhof, 1980), 190. Petersen argued that the revolution must "take the character of a process of structural change . . . a gradual advance rather than an 'all out charge,'" and that the overthrow of capitalism constitutes "the last brick on the wall, rather than the first." The Eurocommunist André Gorz similarly tried to unite the two blocs by advocating a "non-reformist reformism," in which reforms do not just attempt to regulate capitalism but to fundamentally change power relations.

2. Anders Dybdal, "Eduard Bernstein: Politkkens forrang og klassesamarbejde," in *Socialdemokratiske tænkere*, ed. Anders Dybbal (Information, 2014), 85–99.

3. Gunnar Adler-Karlsson, *Funktionsocialisme: Alternativet mellem kommunisme og kapitalisme* (Forlaget Fremad, 1973), 37.

4. Anders Dybdal, introduction to *Socialdemokratiske tænkere*, 12.

5. Adler-Karlsson, *Funktionsocialisme*, 40. This conception of private property was first introduced in the Nordic region by the jurist Nils Karleby in the 1920s but had its origins in earlier republican ideas and the work of Bernstein: "We do not abolish private property, we limit its rights. . . . The decisive point is not the fact that property is being acknowledged, but what kind of property is acknowledged and what rights are connected with property" (quoted in Manfred B. Steger, *The Quest for Evolutionary Socialism: Eduard Bernstein and Social Democracy* [Cambridge, 2006], 147).

6. Magnus E. Marsdal, *FrP-koden: Hemmeligheten bak Fremskrittspartiets suksess* (Forlaget Manifest, 2008).

7. Mette Frederiksen, "How to Save Europe's Centre Left," *Financial Times*, April 12, 2018.

8. Mette-Line Thorup and Rune Lykkeberg, "Mette Frederiksen: Kapitalismen er blevet syg," *Information*, January 28, 2017.

9. Peter Hummelgaard, *Den syge kapitalisme* (Gyldendal, 2018).

10. Hummelgaard, *Den syge kapitalisme*, 109.

11. Hummelgaard, *Den syge kapitalisme*, 26.

12. Thorup and Lykkeberg, "Mette Frederiksen."

13. Laura Friis Wang, "Mette Frederiksen: Vi har 100 års evidens for, at vi kan tøjle kapitalismen," *Information*, April 14, 2018.

14. Hummelgaard, *Den syge kapitalismen*, 195.

15. Aditya Chakraborty, "The Task of Politics Is to Scare the Capitalists as Much as Communism Did," *The Guardian*, November 14, 2019.

16. Hummelgaard, *Den syge kapitalismen*, 195.

17. Rudolf Meidner, *Lötagarfondar* (Tidens Forlag, 1975).

18. According to Meidner, "There is a conflict in keeping private ownership of the means of production and at the same time restricting the right of control. This conflict gives the functional socialist idea the character of an intermediary stage" ("Our Concept of the Third Way: Some Remarks on the Socio-Political Tenets of the Swedish Labour Movement," *Economic and Industrial Democracy* 1 [1980]: 343–69).

19. Henrik Berggren, *Underbara dagar framför oss: En biografi över Olaf Palme* (Norstedt, 2010).

20. Vladmir I. Lenin, *The State and Revolution*," in *Collected Works*, vol. 25 (Progress, 1977), 381–492.

21. Vladmir I. Lenin, "On Dual Power," in *Collected Works*, vol. 24 (Progress, 1977), 38–41.

22. J. K. Gibson-Graham, "Waiting for the Revolution, or How to Smash Capitalism While Working at Home in Your Spare Time," *Rethinking Marxism* 6, no. 2 (1993): 10–24.

23. Apart from their critique of how we view it as all-encompassing, Gibson-Graham also criticizes our tendency to animate capitalism, attribute an organicism and an agency to it as reflected in statements like "capitalism extends itself outward into new areas of society" or "when the Eastern bloc collapsed, capitalism spread like a virus." Gibson-Graham notes that we hardly ever use such language when we speak of socialism or any other economic system, which we regard as having been created by human beings who enacted new laws to effect social change. Just as socialism was invented, so was capitalism. There is no capitalist brain that can make decisions, it has no organic existence. It is instead the result of the daily actions of myriad human beings, and the framework under which such actions take place is determined by political decisions. When capitalism expanded into Eastern Europe it was not by virtue of its own internal dynamic but rather because the conditions had been created for privatization and deregulation. And when market forces enter the public sector, it is not because capitalism itself decided to do so but because of the decisions of politicians. A kind of dialectic is of course at work here, according to which our participation in the system impacts our conception of society and thus also our conduct. But capitalism has no agency, and when we speak as if it does, we attribute to it a nearly supernatural power.

24. See, for example, Karl Marx and Friedrich Engels, *A Contribution to the Critique of Political Economy* (Progress, 1977).

25. In the *Grundrisse* (Penguin, 1973), Marx similarly describes capitalism as an organic and totalizing system: "While in the completed bourgeois system every economic relation presupposes every other in its bourgeois form, and everything posited is thus also a presupposition, this is the case with every organic system. This organic system itself, as a totality, has its presuppositions, and its development to a totality consists precisely in subordinating all elements of society to itself" (278).

26. Paul Mason, *Postcapitalism: A Guide to our Future* (Farrar, Straus and Giroux, 2015), xiii.

27. Gibson-Graham, "Waiting for the Revolution," 21.

28. Gibson-Graham define capitalism as a "social relation, or class process, in which nonproducers appropriate surplus labor in value from free wage laborers." J. K. Gibson-Graham, *The End of Capitalism (As We Knew It)* (University of Minnesota Press, 1996), xxiv.

29. Hummelgaard, *Den syge Kapitalisme*, 28.

30. Nick Warino classifies a series of countries as more or less socialist based on factors such as the extent of democratic ownership and the size of the public sector and compares how they perform on a number of metrics, concluding that more socialist societies like Denmark, Norway, Iceland, and Sweden fare better not only in health, satisfaction, wages, and leisure time but also in wealth and productivity ("The Data Show That Socialism Works," *Current Affairs*, December 7, 2019, https://www.currentaffairs.org/news/2019/12/the-data-show-that-socialism-works.

31. Erik Olin Wright, *How to Be an Anti-Capitalist in the 21st Century* (Verso, 2019), 60.

32. Olin Wright, *How to Be an Anti-Capitalist in the 21st Century*, 62.

33. See note 1 in this chapter for examples of the reform of capitalism and its revolutionary overthrow according to Petersen and Gorz.

34. Danmarks kommunistiske, *Kommunisternes Program: Vedtaget på Danmarks komunistiske partis 25, kongres* (Forlaget Tiden, 1976).

35. F. J. Borgbjerg, "Kooperative foretagender" (Det Kooperative Fællesforbund i Danmark, 1923), 7, 33.

36. Dylan Riley, "An Anti-Capitalism That Can Win," *Jacobin*, January 7, 2016, https://jacobin.com/2016/01/olin-wright-real-utopias-socialism-capitalism-gramsci-lenin-luxemburg/.

Chapter 3. The Communal Economy

1. Thorsten A. Lauritsen, "Andelsbevægelsen fik demokratiet til at blomstre," *Kristeligt Dagblad*, February 17, 2014.

2. Henning Ravnholt, *Andelsbevægelsen: Den folkestyrede Økonomi* (Danske Forlag, 1945), 48.

3. Ravnholt, *Andelsbevægelsen*, 56.

4. Ravnholt, *Andelsbevægelsen*, 56.

5. Ejvind Larsen, *Grundtvig og noget om Marx* (Studenterkredsen, 1974), 61.

6. Claus Bjørn, *Anders Nielsen, Svejstrup Østergaard* (Landbohistorisk Selskab, 1993), 92.

7. Larsen, *Grundtvig og noget om Marx*, 59.

8. Henning Grelle, *Det kooperative alternativ: Arbejderkooperation i Danmark 1852–2012* (Arbejdermuseet, 2012), 101.

9. "Andels-Staten," *Socialist Blade*, 1894. The article is unsigned, but historian Claus Bryld argues that it was mostly likely written by Borgbjerg, given the resemblance to many of his other writings of this period.

10. Anders Lundkvist, *Dansk kapitalisme: Gennembrud, storhed og stagnation* (Gyldendal, 2009), 13.

11. Grelle, *Det kooperative alternative*, 45.

12. Digital tidslinje for brugsforeningsbevægelsen, https://tidslinje.samvirke.dk/tidslinjen.

13. Ravnholt, *Andelsbevægelsen*, 37.

14. Bjørn, *Anders Nielsen, Svejstrup Østergaard,* 74.

15. Grelle, *Det kooperative alternative,* 197.

16. Cited in Mogens Rasmussen, "Direktør: Vi kan da blive 200 år," *Lokalavisen Nyborg,* March 19, 2019.

17. Ravnholt, *Andelsbevægelsen,* 81.

18. Ravnholt, *Andelsbevægelsen,* 81.

19. The Jord, Arbejde og Kapital movement was based on the ideas of American thinker Henry George, who was also the inspiration for the political party Retsforbundet, founded in 1919.

20. Lundkvist, *Dansk kapitalisme,* 67.

21. Matt Bruenig, "Nordic Socialism Is Realer Than You Think," August 5, 2017, https://www.peoplespolicyproject.org.

22. Folketrygdfondet, "Ownership Report 2016," https://www.folketrygdfondet.no/sites/default/files/2022-09/Ownership%20report%202016.pdf.

23. Grelle, *Det kooperative alternative,* 254.

24. Socialministeriet, "Almene boliger i Danmark," *Velfærdspolitisk analyse* 3 (April 2016): 1–8, https://www.ft.dk/samling/20151/almdel/uui/bilag/144/1623394.pdf.

25. Tænketanken Demokratisk Erhverv, "Om Danmarks Demokratiske Virksonheder," https://demokratiskerhverv.dk/danmarks-demokratiske-virksomheder/.

26. Jette Aagard, "Ny maling: 80 procent af danskerne er imod DONG-salget," *B.T.,* January 29, 2014.

27. Finansudvalget, "Beretning om kritisk infrastruktur," April 4, 2019, https://www.ft.dk/samling/20181/almdel/fiu/bilag/128/2044670.pdf.

28. Jordbrugsfonden SamsØkologisk, https://oekologisksamsoe.dk/jordbrugsfonden-oekologisk-samsoe-2/.

29. Tænketanken Demokratisk Erhverv, "Danmarks Demokratiske Virksomheder—Første kortlægning af fuldt demokratiske kontrollerede virksomheder," 2019, https://demokratiskerhverv.dk/wp-content/uploads/2021/03/Kortlaegning_Danmarks-Demokratiske-Virksomheder.pdf.

Chapter 4. Nordic Democratic Socialism

1. Andreas Møller Mulvad, Anton Grau Larsen, and Christoph Ellersgaard, *Tæm eliten: Fra magtelite til borgerdemokrati* (Information, 2017).

2. Elizabeth Anderson, *Private Government: How Employers Rule Our Lives (and Why We Don't Talk About It)* (Princeton, 2017), 37–39. The lecture, Private Government," the second of a two-part series titled "Liberty, Equality, and Private Government," was delivered March 5, 2015, at Princeton University as part of the Tanner Lectures in Human Values.

3. Anderson, *Private Government,* 126–44.

4. Anderson, *Private Government,* 55.

5. Meidner, interview in *Fackföreningsrörelsen* 19, 1975.

6. Ejvind Larsen, *Den satans stat: Det gamle partiers nederlag* (Information, 1974).

7. Marx, *The Civil War in France* (Foreign Languages Press, 2021), 66.

8. Frederick Engels, "The Origins of the Family, Private Property and the State," in *Marx/Engels Selected Works*, vol. 3 (Progress, 1973), 330; Vladmir I. Lenin, *The State and Revolution*, in *Collected Works*, vol. 25 (Progress, 1977), 66.

9. Daron Acemoglu and James A. Robinson, *The Narrow Corridor: States, Societies, and the Fate of Liberty* (Penguin, 2019).

10. Martin Wolf, "The Narrow Corridor: The Fine Line Between Despotism and Anarchy," *Financial Times*, September 26, 2019.

11. Robert A. Dahl, *A Preface to Economic Democracy* (University of California Press, 1985).

12. Ernst Wigforss, *Vision och verklighet: Ett urval av Ernst Wigforss politiska författarskap* (Prisma, 1971).

13. Dahl, *A Preface to Economic Democracy*, 141–42.

14. Dahl, *A Preface to Economic Democracy*, 148.

15. Cooperatives Europe, "Power of Cooperation: Cooperatives Europe Key Figures 2015," April 2016, https://coopseurope.coop/wp-content/uploads/2016/04/The-power-of-Cooperation-Cooperatives-Europe-key-statistics-2015.pdf.

16. Andreas Pinstrup Jørgensen, *Medejer: Kunsten at overhale konkurrenter gennem demokratiske ejerskab* (Gyldendal, 2020), 83.

17. Barney Cotton, "Is Employee Ownership the Future of Business?," *Business Leader*, October 9, 2019.

18. Sophie Nachemson-Ekwall, *Ett Sverige där anställda äger*, Global Utmaning, September 19, 2018, 57–60, 86–91.

19. P2PF Wiki, "Eva," October 30, 2021, https://wiki.p2pfoundation.net/Eva.

20. Kurt Wagner, "Of Course, a Bunch of Twitter Users Want to Buy the Company and Turn It into a Co-Op," *Vox*, September 4, 2017, https://www.vox.com/2017/4/9/15234376/twitter-acquisition-sale-co-op. Sadly it must be noted that Twitter was eventually purchased by noted oligarch Elon Musk.

21. A 1992 study of French, Italian, and Spanish cooperatives concludes that "SCOPs [French worker-owned co-ops], like Italian and Spanish cooperatives, are immune to the main exit process identified in the theoretical literature, namely, self-extinction by underinvestment and degeneration to the capitalist form" (cited in Labour Party, Alternative Models of Ownership, *Report to the Shadow Chancellor of the Exchequer and Shadow Secretary of State for Business, Energy and Industrial Strategy*, 2017, 15).

22. Rosa Luxemburg, *The Essential Rosa Luxemburg: "Reform or Revolution" and "The Mass Strike,"* ed. Helen Scott (Haymarket, 2008), 80–81.

23. Sam Gindin, "Chasing Utopia," *Jacobin*, October 3, 2016, https://jacobin.com/2016/03/workers-control-coops-wright-wolff-alperovitz.

24. See Pinstrup Jørgensen, *Medejer*, 41–62, for a review of the research.

25. Co-Operatives UK, *The UK Co-Operative Economy 2012: Alternatives to Austerity, 2012*, http://staging.community-wealth.org/content/uk-co-operative-economy-2012-alternatives-austerity.

26. Andrew Martins, "Survey Shows Republicans and Democrats Both Want to Work for Employee-Owned Business," *Business News Daily*, May 28, 2019.

27. Niels Dalgaard, "Debatten om økonomisk demokrati i Danmark og Sverige," *Politica* 25, no. 3 (1993): 325.

28. Niels Dalgaard, *Ved demokatriets grænse: Demokratiseringen af arbejdslivet i Danmark 1919–1994* (SFAH, 1995), 204.

29. Niels Dalgaard, *Ved demokatriets grænse*, 200.

30. Niels Dalgaard, *Ved demokatriets grænse*, 213.

31. *Berlingske Tidende*, February 9, 1973 (quoted in Dalgaard, "Debatten om økonomisk demokrati i Danmark og Sverige," 325).

32. In 1979, Social Democratic leader Anker Jørgensen tried again with a new and watered-down proposal now called ØD profit sharing (*overskudsdeling*). But this failed as well. In 1986 the Social Liberals proposed a plan for "obligatory profit sharing, co-ownership, and codetermination" that would not rely on a central fund; instead each individual firm would maintain its own. A majority looked like it could be achieved without the support of the parties of the conservative Schlüter government. But Schlüter could see which way the wind was blowing and deployed both carrot and stick against the Social Liberals, offering a compromise proposal that would give workers more representation in corporate leadership while at the same time threatening new elections, a strategy that worked. The Social Liberals withdrew the proposal, marking the end of the economic democracy project. For a summary of these events, see Dalgaard, *Ved demokatriets grænse*, 239–62.

33. Dalgaard, "Debatten om økonomisk demokrati i Danmark og Sverige," 336.

34. Sveriges Television, "Den svenska modellens fadr avliden," December 9, 2005.

35. Gallup polling revealed that only about one-half of Danish wage earners supported the LO proposal. But when asked about worker co-ownership, a majority were favorable. See Jonas Toubøl and Jonas K. Gielfeldt, "Den fejlslagne kampagne for økonomisk demokrati som faktor i arbejderbevægelsens politiske udvikling," in *Arbejderbevægelsens demokrati*, ed. Rasmus Knold Andersen and Jesper Vestermark Kober (SFAH, 2019).

36. Thomas Larsen, *Lykketoft* (Børsens, 2003), 78.

37. Luke Savage, "Bernie Sanders Wants to Democratize Your Workplace," *Jacobin*, May 31, 2019, https://jacobin.com/2019/05/workplace-democracy-policy-bernie-sanders.

38. Bernie Sanders, "Corporate Accountability and Democracy," berniesanders. com, July 2019, https://berniesanders.com/issues/corporate-accountability-and-democracy/.

39. Saoirse Gowan and Mathew Lawrence, "Democratic Ownership Funds: Creating Shared Wealth and Power," Next System Project, June 12, 2019, https://thenextsystem.org/learn/stories/democratic-ownership-funds-creating-shared-wealth-and-power.

40. Thomas Piketty, *Capital and Ideology* (Harvard University Press, 2020).

41. Martin O'Neill, "James Meade and Predistribution: 50 Years Before His Time," Policy Network, May 28, 2015.

42. Matt Bruenig, "Social Wealth Fund for America," People's Policy Project, 2018, https://www.peoplespolicyproject.org/projects/social-wealth-fund/. In 2017, the British think tank Institute for Public Policy Research presented a similar proposal for a British social wealth fund. Instead of an annual dividend, each citizen would receive a one-time payment of GBP 10,000 at the age of twenty-five that could be used to finance a home or start a business. Like the American proposal, startup capital would be financed by new taxes on capital, including a levy on shareholding. Cary Roberts and Matthew Lawrence, "Our Common Wealth: A Citizen's Wealth Fund for the UK," Institute for Public Policy Research, April 2, 2018, https://www.ippr.org/articles/our-common-wealth.

43. Tim Higginbotham, "Don't Blame the Alaska Permanent Fund Dividend," People's Policy Project, July 18, 2019, https://www.peoplespolicyproject.org/2019/07/18/dont-blame-the-alaska-permanent-fund-dividend/.

44. Leonore Palladino, "Ownership Funds in the U.S.," Common Wealth, May 29, 2019, https://www.common-wealth.org/author/lenore-palladino.

45. As Matt Bruenig explains, "Most production occurs within long value chains that are sliced and diced into different firms. The mining company digs the coal. The trucking company moves it to the coal plant. The electricity generation company burns it for electricity. The electric utility distributes it to customers. These firms all buy supplies from other companies: desks, paper etc. They also probably use various contractors that are not formally employed by their firms. And on and on. The idea that the value-added that formally occurs inside each firm is the sole province of the workers in the firm seems clearly ridiculous when you consider how complicated and arbitrary the organizations of value chains actually are." Matt Bruenig, "The Difficulty of Using the Firm in Socialist Policy," People's Policy Project, June 4, 2019, https://www.peoplespolicyproject.org/2019/06/04/the-difficulty-of-using-the-firm-in-socialist-policy/.

46. Célia Blauel, "Paris Celebrates a Decade of Public Water Success," in *The Future Is Public: Towards Democratic Ownership of Public Services*, ed. Satoko Kishimoto, Lavinia Steinfort, and Olivier Petitjohn (Transnational Institute, 2020), https://www.tni.org/en/publication/the-future-is-public-democratic-ownership-of-public-services.

47. Vitor Gaspar, Paul Medas, and John Ralyea, "State-Owned Enterprises in the Time of COVID-19," IMF Blog, May 7, 2020, https://www.imf.org/en/Blogs/Articles/2020/05/07/blog-state-owned-enterprises-in-the-time-of-covid-19.

48. Thomas M. Hanna, *Our Common Wealth: The Return of of Public Ownership in the United States* (Manchester University Press, 2018), 37.

49. We Own It, *When We Own It: A Model for Public Ownership in the 21st Century*, weownit.org.uk, 2019, https://weownit.org.uk/sites/default/files/attachments/When%20We%20Own%20It%20-%20A%20model%20for%20public%20ownership%20in%20the%2021st%20century.pdf.

50. Cevea, "Forbrugerejet fjernevarme er bedst til prisreduktion," cevea.dk, May 7, 2018, https://cevea.dk/wp-content/uploads/2020/06/Faellesejet-fjernvarme-bedst-til-prisreduktion-endelig.pdf.

51. Ole Helby Petersen, Ulf Hjelmar, Karsten Vrangbæk, and Patricia Thor Larsen, "Effekter ved udlicitering af offentlige opgaver: En forskningsoversigt over danske og international studier fra 2011–2014," vive.dk, November 2014, https://www.vive.dk/media/pure/9023/2042643.

52. Satoko Kishimoto and Olivier Petitjean, *Re-Claiming Public Services: How Cities and Citizens Are Turning Back Privatization*, Transnational Institute, June 2017, https://www.tni.org/files/publication-downloads/reclaiming_public_services.pdf.

53. Møller Mulvad, Grau Larsen, and Ellersgaard, *Tæm eliten.*

54. Socialdemokratiet, *Solidaritet, lighed og trivsel: Principprogram vedtaget på Socialdemokratiets 32, kongres, 1977*, https://www.arbejdermuseet.dk/wp-content/uploads/2016/09/SD1977P.pdf.

55. Quoted in Saoirse Gowan, "Permanently Nationalize the Banks During the Next Crisis," People's Policy Project, July 3, 2018, https://www.peoplespolicyproject.org/2018/07/03/permanently-nationalize-the-banks-during-the-next-financial-crisis/.

56. International Monetary Fund, "Redesigning the Contours of the Future Financial System," IMF staff position note, August 16, 2010, https://www.imf.org/external/pubs/ft/spn/2010/spn1010.pdf.

57. Pelle Dragsted, Nicolai Bentsen, and Poya Pazkad, *En finanssektor, der tjener flertallet*, 2nd ed., (Enhedslisten, 2018), https://bibliotek.dk/materiale/en-finanssektor-som-tjener-flertallet_pelle-dragsted/work-of%3A870970-basis%3A47633079?type=bog.

58. Juliana Broad, "Major Advances in 2019 Toward a More Democratic Economy," Next System Project, December 19, 2019, https://thenextsystem.org/learn/stories/major-advances-2019-toward-more-democratic-economy.

59. The National Bank of Sweden is among those working to create a central bank digital currency. For more on this, see Sveriges Riksbank, "E-Krona," last updated March 25, 2024, https://www.riksbank.se/sv/betalningar--kontanter/e-krona/.

60. Peter Schultz Jørgensen, *Byernes land* (Bogværket, 2019), 275.

61. Mats Magnussen, "Blackstone køber ejendomme gennem skattely," *Ekstra Bladet*, May 30, 2019.

62. The notorious "ghetto law" aimed to reduce the number of immigrants and the poor in public co-op housing, which resulted in eviction and demolition of many units. Cooperative housing construction has for all practical purposes ceased in Copenhagen. In 2017 only 5 percent of new homes were built by co-ops. Schultz Jørgensen, *Byernes land*, 275.

63. Søren Kolstrup, *De røde flertal: Håb, sejre, nederlag* (SFAH, 2017), 53.

64. Schultz Jørgensen, *Byernes land*, 374.

65. It very nearly went this way with the new development in Copenhagen harbor. A 1988 report from the redevelopment committee recommended that the city retain ownership of the harbor area and rent it out on long-term contracts: "The corporation cannot in principle sell off its holdings but can rent them through long-term contracts" (quoted in Schultz Jørgensen, *Byernes land*, 372).

66. Lisa Pelling, *Wienmodellen: Inspiration till en ny social bostadspolitik* (Arena Idé, 2019).

67. A similar right to purchase was included in a 1960s proposal for a new land use law that was never passed.

68. AFP, "Berlin Spends Nearly €1 Billion Buying Back Apartments," *The Local DE*, September 27, 2019, https://www.thelocal.de/20190927/berlin-spends.

69. George Monbiot, ed., "Land for the Many: Changing the Way Our Fundamental Asset Is Used, Owned and Governed," Report to the Labour Party, June 2019, https://landforthemany.uk/.

70. Lars Halskov, "Formand: Udenlandske selskaber kan spekulere i dansk jord," *Politiken*, August 11, 2014.

71. Danmarks statistik, "Udenlandske ejere af landbrug," February 13, 2020, https://www.ft.dk/samling/20191/almdel/mof/bilag/425/2171590.pdf.

72. Danish capitalists also buy land abroad. Best-seller owner Anders Holch Povlsen, for example, has purchased more than 894 square kilometers of Scottish land, which corresponds to an area about half the size of Bornholm. Schultz Jørgensen, *Byernes land*, 206.

73. John Erichsen and Ditlev Tamm, *Grever, baroner of husmænd: Opgøret med de store danske godser 1919* (Gyldendal, 2019).

74. Rasmus Willig and Kim Quist, "Vi har behov for en ny folke bevægelse, hvor vi sammen investerer i vores fælles, dansk jord," *Information*, June 5, 2020.

75. Lasse Skou Andersen, "Kane en venstrefløjsvision fra 1980'erne redde dansk landbrug?," *Information*, September 17, 2016.

76. WHO, "Making the Response to COVID-19 a Public Common Good: Solidarity Call to Action," June 1, 2020, https://www.who.int/initiatives/covid-19-technology-access-pool/solidarity-call-to-action.

77. Ed Silverman, "Pharma Leaders Shoot Down WHO Voluntary Pool for Patent Rights on Covid-19 Products," STAT, May 28, 2020, https://www.statnews.com/pharmalot/2020/05/28/who-voluntary-pool-patents-pfizer/.

78. Mariana Mazzucato, *The Entrepreneurial State: Debunking Public vs. Private Sector Myths* (Penguin, 2018).

79. Pelle Dragsted, "Du betaler for udviklingen af vaccine, medicinalfirmene scorer gevinsten," *Information*, November 19, 2020.

80. Duncan McCann, "Commoning Intellectual Property: Public Funding and the Creation of a Knowledge Commons," Common Wealth, July 29, 2020, https://www.common-wealth.org/publications/commoning-intellectual-property.

81. Rosie Collington, "Digital Public Assets: Rethinking Value, Access and Control of Public Sector Data," Common Wealth, November 1, 2019, https://

www.common-wealth.org/publications/digital-public-assets-rethinking-value-access-and-control-of-public-sector-data-in-the-platform-age.

82. Amy Lewin, "Barcelona's Robin Hood of Data: Francesca Bria," *Sifted*, September 16, 2018, https://sifted.eu/articles/barcelonas-robin-hood-of-data-francesca-bria.

83. Ben Tarnoff, "Big Data for the People: It's Time to Take It Back from Our Tech Overlords," *The Guardian*, March 14, 2018.

84. Simon Borkin, "Platform Co-operatives: Solving the Capital Conundrum," Nesta, February 2019, https://media.nesta.org.uk/documents/Nesta_Platform_Report_FINAL-WEB_b1qZGj7.pdf.

85. Despite its name, the bank was not cooperative but owned by a group of large investors. Finansiel Stabilitet, "Finansiel Stabilitet overtager kontrollen med Københavns Andelskasse," September 13, 2018, https://www.fs.dk/nyheder/meddelelser/finansiel-stabilitet-overtager-kontrollen-med-koebenhavns-andelskasse.

86. Gunnar Adler-Karlsson, *Funktionsocialisme: Alternativet mellem kommunisme og kapitalisme* (Forlaget Fremad, 1973), 39.

87. Adler-Karlsson, *Funktionsocialisme*, 15.

88. Piketty, *Capital and Ideology* (Harvard University Press, 2020).

89. David Schweikert, *After Capitalism* (Rowman and Littlefield, 2011).

90. Adrienne Buller, Mathew Lawrence, Sandy Brian Hager, and Joseph Baines, "Commoning the Company," Common Wealth, April 17, 2020, https://www.common-wealth.org/publications/commoning-the-company.

91. Piketty, *Capital and Ideology*.

92. Isabelle Ferreras, *Firms as Political Entities: Saving Democracy through Economic Bicameralism* (Cambridge, 2017).

93. Jens Otto Krag, "Begrebet Planøkonomi," *Socialdemokraten*, December 28, 1943.

94. Christian O. Christiansen, "Karl Polanyi og utopian om det fri marked: En introduktion til Karl Polanyi's *The Great Transformation*," *Slagmark* 64 (2012): 131–45.

95. "The veil is not removed from the countenance of the social life-process, that is, the process of material production, until it becomes production by freely associated men, and stands under their conscious and planned control." Karl Marx, *Capital*, vol. 1 (Vintage, 1977), 173.

96. Vladmir I. Lenin, "Can the Bolsheviks Retain State Power," in *Collected Works*, vol. 26 (Progress, 1977), 107.

97. Leigh Phillips and Michael Rozworski, *The People's Republic of Walmart* (Verso, 2019), 158.

98. Hans Aage, "Planøkonomis genkomst," *Information*, February 3, 2012.

99. Alec Nove, *The Economics of Feasible Socialism Revisited* (HarperCollins Academic, 1991), 83.

100. Ernst Mandel, "The Myth of Market Socialism," *New Left Review* 169 (May/June 1988): 109–20.

101. Nove, *The Economics of Feasible Socialism Revisited*, 83.

102. The concept of market socialism is also used to describe theoretical models for a planned economy that attempts to imitate market forces. Such models were the subject of the "socialist calculation debate" that pitted Marxist Oskar Lange against market fundamentalist Ludvig von Mises. A fine introduction to this debate can be found in Phillps and Rozworski, *The People's Republic of Walmart*, who note that these models have found new life among socialist theorists advocating a data-driven form of planning. But since this iteration of market socialism is not relevant to this book, I use the term to describe a socialist society that makes use of markets rather than a planned economy imitating market forces.

103. P. H. Liotta, "Paradigm Lost: Yugoslav Self-Management and the Economics of Disaster," *Balkanologie* 1–2 (2001): 1–18.

104. János Kornai, "The Soft Budget Constraint," *Kyklos* 39 (February 1986).

105. Nove, *The Economics of Feasible Socialism*, 133–41.

106. Schweikert, *After Capitalism.*

107. John E. Roemer, *A Future for Socialism* (Verso, 1994).

108. Nove, *The Economics of Feasible Socialism*; Robin Hahnel and Erik Olin Wright, *Alternatives to Capitalism: Proposals for a Democratic Economy* (Verso, 2016); Richard Wolff, *Democracy at Work: A Cure for Capitalism* (Haymarket, 2012).

109. Participatory economics operates according to the principle of equal pay for equal work.

110. Hahnel and Olin Wright, *Alternatives to Capitalism.*

111. Hahnel and Olin Wright, *Alternatives to Capitalism.*

112. Phillips and Rozworski, *The People's Republic of Walmart.*

113. Other socialist theorists like Paul Mason argue that the market economy will eventually undermine and erode itself as the information economy continues to develop. In *Postcapitalism*, Mason notes that the precondition of the market economy is that the physical products exchanged are made from scarce resources. But information and knowledge, which increasingly drive the economy, are not scarce and have no marginal costs. The price mechanism can thus only be maintained by increasingly desperate measures to protect intellectual property, which limits the possibilities to make use of such resources. He thus views Wikipedia as a kind of model for a future communist economy.

114. This account is inspired by Seth Ackerman, "The Red and the Black," *Jacobin*, December 20, 2012, https://jacobin.com/2012/12/the-red-and-the-black.

115. Nove, *The Economics of Feasible Socialism*, 219.

116. Preben Wilhjelm, *Krisen og den udeblevne systemkritik* (Politisk Revy, 2012), 17–18. In my view, however, neither Wilhjelm nor Nove properly appreciate how much consumer behavior is influenced by advertising. And with the development algorithmic-targeted advertising, it is longer so clear how "free" our choices really are.

117. Theorists like Roemer and Schweickart have already developed comprehensive models for a market socialist economy, models that can serve as inspiration in our efforts to find the correct balance. But as I have noted, I do not think it is realistic or desirable to seek to implement an entirely new economic approach all

at once, even of the kind Roemer and Schweikart recommend so long as a more gradual, trial-and-error-based transition remains viable.

118. Kate Raworth, *Doughnut Economics: Seven Ways to Think Like a 21st-Century Economist* (Chelsea Green, 2017).

119. Cited in Hanna, *Our Common Wealth*, 79.

120. Hahnel and Olin Wright, *Alternatives to Capitalism*, 199.

121. Hahnel and Olin Wright, *Alternatives to Capitalism*, 135.

122. The central idea I have presented here, that of a democratic pluralistic socialism that combines various ownership forms and seeks a fine-tuned balance between markets and planning, was also popular among East European reform economists of the 1970s and 1980s such as Włodzimierz Brus, Ota Šik, and Alec Nove, all of whom sought a third way between capitalism and state socialism. Nove's discussion of Brus and Šik in *The Economics of Feasible Socialism* is highly recommended. It is unfortunate that the ideas of these reform economists did not win the day after the collapse of the Soviet bloc and that they have unjustly been forgotten even though they could enliven current debates on alternatives to capitalism.

Chapter 5. Ten Reforms Toward a Democratic Nordic Socialism

1. John Duda, "The Italian Region Where Co-ops Produce a Third of Its GDP," *Yes! Magazine*, July 5, 2016, https://www.yesmagazine.org/economy/2016/07/05/the-italian-place-where-co-ops-drive-the-economy-and-most-people-are-members.

2. For a useful discussion of platform co-ops, see Peter Westermann and Lisbeth Bech Poulsen, *Oprør for fremtiden. Manifest for frihed og fællesskab: Midt i en tech-tid* (Gyldendal, 2018).

3. The author thanks Lars Engberg for this idea, first articulated in "Grønt lys til at ændre ejerforholdene i Danmark," *Information*, December 15, 1988.

4. For more on the *kommunalfuldmagt*, see https://www.kl.dk/oekonomi-og-administration/kommunaljura/kommunalfuldmagten.

5. Requiring banks and other financial institutions to adopt the bicameral system, with customers replacing the employees in the second chamber, is also a possibility. This would ensure a better balance between the interests of customers and shareholders. In *Tæm eliten: Fra magtelite til borgerdemokrati* (Information, 2017), Andreas Møller Mulvad, Anton Grau Larsen, and Christoph Ellersgaard further suggest that all large concerns be required to include a "citizen representative," chosen by lot on their boards who addresses societal concerns.

6. The ideas in this section are largely the result of my work with my colleagues in Enhedslisten during the period in which I served as the party's finance and business spokesperson. See Pelle Dragsted, Nicolai Bentsen, and Poya Pazkad, *En finanssektor, der tjener flertallet*, 2nd ed. (Enhedslisten, 2018), https://bibliotek.dk/materiale/en-finanssektor-som-tjener-flertallet_pelle-dragsted/work-of%3A870970-basis%3A47633079?type=bog.

7. Enhedslisten proposed such a fund in 2016. Søren Egge Rasmussen, "Forslag til folketingsbeslutning om oprettelse af Danmarks Økologiske Jordbrugerfond,"

Folketingstidende, 2016–17, https://www.folketingstidende.dk/samling/20161/beslutningsforslag/B59/index.htm.

8. Danmarks Statistik, "Det offentlige forskningsbudget sætter rekord," Nyt fra Danmarks Statistik, May 14, 2020, https://www.dst.dk/da/Statistik/nyheder-analyser-publ/nyt/NytHtml?cid=30295.

9. Casey O'Brien, "15 Amazing Things You Can Check Out from the Library (Besides Books)," Shareable, August 12, 2019, https://www.shareable.net/15-amazing-things-you-can-check-out-from-the-library-besides-books/?gad_source=1&gclid=CjwKCAjwooq3BhB3EiwAYqYoEh8308tfptml_K8uJpVEOjfoAsjkxRXGGjrhCN28lOas4SijBbqd_RoCJV4QAvD_BwE.

10. Adam Tooze, "The Death of the Central Bank Myth," *Foreign Policy*, May 13, 2000, https://foreignpolicy.com/2020/05/13/european-central-bank-myth-monetary-policy-german-court-ruling/.

11. Alternative methods of maintaining full employment are reducing the length of the work week during periods of higher unemployment or instituting special family leave or early retirement options when unemployment passes a certain benchmark.

Epilogue

1. For a comprehensive review of the research, see Andreas Pinstrup Jørgensen, *Medejer: Kunsten at overhale konkurrenter gennem demokratiske ejerskab* (Gyldendal, 2020).

2. Gallup International, *State of the Global Workplace, 2017*, https://www.slideshare.net/slideshow/state-of-the-global-workplace-gallup-report-2017/111021420.

3. Jim Harter, "Dismal Employee Engagement Is a Sign of Global Mismanagement," Global Project Engineering Group, December 20, 2017, https://globalprojectengineering.ch/dismal-employee-engagement-is-a-sign-of-global-mismanagement/.

4. Blakeley, *Stolen*, 115–16.

5. In my view, the concept of identity politics, conceived as the struggle for formal equality and minority rights, is not particularly useful, since it implies that such struggles are rooted solely in identity and the culture wars and thus neglects the matter of material conditions. Identity politics are even all too often portrayed as in conflict with class struggle. But the class struggle itself also possesses an identitarian component in that the acknowledgment of our identity as a class is a precondition for collective struggle.

Index